JN093818

English

vocabulary explained in English

Elementary Level

英語を英語で理解する

英英英単語®

初級編

ジャパンタイムズ出版 英語出版編集部
&ロゴポート 編

英英英単語 SERIES

the japan times出版

はじめに

本書は、『英語を英語で理解する 英英英単語 上級編／超上級編』の続編です。英語学習の基礎となる、初級レベルの語彙1,000語を取り上げています。

既刊の『上級編／超上級編』は、英語による見出し語の語義説明を掲載することで、英語のニュアンスを正しく捉え、かつ自分の考えを平易な言葉で伝える力をつけることを目的とした、新しい単語集でした。幸い、この2冊は多くの方に好意的に迎えていただくことができましたが、取り上げた語彙のレベルが高かったため、より重要度の高い初級レベルの語彙を扱った続編を求める声が多く寄せられました。そこで誕生したのが、本書『英語を英語で理解する 英英英単語 初級編』です。

*Longman Dictionary of Contemporary English*や*Oxford Advanced Learner's Dictionary*といった学習者用の英英辞典は、平易な単語で語義を説明しているので、見出し語のニュアンスが捉えやすく、言いたいことをシンプルな語句で表現する際の参考にもなる、優れた英語学習ツールです。一方、辞書であるために情報が多すぎて語彙学習には使いづらく、語義説明の理解が不十分だと英和辞典を引き直す手間がかかってしまう、というデメリットもあります。

『英英英単語』シリーズは、こうした問題をクリアすべく作られています。本書では、大学入試*や英検®2級・準2級の過去問データなどを基に、大学受験生だけでなく、一般の英語学習者の役にも立つ基礎レベルの語彙1,000語を厳選しました（iWebコーパス**の頻度順位で平均約2,100位レベル）。そして、各種の英英辞典を参考に、ネイティブが書きおろしたオリジナルの英語の語義説明と、見出し語の典型的な使い方を示した例文を付けました。学習効率の向上のため、あえて見出し語の訳語、例文の和訳も掲載しています。また語法情報を充実させ、適宜、語源情報も掲載しました。類義語、反意語、派生語などを含め、約2,140語を収録しています。

このように、本書を学習すれば、あらゆる英語学習者に必要な初級レベルの語彙を英語で理解し、その具体的な使い方を知ることができるようになっています。

008ページでは、本書を使った学習法をいくつかご紹介しています。それらを参考に、本書を読み込み、そして使い倒してください。少しずつ頭の中に英語回路が形成され、一般的な単語集では手に入らない単語のニュアンスの知識とパラフレージング力が身につくでしょう。

本書が読者の皆さまの語彙力向上の一助になれば、これに過ぎる喜びはありません。

編者

* 青山学院大学、学習院大学、中央大学、法政大学、明治大学、立教大学の過去問3年分などを分析。

** アメリカのBrigham Young UniversityのMark Davies教授が構築した140億語のコーパス（The Intelligent Web-based Corpus）を指す。

目次

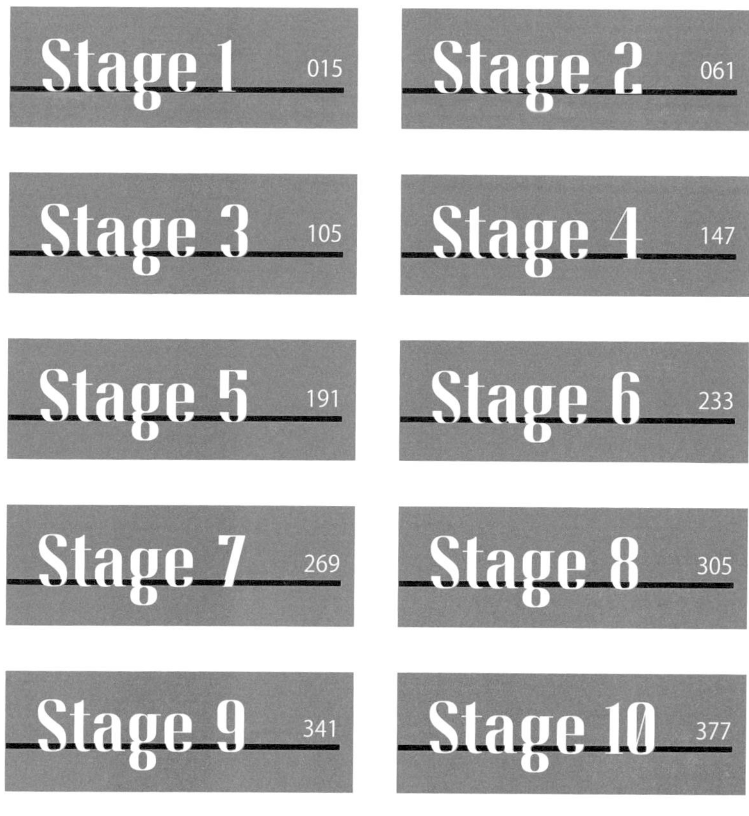

ナレーション：Josh Keller（米）／ Rachel Walzer（米）
録音・編集：ELEC録音スタジオ
音声収録時間：約4時間15分

カバー・本文デザイン：竹内雄二
イラスト：矢戸優人
DTP組版：株式会社 創樹

本書の構成

本書では、初級レベルの単語1,000語を、100語ずつ10のSTAGEに分けて掲載しています。

MP3 0070-0072
10
STAGE 1
0072
1
common
2
/ kɑ́ːmən /
副 commonly 一般的に
3
4
形 not unusual and happening or existing a lot
普通の、一般的な
5
6
≒ ordinary
⇔ rare, uncommon
8
〈com-（共に）+mon（義務を負わされた）〉
7
i common sense（常識、良識）という表現も覚えておこう。
9
例 Eating turkey on Thanksgiving is **common** in the U.S.
感謝祭に七面鳥を食べるのは、アメリカでは一般的だ。
本書で使われている記号
〈 〉…他動詞の目的語、自動詞・形容詞の主語にあたる訳語であることを表します。
（ ）…訳語の補足説明／省略可能であることを表します。
[ ]…訳語の注記／言い換え可能であることを表します。
《 》…通例その形で使われる語義であることを表します。
動…このアイコンは見出し語の品詞を表しています。
動…このアイコンは派生語の品詞を表しています。
動…動詞、名…名詞、形…形容詞、副…副詞、接…接続詞、前…前置詞

1 見出し語

米つづりを採用しています。英つづりが異なる場合は注記に挙げています。

2 発音記号

米発音を採用しています。品詞によって発音が変わる語の場合、本書に掲載した品詞の発音のみを挙げています。

3 派生語

見出し語と派生関係にある語を掲載しています。

4 品詞と英語の語義説明

見出し語の品詞を示し、語義を英語で説明しています。特によく使われる語義、学習者が覚えておくと役に立つ語義を選んで掲載しています。

※大きく語義の異なるものは一般の辞書では別見出しにすることがありますが、本書では適宜1つの見出しにまとめています。

※語義説明では英英辞典にならい、総称人称のyou（人一般を表すyou)、singular they (he or sheの代用）を使っている場合があります。

5 訳語

見出し語の訳語です。赤フィルターで隠すことができます。

6 類義語と反意語

≒の後ろに掲載されているのは見出し語の類義語、⇔の後ろに掲載されているのは見出し語の反意語です。

7 注記

ⓘの後ろには、見出し語の語法、関連語、同語源語、発音・アクセントの注意事項など、幅広い補足情報を掲載しています。

8 語源

🔑の後ろには、語源に関する情報を掲載しています。

9 例文と訳

見出し語を使った例文とその訳です。英文中の見出し語相当語は太字になっています。訳は赤フィルターで隠すことができます。

※go see the movies（映画を見にいく）のような、ネイティブにとって自然な語法を使っている場合があります。

10 音声のトラック番号

付属音声には各項目の見出し語、英語の語義説明、例文（英文）が収録されています。音声はアプリまたはPCでダウンロードすることができます。ご利用方法は010ページをご覧ください。

章末ボキャブラリーチェック

各STAGEの終わりに、確認のための問題を用意しています。赤フィルターでページを隠し、本文にあった語義説明（複数ある場合は1つ目の語義）を見て、ヒントを参考に見出し語を答えましょう。間違えた場合は元のページに戻って復習しましょう。

本書を使った効果的な学習法

本書を使った学習法をいくつかご紹介します。これらを参考に、ご自分に合ったオリジナルの学習法もぜひ考えてみてください。

◉基本的な使い方

1 訳を見ながら〈見出し語→語義説明→例文〉の順に読み進める

〈見出し語→語義説明→例文〉の順番に読んでいきましょう。音声を聞いて、自分でも発音してみるとより身につきます。この方法で一度本書を読み終えたら、2の学習法でもう1周すると、英語を英語で理解する力がしっかりとつきます。

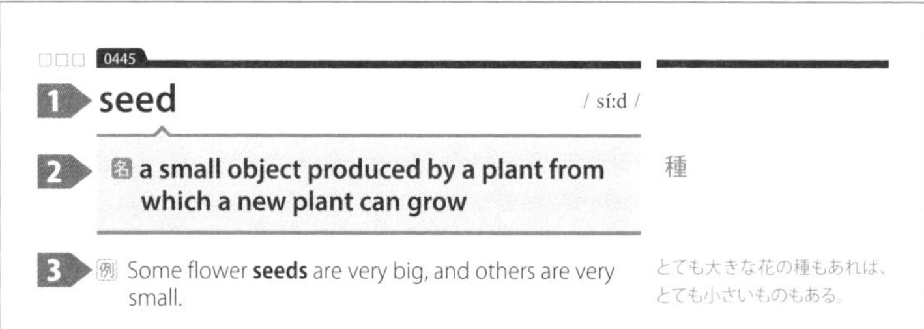

2 赤フィルターを使って英語だけで読み進める

最初から赤フィルターで日本語部分を隠して〈見出し語→語義説明→例文〉の順に読み進める方法もあります。訳は確認に使います。やはり音声を聞いて、自分でも発音してみると、より内容が身につきます。

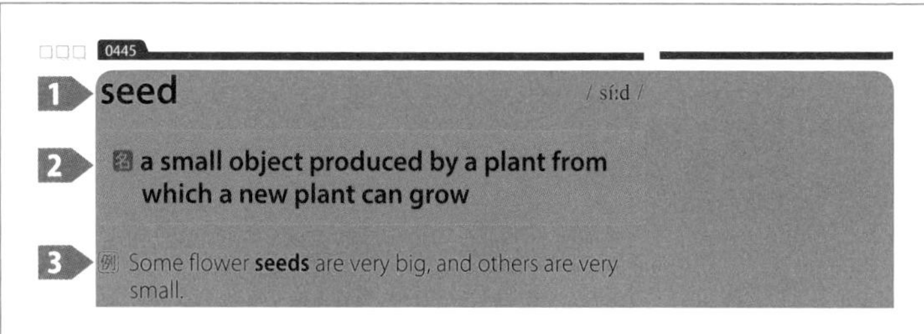

3 テキストを見ずに耳で読む

テキストを見ずに、〈見出し語→語義説明→例文〉が収録された音声を聞く学習法です。前述の1あるいは2で学習した後に、この方法を試すと、さらに内容が頭に入り、リスニング力の強化にもつながります。

4 章末ボキャブラリーチェックを繰り返し解く

完ぺきに正解できるようになるまで、章末ボキャブラリーチェックを繰り返し解きましょう。語義説明を何度も読むことは、パラフレージング力の強化につながります。

◉応用的な使い方

5 英語の語義説明の自分なりの訳語を考える

本書の英語の語義説明をもとに、辞典編集者になったつもりで、自分ならどんな訳語をあてるか考えてみましょう。この作業は英語のニュアンスを深く掘り下げることにつながります。

◉本書を使った後の学習法

6 英英辞典の利用を習慣化する

本書で英語の語義を読むことに慣れたら、普段の学習でも英英辞典を使ってみましょう。オンライン辞書でも紙の辞書でもかまいません。これができるようになれば、「英英英単語」は卒業です。

音声のご利用案内

本書の音声は、スマートフォン(アプリ)やパソコンを通じてMP3形式でダウンロードし、ご利用いただくことができます。

スマートフォン

1. ジャパンタイムズ出版の音声アプリ「OTO Navi」をインストール

2. OTO Naviで本書を検索

3. OTO Naviで音声をダウンロードし、再生

3秒早送り・早戻し、繰り返し再生などの便利機能つき。学習にお役立てください。

パソコン

1. ブラウザからジャパンタイムズ出版のサイト「BOOK CLUB」にアクセス
https://bookclub.japantimes.co.jp/book/b525049.html

2. 「ダウンロード」ボタンをクリック

3. 音声をダウンロードし、iTunesなどに取り込んで再生

※音声はzipファイルを展開(解凍)してご利用ください。

ウォーミングアップQuiz

本文を読み始める前に、まずはウォーミングアップQuizを解いてみましょう。
次の単語のかけ算とイラストをヒントに、右の頭文字で始まる英単語を考えてみてください。
クイズなので気楽に挑戦してみましょう。

(1) train × underground = s________

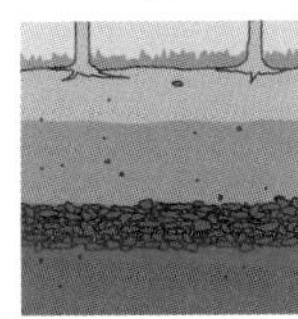

(2) teeth × doctor = d________

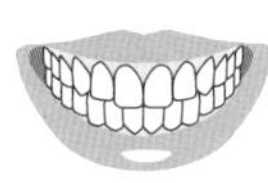

(3) letter × container = e________

(4) fish × building = a________

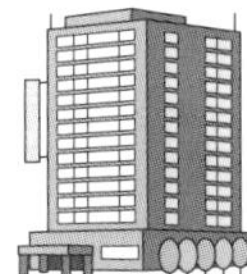

どうでしたか？　解けましたか？　それでは解答です。

(1)　train　×　underground　=　subway

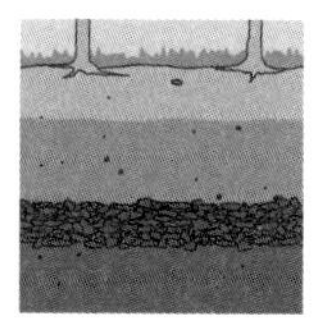

(2)　teeth　×　doctor　=　dentist

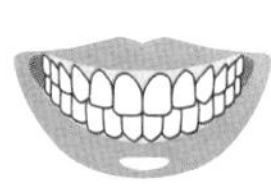

(3)　letter　×　container　=　envelope

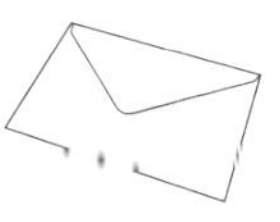

(4)　fish　×　building　=　aquarium

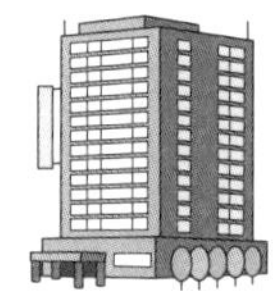

では、一つずつ確認していきましょう。
英英辞典を引いているつもりで、読んでみてください。

(1)

train（列車）とunderground（地下の）をかけ合わせたら？ という問題。正解はsubway（地下鉄）です。subwayを英語で説明すると、an underground train system in a big city（大都市の地下の鉄道システム）のような感じになります。
sub-は「下の」を意味する接頭辞で、suburb（郊外）、subconscious（潜在意識の）、submarine（潜水艦）などにも含まれています。wayは「道」という意味ですね。なお、「地下鉄」はイギリス英語ではtubeと言うこともあります。

(2)

teeth（歯）とdoctor（医師）をかけ合わせたら？ という問題。正解はdentist（歯科医）です。日本語だとほぼ2語をつなげただけですが、英語ではまったく別の語になります。dentistを英語で説明すると、a doctor who takes care of the teeth and mouth（歯や口の手入れをする医師）のような感じです。
dentは「歯」を意味する語根で、dental（歯の）という形容詞にも含まれています。少し形の違うdanもdentと同じように「歯」を表す語根で、dandelion（タンポポ）は「ライオンの歯」という意味です。タンポポの葉がライオンの歯に似ていることから、この名前がつきました。

(3)

letter（手紙）とcontainer（入れ物、容器）をかけ合わせたら？ という問題。正解はenvelope（封筒）です。envelopeを英語で説明すると、a flat paper container usually used to mail letters（ふつう手紙を送るための平らな紙の入れ物）のような感じになります。

velopは「包む」を意味する語根で、envelop（～を包む）やdevelop（発達する）にも含まれています。en-は「中に」を意味する接頭辞です。envelop [ɪnvéləp] は「～を包む」という意味の動詞、envelope [énvəlòʊp] は「封筒」という意味の名詞で、発音も異なります。混同しないように注意してくださいね。

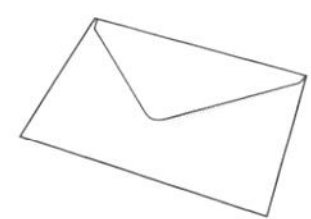

(4)

fish（魚）とbuilding（建物）をかけ合わせたら？ という問題。正解はaquarium（水族館）です。aquariumを英語で説明すると、a building that you can visit to see fish and other sea animals（人が魚やその他の海洋動物を見に行く建物）のような感じになります。

aquariumには「水槽」という意味もあります。aquaは「水」を意味する語根で、aquatic（水生の）という形容詞にも含まれています。一方-riumは「場所」を表す接尾辞で、auditorium（講堂）やplanetarium（プラネタリウム）などにも含まれています。

このように、英単語はやさしい英語で説明することができます。
こうした説明を読むことで、英単語のニュアンスがわかり、
パラフレージング力も身につきます。
それでは、次のページから、1,000語の初級レベルの単語を、
英語の語義説明と例文とともに学習していきましょう！

Stage 1

There's no time like the present.
思い立ったが吉日。

0001

will

/ wíl /

名 **the determination or desire to do something**

意志

ⓘ 原義は「望む、欲する」。そこから助動詞や「意志」を表す用法が派生した。

例 Mary has the **will** to succeed in anything she wants to do.

メアリーは自分がしたいと思うどんなことにおいても成功しようとする意志を持っている。

0002

leave

/ lí:v /

動 ① **to forget or choose not to take something with you when you go away from a place**

～を残す、置き忘れる

ⓘ leave-left-leftと活用する。

例 He **left** his homework at home again.

彼はまた宿題を家に忘れてきた。

② **to keep something or someone in a specific condition or position**

～を…のままにしておく

例 The man **left** the door unlocked for his wife.

男性は妻のためにドアに鍵をかけないままにしておいた。

名 **a period of time when someone is allowed to be away from their job**

休暇、休み

ⓘ「1日休みを取る」と言う場合はtake [get] a day offと言う。

例 After having a baby, most women take maternity **leave**.

出産後、ほとんどの女性が産休を取る。

□□□ 0003

chance

/ tʃǽns /

名 **an opportunity for someone to do something**

機会、チャンス

≒ occasion

ⓘ「チャンス」はカタカナ語にもなっている。「見込み、可能性」という意味もある。

例 The scholarship she won gave her the **chance** to study abroad in Europe.

彼女が得た奨学金は、ヨーロッパへ留学するチャンスを彼女に与えた。

□□□ 0004

point

/ pɔ́ɪnt /

名 ① **something used to count a score in a game, match, etc.**

得点

例 The home team is ahead by 12 **points**.

ホームチームが12点リードしている。

② **an idea that you want others to understand and accept**

要点

例 Nobody could understand the **point** the man was trying to make.

その男性が伝えようとしている要点を誰も理解できなかった。

動 **to move your finger or something in your hand in the direction you want someone to look**

指さす

ⓘ point out（～を指摘する）という表現も覚えておこう。

例 The little girl smiled and **pointed** at Mt. Fuji from inside the car.

小さな女の子は微笑んで車の中から富士山を指さした。

0005

case

/ kéɪs /

名 ① **a particular situation, or a particular type of situation**

状況、場合

例 In some **cases**, you will have to wait over one month to have a book delivered from overseas.

海外から本を届けてもらうのに1か月以上待たなければならない場合もある。

② **a situation that is being officially looked at or managed by someone, especially a police officer**

事件

例 There have been three **cases** of theft at the store since it opened last month.

その店が先月オープンしてから、盗難事件が3件あった。

0006

clear

/ klíər /

副 clearly はっきりと
名 clarity 明快さ
動 clarify ～を明らかにする

形 **easy to see (through)**

澄んだ、きれいな

≒ transparent

例 The water was so **clear** that you could see all the way to the bottom.

その水はとても澄んでいて、水底までずっと見通すことができた。

0007

though

/ ðóʊ /

接 **used to add information that does not match or is less important than what was already said**

～だけれども

≒ although

例 **Though** it is sunny, the wind is very cold.

晴れてはいるが、風はとても冷たい。

□□□ 0008

even

/ íːvn /

副 evenly 平らに

副 **used to show that something is not likely or is surprising**

〜さえ

例 She didn't like anything she ate at the restaurant, not **even** their famous cheesecake.

彼女はそのレストランで食べたものがどれも好きではなく、その店の有名なチーズケーキでさえも好みでなかった。

形 ① **having a surface that is flat or smooth**

平らな

≒ level

例 It is safer to play soccer where the ground is **even**.

地面が平らなところでサッカーをした方が安全だ。

② **able to be divided into two whole numbers**

偶数の

⇔ odd

ⓘ whole number（整数）、even number（偶数）、odd number（奇数）、decimal（小数）、fraction（分数）もあわせて覚えておこう。

例 She baked an **even** number of cookies so her two kids wouldn't fight over them.

2人の子どもたちがけんかにならないように彼女はクッキーを偶数個焼いた。

□□□ 0009

dangerous

/ déɪndʒərəs /

名 danger 危険
副 dangerously 危険なほどに

形 **not safe**

危険な

≒ risky

〈danger(危険)+-ous(満ちた)〉

例 Playing basketball in the street is **dangerous**.

通りでバスケットボールをするのは危険だ。

□□□ 0010

free

/ fríː /

副 freely 自由に
名 freedom 自由

形 ① **costing no money**

無料の

ⓘ for free, free of charge（無料で）という表現も覚えておこう。

例 The fast-food restaurant gives out **free** coffee sometimes.

そのファストフード店ではときどき、無料のコーヒーを提供している。

② **having nothing that needs to be done and time to do what you want to do**

暇な

⇔ busy

例 He spends most of his **free** time playing video games.

彼は暇な時間の大半をテレビゲームをして過ごす。

□□□ 0011

real

/ ríː(j)əl /

副 really 本当に
名 reality 現実性

形 ① **actually existing or happening and not just in your mind**

現実の、実在する

≒ actual

⇔ fake

〈re（物）+-al（形容詞）〉

例 A dragon is not a **real** animal.

竜は実在する動物ではない。

② **not being a copy of something or fake**

本物の

≒ true

⇔ false

例 The necklace was made with **real** diamonds, so it was very expensive.

そのネックレスは本物のダイヤでできていたので、とても高価だった。

□□□ 0012

change

/ tʃéɪndʒ /

動 **to make someone or something different, or to become different**

～を変える，変わる

≒ alter

例 The company has **changed** its logo several times over the last few decades.

その会社はこの数十年のうちにロゴを何度か変えた。

名 **money in the form of coins, or the money that is given back to you after you pay for something**

小銭、釣り銭

例 She gave the taxi driver 20 dollars and told him to keep the **change**.

彼女はタクシーの運転手に20ドル渡し、釣りはとっておくように言った。

□□□ 0013

lead

/ líːd /

名 leader リーダー、指導者
形 leading 主要な

動 ① **to guide or instruct someone**

～を率いる、先導する

⇔ follow

ⓘ lead-led-ledと活用する。「鉛」という名詞の意味もあるが、その場合は発音は[léd]。

例 She **led** the children into the store so that they could use the bathroom.

彼女は、子どもたちがトイレを使えるように、その店の中へ子どもたちを連れて入った。

② **to result in something**

引き起こす

ⓘ lead to（～を引き起こす）の形で押さえておこう。

例 Her interest in anime **led** to her moving to Japan.

アニメへの興味から、彼女は日本へ渡ることにした。

□□□ 0014

order

/ ɔ́ːrdər /

動 ① to ask for something that you want to buy (often at a restaurant)

（～を）注文する

ⓘ「キャンセルする」はcancel、「発送する」はshipと言う。

例 Jack **ordered** a large pizza for the party.

ジャックはパーティー用に大きなピザを注文した。

② to use your power to tell someone to do something

〈人〉に命令する

ⓘ〈order A to *do*〉（Aに～するよう命令する）の形で押さえておこう。

例 The man **ordered** his staff to get ready for the meeting with the prime minister.

男性はスタッフに、首相との面会の準備をするよう命じた。

名 the way that things are organized into a list, series, etc.

順序

ⓘ〈in order to *do*〉（～するために）という表現も覚えておこう。

例 The children lined up in **order** of height, with the tallest kids at the back.

子どもたちは一番背の高い子が後ろになるようにして背の順に並んだ。

□□□ 0015

art

/ ɑ́ːrt /

名 artist 芸術家

名 a creation by a person that is beautiful or expresses important ideas or feelings

美術、芸術

ⓘ 複数形artsは、自然科学に対する「人文科学」という意味でも使われる。

例 There are many museums in Tokyo where you can view **art** from all over the world.

東京には、世界中の芸術作品を見ることができる美術館がたくさんある。

□□□ 0016

mind

/ máɪnd /

動 **to not like something or be bothered by it**

…を気にする、嫌だと思う

ⓘ「～するのを嫌だと思う」は〈mind *doing*〉の形。〈mind to *do*〉は誤りなので注意。

例 I don't **mind** the heat in summer at all.

私は夏の暑さがまったく気にならない。

名 **the part of you that thinks and feels**

考え、気持ち

例 Going for a walk helps him clear his **mind** and relax.

散歩に出かけると、彼は気持ちをすっきりさせてリラックスできる。

□□□ 0017

face

/ féɪs /

形 facial 顔の

動 **to encounter something that is not good**

〈困難など〉に直面する

≒ confront

ⓘ「顔」「表面」などの名詞の意味もある。

例 Clark is **facing** criminal charges for his role in the robbery.

クラークはその強盗事件で担った役割で刑事責任を問われている。

□□□ 0018

ready

/ rédi /

形 **having finished everything that needs to be done before doing something else**

準備ができた

≒ prepared

ⓘ〈be ready to *do*/for A〉（～する／Aの準備ができている）の形で押さえておこう。

例 She was **ready** to go to the airport several hours before her flight.

彼女はフライトの数時間前に空港に行く準備ができた。

□□□ 0019

practice

/ prǽktɪs /

形 practical 実践的な

動 to do something as part of your everyday life

～を行う、実践する

ⓘ イギリス英語では動詞はpractiseともつづる。「～を練習する」という意味もある。

例 She **practices** yoga every day to reduce her stress.

彼女はストレスを緩和するために毎日ヨガをしている。

名 something that you do regularly

習慣

≒ routine, habit

ⓘ 「練習」「(社会的) 慣習」「実践」という意味もある。

例 It is the couple's **practice** to clean their apartment together every weekend.

毎週末にアパートを一緒に掃除するのがその夫婦の習慣だ。

□□□ 0020

lose

/ lúːz /

名 loss 喪失;敗北

動 ① to not be able to find someone or something

～をなくす

⇔ discover

ⓘ lose-lost-lostと活用する。

例 He **loses** his keys at least once a week.

彼は少なくとも週に1回は鍵をなくす。

② to not win in an activity or contest

〈試合など〉に負ける

例 The soccer team did their best, but they still **lost** the game.

そのサッカーチームはベストを尽くしたが、それでも試合には負けてしまった。

0021

department

/ dɪpɑ́ːrtmənt /

名 **a part of an organization**

（会社などの）部署、部門

≒ division

〈de-(離れて)+part(分ける)+-ment(名詞)〉

例 Abby joined the marketing **department** of the company after she graduated from university.

アビーは大学を卒業した後、その会社のマーケティング部に入った。

0022

post

/ póʊst /

動 **to write a message or share something online for other people to see**

（インターネットに）～を投稿する

ⓘ「郵便」「地位、職」「支柱」など、いろいろな名詞の意味もある。

例 The man **posts** pictures of his pet rabbit on Instagram every day.

その男性は毎日インスタグラムにペットのウサギの写真を投稿している。

0023

spend

/ spénd /

動 ① **to use money to buy something**

〈金〉を使う

ⓘ spend-spent-spentと活用する。〈spend A on B〉（AをBに費やす）の形で押さえておこう。

〈s-（外に）+pend（支払う）〉

例 His mother couldn't believe that he had **spent** 100 dollars on a pair of sunglasses.

彼がサングラス1つに100ドルも使ったなんて、彼の母は信じられなかった。

② **to let time pass while doing a particular activity**

〈時〉を過ごす

例 **Spending** time with family is an important part of the holiday season.

家族と時間を過ごすことは、休暇シーズンの重要な一部だ。

□□□ 0024

save

/ séɪv /

名 savings 預金

動 ① **to make sure people and things are safe and help them when they are in trouble**

～を救う

≒ rescue

例 Every year, volunteers work to **save** animals from forest fires.

毎年、ボランティアが森林火災から動物を救うために活動している。

② **to not spend money so that you will have it to use in the future**

〈金〉を蓄える

例 The little boy is **saving** his money to buy a new video game.

その小さな男の子は、新しいテレビゲームを買うためにお金を貯めている。

③ **to keep something from being lost or used without need**

～を節約する

例 She **saved** water by taking a shower instead of having a bath.

彼女は風呂に入る代わりにシャワーを浴びることで水を節約した。

□□□ 0025

receive

/ rɪsíːv /

名 receipt 領収書
名 reception 受け取ること；受付

動 **to get or be given something**

～を受ける

⇔ give

ⓘ 球技の「レシーブ」もこのreceive。

例 You will **receive** a prize if you win the contest.

コンテストで優勝したら、賞品がもらえる。

□□□ 0026

last

/ lǽst /

動 **to continue or stay in good condition over a period of time**

続く、長持ちする

例 This laptop should **last** at least five years.

このノートパソコンは少なくとも5年はもつはずだ。

□□□ 0027

decide

/ dɪsáɪd /

名 decision 決定
形 decisive 決定的な

動 **to think about something and make a choice**

～を決める

≒ determine

〈de-（離れて）+cide（切る）〉

ⓘ 〈decide (that)...〉（…と決める）、〈decide to *do*〉（～することに決める）の形で押さえておこう。

例 They **decided** they would go to Hawaii for their vacation.

彼らは休暇にハワイへ行くことに決めた。

□□□ 0028

fine

/ fáɪn /

形 **good or acceptable**

申し分ない、十分な

ⓘ finは「終わり」を意味する語根で、finish（終わる）やfinite（有限な）などと同語源語。

例 The house looks **fine** from far away, but when you get close it's ugly.

その家は遠く離れて見てみると申し分なく見えるが、近づいてみると見苦しい。

名 **money that you must pay when you break a law or rule**

罰金

≒ penalty

例 The man was given a **fine** for driving too fast.

男性はスピード違反で罰金を科された。

□□□ 0029

ground

/ gráund /

名 ① **the land that is the surface of the earth** 地面

ⓘ「運動場、グラウンド」の意味もあるが、アメリカ英語では a soccer field（サッカー場）のようにfieldを使うことが多い。

例 The child dropped her ice cream on the **ground**.

その子どもは地面にアイスクリームを落とした。

② **the reason for thinking or doing something** 根拠

≒ basis

例 Her application was not accepted on the **grounds** that it wasn't written correctly.

彼女の申請は、正しく記述されていなかったという理由で、受けつけられなかった。

□□□ 0030

rule

/ rú:l /

名 ruler 支配者；定規

名 **something that tells what you are or are not allowed to do** 規則、ルール

≒ regulation

ⓘ as a rule（ふつうは、概して）という表現も覚えておこう。

例 Students must follow the school **rules**.

生徒たちは校則に従わなければならない。

動 **to have control and power over what happens in an area or group** ～を統治する

≒ govern

例 Emperor Meiji **ruled** Japan for 45 years.

明治天皇は45年間日本を統治した。

□□□ 0031

enter

/ éntər /

名 entrance 入り口、入学

動 ① **to go inside something or somewhere** 〜に入る

⇔ exit

例 The dog **entered** the room quietly. その犬は静かに部屋に入った。

② **to join an event officially** 〈競技など〉に参加する

例 She decided to **enter** the London Marathon this year. 彼女は今年のロンドンマラソンに参加することに決めた。

□□□ 0032

note

/ nóut /

名 **a short message that is written to help someone remember something** 覚書、メモ

ⓘ notは「印をつける」を意味する語根で、notable（著しい）、notice（知らせ）などと同語源語。「筆記帳」の意味の「ノート」はnotebook。

例 His wife left him a **note** to tell him that she would be late for dinner. 妻は夕食に遅れることを彼に伝えるためにメモを残した。

□□□ 0033

wear

/ wéər /

動 **to have clothing or accessories on your body** 〜を身につけている

ⓘ wear-wore-wornと活用する。着る動作はput onと言う。また「すり切れる；〜をすり減らす」という意味もある。It has only been a few years, but the carpets are already starting to wear.（まだ2、3年しかたっていないのに、カーペットがもうすり切れ始めた）

例 The girl **wears** blue sneakers to school every day. その女の子は毎日青いスニーカーを履いて学校に行く。

□□□ 0034

own

/ óʊn /

名 owner 所有者

形 belonging to a particular person

自分自身の、独自の

ⓘ on *one's* own（一人で；独力で）という表現も覚えておこう。

例 Her grandfather built their house with his **own** two hands.

彼女の祖父は自らの手で家を建てた。

動 to have something that belongs to you

～を所有している

≒ possess

ⓘ have（～を持っている）と同様、進行形にしない。

例 That family **owns** all of the restaurants in this neighborhood.

その家族は、この近所にあるすべてのレストランを所有している。

□□□ 0035

cover

/ kʌ́vər /

名 coverage 範囲

動 ① to relate to or include something

〈範囲〉を覆う、含む

ⓘ「(物理的に)〈もの〉を覆う」「～を報道する、取材する」という意味もある。また、「覆い、カバー」という名詞の意味もある。

例 The word "blue" **covers** many different colors.

「青」という語はさまざまな色を含む。

② to provide the money needed to pay for something

〈費用など〉をまかなう

例 His New Year's money **covered** the cost of buying a new stereo.

彼はお年玉で新しいステレオを買う費用をまかなった。

□□□ 0036

sound
/ sáʊnd /

動 **to seem to be a certain way (when heard)**
(〜に) 思われる、聞こえる

≒ appear

例 The baby **sounds** like she needs a nap.
その赤ちゃんは昼寝が必要そうだ。

名 **something that can be heard**
音

例 The **sound** of the train woke him up every morning.
彼は毎朝、電車の音で起こされた。

□□□ 0037

pick
/ pík /

動 ① **to take a piece or part of something from another thing, especially with your fingers**
〜を摘む

例 His daughter always **picks** the nuts off the top of her cookies.
彼の娘はいつもクッキーにのったナッツをつまみ取る。

② **to make a choice about who or what will do something**
〜を選ぶ

≒ choose

ⓘ 選び出すことをカタカナ語で「ピックアップする」と言うが、英語ではpick outと言う。英語のpick upには「〜を拾い上げる」「〜を車で迎えに行く」など多様な意味がある。

例 He let his son **pick** which restaurant they would eat at that weekend.
彼はその週末に食事をするレストランを息子に選ばせた。

□□□ 0038

state

/ stéɪt /

名 **the physical, mental, or emotional condition of someone or something**

状態

例 The country's economy is in a **state** of decline.

その国の経済は衰退の状態にある。

動 **to say something formally in speech or writing**

～を述べる

例 The professor **stated** his research findings at a major conference.

その教授は大きな会議で研究結果を述べた。

□□□ 0039

area

/ éəriə /

名 **a place that is part of a bigger place**

地域

≒ zone, region

例 Many young people live in the **area** because there is a university nearby.

近くに大学があるので、その地域には多くの若者が住んでいる。

□□□ 0040

letter

/ létər /

名 **a symbol or mark that is made in a language to represent the sounds of speech**

文字

ⓘ Chinese characters（漢字）のように表意文字にはcharacterを使う。

例 There are 26 **letters** in the English alphabet.

英語のアルファベットは26文字ある。

□□□ 0041

present

/ 動 prɪzént 形 préznt /

名 presentation 発表

動 **to talk about something you have written or studied to a large group of people (usually in a formal situation)**

～を発表する、提案する

ⓘ 「贈り物；～を贈る」という意味もある。

例 The scientist **presented** his research to the whole department.

その科学者は学科全体に向けて彼の研究について発表した。

形 **existing now and not in the past or future**

現在の

ⓘ 「出席している」という意味も重要。「現在」という名詞の意味もある。

例 There are no new updates on the situation at the **present** time.

現時点では、状況について新たな更新情報はない。

□□□ 0042

popular

/ pá:pjələr /

名 popularity 人気

形 **liked by a lot of people**

人気がある

ⓘ pop culture（大衆文化）のpopはpopularの短縮語。

〈popul（人々）+-ar（形容詞）〉

例 The TV show is especially **popular** among young boys and girls.

そのテレビ番組は少年少女の間で特に人気がある。

□□□ 0043

worry

/ wə́:ri /

動 **to think about something and feel fear or concern about it**

～を心配する

ⓘ be worriedも「心配させられる＝心配する」の意味。

例 Bella spent the whole night **worrying** that she would fail her exam.

ベラは試験に落ちるのではないかと一晩中心配していた。

0043語

□□□ 0044

matter

/ mǽtər /

名 **a subject or situation that you talk about, think about, or deal with** — 問題

≒ issue

例 The man left work early to deal with a few personal **matters**. — その男性は私用を片づけるために仕事を早退した。

動 **to be important** — 重要である

≒ count

例 The color of her hair doesn't **matter** to me. — 彼女の髪が何色だろうと私にはどうでもいいことだ。

□□□ 0045

lot

/ lɑ́:t /

名 **a small area of land that is or could be used to build something** — 区画、用地

ⓘ 同じつづりで「たくさん、多く」という意味の名詞もあり、a lot of（多くの～）などの表現で使われる。

例 Many stray cats live in the empty **lot** next door. — 隣りの空き地には野良猫がたくさん住んでいる。

□□□ 0046

million

/ míljən /

名 **the number 1,000,000** — 100万

ⓘ「100万（人・個）の」という形容詞の意味もある。mil(l)は「千」を意味する語根で、millennium（1000年（間）、千年紀）などと同語源語。

例 The population of the city is around one **million**. — その市の人口は100万人ほどだ。

0047

return

/ rɪtə́ːrn /

動 ① **to bring something back to its original place because you do not want it, cannot use it, or no longer need it**

～を返す

〈re- (元に) +turn (曲がる)〉

例 After Sarah finished reading the book, she **returned** it to her friend.

サラはその本を読み終えた後、友人に返した。

② **to go back to the place where you were before**

帰る

例 He **returned** home after a fun day at the beach.

彼はビーチで楽しい1日を過ごした後、家に帰った。

0048

actually

/ ǽktʃuəli /

形 actual 実際の

副 **used to talk about what is true, especially when compared to something that is not**

実は

≒ in fact

例 He had **actually** planned to go camping today, but he got sick.

彼は実は今日キャンプに行く予定だったが、体調を崩してしまった。

0049

local

/ lóʊkl /

動 locate〈建物など〉を置く
名 location 位置

形 **belonging to the particular place or area being talked about or lived in**

地元の

ⓘ「全国的な」はnational。

〈loc (場所) +-al (形容詞)〉

例 You can help the environment by supporting **local** farmers.

地元の農家を支えることで、環境保護の役に立つことができる。

□□□ 0050

experience

/ ɪkspíəriəns /

形 experienced 経験豊かな

名 **something that has happened to you or been done by you**

経験

ⓘ アクセントはpeの位置。

例 Volunteering at the hospital was a good **experience** for the students.

病院でのボランティアは学生たちにとってよい経験だった。

動 **to do something or have something happen to you**

～を経験する

例 She **experienced** a variety of cultures when she was in Europe.

彼女はヨーロッパにいたとき、さまざまな文化を体験した。

□□□ 0051

air

/ éər /

名 **the mixture of gases surrounding the Earth that people and animals breathe**

空気

ⓘ「空の」という意味もあり、airplaneは「飛行機」、airportは「空港」。

例 When spring comes, the **air** smells like flowers.

春が来ると、空気は花のような香りがする。

動 **to present something on radio or television**

～を放送する

≒ broadcast

例 The TV station **airs** a special history show every Wednesday.

そのテレビ局は毎週水曜日に特別な歴史番組を放送している。

□□□ 0052

miss

/ mís /

動 ① **to fail to do, make, have, use, or take something**

～を逃す、～に乗り遅れる

ⓘ「誤り」の意味の「ミス」は英語ではmistakeと言う。

例 He overslept and **missed** his first class.

彼は寝過ごして、1時間目の授業に出られなかった。

② **to feel sad because someone or something is not with you**

～がいなくて寂しく思う

例 During his study abroad he really **missed** his pet hamster.

留学中、彼はペットのハムスターがいなくて本当に寂しかった。

□□□ 0053

race

/ réɪs /

名 ① **a contest between people, cars, etc. to see who or what is the fastest**

競走、レース

ⓘ「レース」はカタカナ語にもなっている。布の「レース」はlace。

例 Their family goes to the horse **races** every weekend.

彼らの家族は毎週競馬へ出かける。

② **one of the groups that people are put into based on what they look like (especially on skin color)**

人種

例 It is wrong to be unkind to people because of their **race**.

人種を理由に人々に不親切にするのは間違っている。

0054

law

/ lɔ́ː /

名 lawyer 弁護士

名 ① **the rules that are made by a government**

法律

例 It is now against the **law** to smoke in restaurants.

飲食店での喫煙は今では法律違反だ。

② **the fact that something works in a certain way in the natural world**

（科学などの）法則、原理

例 Scientists criticized the film for showing things that break the **laws** of physics.

科学者たちは、その映画が物理法則に反する事象を描いていると言って批判した。

0055

add

/ ǽd /

名 addition 追加
形 additional 追加の

動 **to put two or more things together (including numbers in math)**

～を加える、足す

⇔ subtract

i ad（広告）と同音。

例 She wants to **add** some new books to her comic book collection.

彼女は漫画本のコレクションに新しい本を何冊か追加したい。

0056

reason

/ ríːzn /

名 **something that explains why things happen, get done, or are a certain way**

理由

i for this reason（このようなわけで）という表現も覚えておこう。

例 The woman has many **reasons** for wanting to change her job.

その女性が仕事を変えたい理由はたくさんある。

0057

sign

/ sáɪn /

名 signature 署名、サイン

名 **something that is displayed to give information about something**

標識、看板

i 発音に注意。

例 The **sign** in the store window said that the shop was closed.

その店のショーウィンドーの看板には、閉店したと書かれていた。

動 **to write your name on something to show that you agree with or confirm something**

～に署名する

i 書類の「署名、サイン」はsignature、有名人の「サイン」はautographと言う。

例 You will not be able to use your credit card if you don't **sign** the back of the card.

クレジットカードの裏側に署名していないと、カードを使うことはできない。

0058

care

/ kéər /

動 **to feel concerned about or interested in something**

～を気にかける

i care about（～を気にかける）の形も重要。

例 He doesn't **care** what anybody thinks of him.

彼は誰かが彼についてどう思おうと気にしない。

名 **the actions that are done to make sure someone or something is safe and healthy**

世話

例 Dental **care** is an important part of keeping healthy.

歯の手入れは健康維持の一環として重要だ。

□□□ 0059

support

/ səpɔ́ːrt /

名 supporter 支持者、サポーター

動 **to help someone or something with something**

～を支持する、支援する

〈sup-（下で）+port（支える）〉

例 That group **supports** people that need to find a new job.

そのグループは、新しい仕事を見つける必要のある人たちを支援している。

名 **the act of helping someone by giving them something, such as love, encouragement, money, or information**

支援

例 Cindy showed her son **support** by going to all his soccer games.

シンディは息子のサッカーの試合すべてに行くことで、彼への応援の気持ちを示した。

□□□ 0060

memory

/ méməri /

形 memorial 記念の、追悼の
動 memorize ～を記憶する

名 ① **something that you remember**

記憶、思い出

ⓘ コンピュータの「記憶容量、メモリー」の意味もある。

例 The family has many good **memories** of their vacation to Guam.

その家族はグアムでの休暇旅行の楽しい思い出がたくさんある。

② **the ability to remember something that you have learned before**

記憶力

例 Our **memory** often gets worse as we age.

私たちの記憶力は年を取るにつれて低下することが多い。

□□□ 0061

continue

/ kəntínjuː /

形 continuous 絶え間ない
形 continual 断続的な

動 to keep going and not stop

続く

≒ last

ⓘ 〈continue to *do*〉または〈continue *doing*〉で「～し続ける」の意味。

例 It **continued** to snow for the rest of the night.

その夜はその後ずっと雪が降り続いた。

□□□ 0062

product

/ práːdəkt /

動 produce ～を生産する
名 production 製造、生産

名 something made or grown by someone to be used or sold

製品、生産物

〈pro-(前に)+duct(導かれた)〉

例 The company's new pet cleaning **products** are not selling well.

その会社の新しいペット用クリーニング製品はあまり売れていない。

□□□ 0063

act

/ ǽkt /

名 action 行動
形 active 活動的な

動 to do something

行動する

例 The firefighters had to **act** quickly to save the house.

消防士たちはその家を守るために迅速に行動しなければならなかった。

名 a law made by a group of people in the government

法令

例 The Customs **Act** for Canada has over 200 pages.

カナダの関税法は200ページを超える。

0064

death

/ déθ /

動 die 死ぬ
形 dead 死んだ

名 **the state of not being alive, or the time when someone or something stops being alive**

死

⇔ birth

例 The **death** of her uncle made her very sad.

彼女は、おじの死でとても悲しくなった。

0065

event

/ ɪvént /

名 **something that happens (either planned or not)**

出来事、イベント

ⓘ アクセントはveの位置。

例 The school **event** was canceled because of the typhoon.

その学校のイベントは台風のため中止された。

0066

follow

/ fá:loʊ /

名 follower 信奉者、（SNSの）フォロワー

動 ① **to do what someone or something says should be done**

〈忠告・命令など〉に従う

≒ obey

例 Soldiers must learn to **follow** orders from their superiors.

兵士は上官の命令に従うようにならなければならない。

② **to happen after something else has happened**

～に後続する

例 The hockey game was **followed** by a huge party when the team won.

そのホッケーチームが優勝すると、試合に続いて大規模なパーティーが開かれた。

□□□ 0067

view

/ vjúː /

名 ① **the things that can be seen around you from where you are**

眺め

≒ scenery

ⓘ point of view（観点）という表現も覚えておこう。

例 The **view** from the top of Tokyo Tower is beautiful.

東京タワーのてっぺんからの眺めは美しい。

② **what you think about something**

意見、見解

例 The man doesn't like to share his political **views** with other people.

その男性は、自分の政治的な意見を他人に話すのが好きではない。

□□□ 0068

especially

/ ɪspéʃəli /

副 **used to show that something is special and should get more attention**

特に

≒ particularly

⇔ generally

例 The cake at this café is **especially** good.

このカフェのケーキは特においしい。

□□□ 0069

period

/ píəriəd /

形 periodic 定期的な
名 periodical 定期刊行物

名 **a length of time during which something happens or happened**

期間

ⓘ 英文の文末に書く「ピリオド」(.) もこの period。

〈peri (周りに) +od (道)〉

例 Three earthquakes hit the city in the **period** of a few hours.

その市は、数時間の間に3度の地震に見舞われた。

□□□ 0070

age
/ éɪʤ /

名 ① **the length of time that someone or something has lived or existed**

年齢

例 His grandmother had a long life and lived to the **age** of 98.

彼の祖母は長生きして、98歳という年齢まで生きた。

② **a specific period of time in history**

時代

≒ era

例 In the **age** of computers, it is easy to learn new things.

コンピュータの時代には、新しい物事を学ぶのは簡単だ。

□□□ 0071

whole
/ hóʊl /

形 **having all the parts of something**

全部の

≒ entire

ⓘ hole（穴）と同音。

例 Carl ate the **whole** can of beans by himself.

カールは豆の缶詰を全部ひとりで食べた。

□□□ 0072

common
/ kɑ́:mən /

副 commonly 一般的に

形 **not unusual and happening or existing a lot**

普通の、一般的な

≒ ordinary

⇔ rare, uncommon

ⓘ common sense（常識、良識）という表現も覚えておこう。

〈com-（共に）+mon（義務を負わされた）〉

例 Eating turkey on Thanksgiving is **common** in the U.S.

感謝祭に七面鳥を食べるのは、アメリカでは一般的だ。

0073

board

/ bɔ́ːrd /

動 **to get on or in something that will take you somewhere** 乗る、搭乗する

ⓘ on board (〈船・飛行機など〉に乗って) という表現も覚えておこう。

例 The sisters **boarded** the train right before it left the station.
その姉妹は、電車が駅を出る直前にそれに乗った。

名 **a group of people who manage an organization or gather together to learn information and fix problems** 委員会

例 The new principal of the school will be selected by the members of the school **board**.
新しい校長は教育委員会の委員たちによって選ばれる。

0074

human

/ hjúːmən /

名 humanity 人間性

形 **of or relating to people and not animals, machines, or gods** 人間の

ⓘ human being (人間) という表現も覚えておこう。

例 The **human** body is very hard to understand.
人体は理解するのが大変難しい。

0075

moment

/ móumənt /

形 momentary 瞬時の

名 **a period of time that does not last long** 瞬間

≒ instant

例 It only took a **moment** for the mechanic to fix the car.
その修理工が車を直すには一瞬しかかからなかった。

□□□ 0076

cause

/ kɔ́ːz /

動 **to make something happen or be the reason that something happens**

〜を引き起こす

例 The train delay was **caused** by a broken signal light.

電車の遅延は、信号機の故障によって引き起こされた。

名 **something or someone that makes something happen**

原因

i cause and effect（原因と結果）という表現も覚えておこう。

例 A mouse chewing through a wire was the **cause** of the fire.

ネズミが電線をかみ切ったことが火事の原因だった。

□□□ 0077

perhaps

/ pərhǽps /

副 **possibly but not for sure**

もしかすると

≒ maybe

〈per-（〜によって）+hap(s)（偶然）〉

例 **Perhaps** we'll meet again someday.

またいつかお会いするかもしれませんね。

□□□ 0078

check

/ tʃék /

動 **to look at something to make sure that there are no problems with it**

（〜を）確かめる、チェックする

≒ review

i 「（ホテルで）チェックイン［アウト］する」は英語でもcheck in [out]。

例 It is important to **check** your answers before handing in a test.

テストを提出する前に答えを確認するのは重要だ。

□□□ 0079

appear

/ əpíər /

名 appearance 外見

動 ① **to start to be seen**

現れる、姿を現わす

≒ emerge

⇔ disappear

ⓘ 打ち消しを意味するdis-がついたdisappearは「いなくなる、見えなくなる」。

例 The bird **appeared** in front of them suddenly.

その鳥は突然彼らの前に姿を現した。

② **to be like something or make someone think that someone or something is like something**

(のように) 見える

≒ seem

ⓘ 〈appear to *do*〉(～するように見える) の形で押さえておこう。

例 The boy **appears** to be angry about something.

その男の子は何かに怒っているように見える。

□□□ 0080

develop

/ dɪvéləp /

名 development 開発、発達

動 ① **to make a new thing over a period of time**

～を開発する

ⓘ 「〈病気〉を患う」という意味も覚えておこう。

〈de-(離れて)+velop(包む)〉

例 The new smartphone took many years to **develop**.

その新しいスマートフォンは開発するのに何年もかかった。

② **to grow or get better gradually over a period of time**

成長する、発達する

例 He has **developed** into a smart young man.

彼は賢い青年に成長した。

□□□ 0081

interest

/ íntərəst /

形 interesting 面白い
形 interested 興味を持った

名 ① **the feeling of wanting to know more about something**

興味、関心

〈inter-(間に)+est(存在する)〉

例 Catherine has a deep **interest** in Russian dolls.

キャサリンはロシアの人形に深い関心がある。

② **the extra money you have to pay after borrowing money or that you get from investing money**

利子

例 The bank gave them a very low **interest** rate on the home loan.

銀行は彼らにとても低い利率で住宅ローンを組ませてくれた。

□□□ 0082

serve

/ sə́ːrv /

名 service 接客、サービス

動 ① **to help a customer with something**

～に仕える

i テニスなどの「サーブ（する）」の意味もある。

例 There are never enough staff at the shop to **serve** all the customers quickly.

その店に、すべての顧客に迅速に対応できるだけのスタッフがいたことは一度もない。

② **to bring food, drinks, and so on to someone, especially at a restaurant**

〈食べ物など〉を出す

例 A waiter's job is to take orders and **serve** food to customers.

ウエイターの仕事は、客から注文を取って料理を出すことだ。

0083

shape

/ ʃéɪp /

名 the form or outline of something — 形

ⓘ 「〜を形作る」という動詞の意味もある。「色」はcolor、「大きさ」はsize。

例 She made the cake into the **shape** of a heart. — 彼女はケーキをハート型にした。

0084

pull

/ púl /

動 to hold someone or something and move it toward you — 〜を引く、引っ張る

⇔ push

例 The teacher **pulled** open the door and entered the classroom. — その教師はドアを引いて開け、教室に入った。

0085

apply

/ əpláɪ /

名 application 申し込み
名 applicant 志願者

動 ① to use something in a specific situation — 〜を適用する

〈ap-（〜に）+ply（たたむ）〉

例 Not everything learned at school can be **applied** to everyday life. — 学校で学んだことのすべてが、毎日の生活に適用できるわけではない。

② to ask for something, usually by filling out a form — 申請する

例 The girl **applied** to work at the coffee shop for her first job. — その女の子は初めての仕事として、そのコーヒーショップでの仕事に申し込んだ。

□□□ 0086

standard

/ stǽndərd /

動 standardize ～を規格化する

名 **a level of something that is accepted to be correct or desirable**

標準

ⓘ「JISマーク」のJISは、Japan Industrial Standard（日本工業規格）の略。

例 By American **standards**, Japanese houses are too small.

アメリカの標準からすると、日本の家は小さすぎる。

□□□ 0087

attack

/ ətǽk /

動 **to act against someone or something to try to hurt or destroy them**

～を攻撃する

⇔ defend

例 The dog **attacked** the robber who entered the house.

その犬は、家に入った泥棒を攻撃した。

□□□ 0088

character

/ kǽrəktər /

形 characteristic 特有の

名 ① **the parts of you that make your personality**

性格

ⓘ「キャラクター」というカタカナ語にもなっている。アクセントはchaの位置。

例 He is known to have an honest **character**.

彼は誠実な性格で知られている。

② **a person inside a story**

登場人物

例 Bart's favorite **character** in the TV show is the detective.

そのテレビ番組で、バートのお気に入りの登場人物は探偵だ。

□□□ 0089

certain

/ sə́ːrtn /

副 certainly 確かに
名 certainty 確実性

形 ① used to talk about something or someone that is not named clearly

ある、一定の

例 Each family member will get a **certain** amount of the lottery money.

家族一人ひとりが一定額の宝くじの当選金をもらえる。

② sure to be true or correct

確かな

例 Without their top player, it is almost **certain** that the basketball team will lose.

チームのトッププレーヤーがいなければ、そのバスケットボールチームが負けるのはほとんど確実だ。

③ being very confident about something

確信して

例 The man was **certain** that his daughter would win the gymnastics competition.

その男性は、娘が体操の大会で優勝するだろうと確信していた。

□□□ 0090

professional

/ prəféʃənl /

名 profession 職業

形 doing something as your job and not as a hobby

プロの

⇔ amateur

ⓘ「プロ選手」という名詞の意味もある。英語でもpro（プロ（の））と短縮することがある。

例 When the little girl grows up, she wants to be a **professional** wrestler.

その小さな女の子は大人になったらプロレスラーになりたいと思っている。

□□□ 0091

rest

/ rést /

名 ① **what is left when other things or people have been used, are gone, etc.**

残り

≒ remains

例 His mother put the **rest** of the chicken in the fridge.

彼の母は鶏肉の残りを冷蔵庫に入れた。

② **a period of time during which you relax, sleep, or recover your energy**

休息

例 After working all afternoon, the woman needed a **rest**.

午後ずっと働いた後、その女性は休息が必要だった。

□□□ 0092

effort

/ éfərt /

名 **a serious attempt to do something**

努力

ⓘ アクセントはeの位置。「努力家」はhard workerと言う。

〈ef-（外に）+fort（力）〉

例 It took all her **effort** not to eat the cookies.

彼女がそのクッキーを食べないようにするには、あらゆる努力を要した。

□□□ 0093

explain

/ ɪkspléɪn /

名 explanation 説明
形 explanatory 説明的な

動 **to talk about something so others can understand it**

～を説明する

〈ex-（完全に）+plain（平らにする）〉

例 The P.E. teacher **explained** the rules of the game to the class.

その体育教師はクラスに試合のルールを説明した。

□□□ 0094

scene

/ síːn /

名 scenery 風景、景色

名 ① **a part of a story in which something happens**

（映画・小説などの）場面

i see（～を見る）の過去分詞seenと同音。

例 The best **scene** in the movie is when the dog saves her owner.

その映画の最高の場面は、犬が飼い主を助けるところだ。

② **the place where something happened**

（事件などの）現場

例 The police were late to arrive to the **scene** of the crime.

警察は、犯行現場に遅れて到着した。

□□□ 0095

agree

/ əgríː /

名 agreement 同意、合意

動 ① **to think the same thing or share a view with someone**

同意見である

⇔ disagree

i アクセントはreeの位置。〈agree (that)...〉（…ということで意見が一致する）の形で押さえておこう。

例 Critics **agreed** that the book was the author's best work yet.

評論家たちは、その本が著者のこれまでの最高傑作だということで意見が一致した。

② **to say that you will do or accept something that another person asks of you**

～することに同意する

i 〈agree to *do*〉（～することに同意する）、〈agree (that)...〉（…ということに同意する）の形で押さえておこう。

例 The parents **agreed** to buy their children new bicycles for Christmas.

両親は、クリスマスに新しい自転車を子どもたちに買うことに同意した。

□□□ 0096

nature

/ néɪtʃər /

形 natural 自然の、当然の
副 naturally 自然に、当然

名 ① **the world and everything in it that people did not make**

自然

〈nat (生まれる) +-ure (こと)〉

例 Rio loves **nature** and wants to study it when she grows up.

リオは自然が大好きで、大きくなったら自然を研究したいと考えている。

② **the way someone or something acts**

性質

例 It is not in a lion's **nature** to be nice to other animals.

ほかの動物たちに優しくするということは、ライオンの性質にはない。

□□□ 0097

remove

/ rɪmúːv /

名 removal 除去

動 **to take something away from somewhere**

～を取り除く

〈re (再び) +move (動かす)〉

例 The chairs were **removed** from the room to make more standing space.

立つスペースを増やすために、いすが部屋から撤去された。

□□□ 0098

attention

/ əténʃən /

動 attend 注意を向ける

名 **the interest or notice that is given to something**

注目

ⓘ Attention, please.（お知らせいたします）はアナウンスの最初に言う決まり文句。pay attention to（～に注意を払う）という表現も覚えておこう。

例 The author got a lot of **attention** for winning the Nobel Prize.

その作家はノーベル賞を受賞したことで多くの注目を集めた。

□□□ 0099

result

/ rɪzʌ́lt /

名 something that has happened because of something that was done before

結果

⇔ cause

〈re-(元に)+sult(跳ね返る)〉

例 His flight was canceled because of bad weather, and as a **result** he missed the concert.

彼の乗る飛行機は悪天候により欠航となり、その結果、彼はコンサートに行けなかった。

動 to happen or be caused by something that has happened before

結果として生じる

例 Using a phone while driving can **result** in an accident.

運転中の携帯電話の使用は、結果として事故につながることがある。

□□□ 0100

value

/ vǽljuː /

形 valuable 価値のある

名 the price or importance of something

価値、重要性

例 Antiques gain more **value** the longer time passes.

骨董品は、時間が長く経っているほど価値が上がる。

動 to decide how much something is worth or think that someone or something is important

～(の価値)を評価する

≒ appreciate

例 Living far away from home teaches you to **value** your family.

家から遠く離れて住むと、家族の価値がわかるようになる。

章末ボキャブラリーチェック

次の語義が表す英単語を答えてください。

語義	解答	連番
❶ to feel concerned about or interested in something	care	0058
❷ doing something as your job and not as a hobby	professional	0090
❸ a period of time that does not last long	moment	0075
❹ something that happens (either planned or not)	event	0065
❺ an opportunity for someone to do something	chance	0003
❻ the parts of you that make your personality	character	0088
❼ the land that is the surface of the earth	ground	0029
❽ a short message that is written to help someone remember something	note	0032
❾ something that has happened because of something that was done before	result	0099
❿ having finished everything that needs to be done before doing something else	ready	0018
⓫ something used to count a score in a game, match, etc.	point	0004
⓬ to make sure people and things are safe and help them when they are in trouble	save	0024
⓭ a part of a story in which something happens	scene	0094
⓮ something that tells what you are or are not allowed to do	rule	0030
⓯ of or relating to people and not animals, machines, or gods	human	0074
⓰ the price or importance of something	value	0100
⓱ something made or grown by someone to be used or sold	product	0062
⓲ to make someone or something different, or to become different	change	0012
⓳ used to show that something is not likely or is surprising	even	0008
⓴ a subject or situation that you talk about, think about, or deal with	matter	0044

語義	解答	連番
㉑ used to show that something is special and should get more attention	especially	0068
㉒ possibly but not for sure	perhaps	0077
㉓ something that has happened to you or been done by you	experience	0050
㉔ used to talk about something or someone that is not named clearly	certain	0089
㉕ something that is displayed to give information about something	sign	0057
㉖ not unusual and happening or existing a lot	common	0072
㉗ the number 1,000,000	million	0046
㉘ to put two or more things together (including numbers in math)	add	0055
㉙ the physical, mental, or emotional condition of someone or something	state	0038
㉚ to get on or in something that will take you somewhere	board	0073
㉛ to talk about something you have written or studied to a large group of people (usually in a formal situation)	present	0041
㉜ to ask for something that you want to buy (often at a restaurant)	order	0014
㉝ a serious attempt to do something	effort	0092
㉞ actually existing or happening and not just in your mind	real	0011
㉟ to not like something or be bothered by it	mind	0016
㊱ something that explains why things happen, get done, or are a certain way	reason	0056
㊲ to start to be seen	appear	0079
㊳ a part of an organization	department	0021
㊴ the form or outline of something	shape	0083
㊵ a particular situation, or a particular type of situation	case	0005
㊶ to relate to or include something	cover	0035

語義	解答	連番
㊷ to make something happen or be the reason that something happens	cause	0076
㊸ to make a new thing over a period of time	develop	0080
㊹ to continue or stay in good condition over a period of time	last	0026
㊺ belonging to the particular place or area being talked about or lived in	local	0049
㊻ used to add information that does not match or is less important than what was already said	though	0007
㊼ to do something as part of your everyday life	practice	0019
㊽ to think about something and make a choice	decide	0027
㊾ to think about something and feel fear or concern about it	worry	0043
㊿ a length of time during which something happens or happened	period	0069
51 to get or be given something	receive	0025
52 to bring something back to its original place because you do not want it, cannot use it, or no longer need it	return	0047
53 to encounter something that is not good	face	0017
54 the determination or desire to do something	will	0001
55 a level of something that is accepted to be correct or desirable	standard	0086
56 to use something in a specific situation	apply	0085
57 easy to see (through)	clear	0006
58 liked by a lot of people	popular	0042
59 the length of time that someone or something has lived or existed	age	0070
60 to act against someone or something to try to hurt or destroy them	attack	0087
61 a symbol or mark that is made in a language to represent the sounds of speech	letter	0040
62 what is left when other things or people have been used, are gone, etc.	rest	0091

語義	解答	連番
(63) the mixture of gases surrounding the Earth that people and animals breathe	air	0051
(64) costing no money	free	0010
(65) belonging to a particular person	own	0034
(66) to use money to buy something	spend	0023
(67) to look at something to make sure that there are no problems with it	check	0078
(68) a place that is part of a bigger place	area	0039
(69) a contest between people, cars, etc. to see who or what is the fastest	race	0053
(70) a creation by a person that is beautiful or expresses important ideas or feelings	art	0015
(71) to go inside something or somewhere	enter	0031
(72) to think the same thing or share a view with someone	agree	0095
(73) the interest or notice that is given to something	attention	0098
(74) to help someone or something with something	support	0059
(75) to fail to do, make, have, use, or take something	miss	0052
(76) to take a piece or part of something from another thing, especially with your fingers	pick	0037
(77) having all the parts of something	whole	0071
(78) to keep going and not stop	continue	0061
(79) to not be able to find someone or something	lose	0020
(80) the state of not being alive, or the time when someone or something stops being alive	death	0064
(81) to do what someone or something says should be done	follow	0066
(82) good or acceptable	fine	0028
(83) to seem to be a certain way (when heard)	sound	0036
(84) a small area of land that is or could be used to build something	lot	0045
(85) to guide or instruct someone	lead	0013

語義	解答	連番
(86) the things that can be seen around you from where you are	view	0067
(87) to help a customer with something	serve	0082
(88) to write a message or share something online for other people to see	post	0022
(89) the feeling of wanting to know more about something	interest	0081
(90) to have clothing or accessories on your body	wear	0033
(91) to talk about something so others can understand it	explain	0093
(92) to hold someone or something and move it toward you	pull	0084
(93) not safe	dangerous	0009
(94) to forget or choose not to take something with you when you go away from a place	leave	0002
(95) the rules that are made by a government	law	0054
(96) something that you remember	memory	0060
(97) to do something	act	0063
(98) to take something away from somewhere	remove	0097
(99) used to talk about what is true, especially when compared to something that is not	actually	0048
(100) the world and everything in it that people did not make	nature	0096

Stage 2

A journey of a thousand miles begins with a single step.
千里の道も一歩から。

□□□ 0101

global

/ glóubl /

名 globe 地球

形 **involving the whole world**

地球規模の、世界的な

ⓘ「グローバル」はカタカナ語にもなっている。

例 The **global** economy suffered greatly in 2008.

世界経済は2008年にひどい苦境を経験した。

□□□ 0102

touch

/ tʌ́tʃ /

動 **to put a part of your body, such as your hand, on someone or something**

～に触れる、触る

ⓘ「接触、触ること」という名詞の意味もある。keep [stay] in touch with（～と連絡［交際］を続ける）という表現も覚えておこう。

例 Visitors are not allowed to **touch** the paintings at the museum.

その美術館では、来館者は絵画に触れてはならない。

□□□ 0103

figure

/ fígjər /

名 ① **a number that represents a particular amount**

数字

ⓘ「図形」の意味もあり、「フィギュアスケート」のfigureはその意味。

例 The company's latest sales **figures** are higher than they have ever been.

その会社の最新の売上高は史上最高だ。

② **something, such as a drawing or sculpture, that is made to look like a person or animal**

例 She has a collection of cartoon **figures** in her room.

彼女は自分の部屋に漫画のフィギュアのコレクションがある。

0104

purpose
/ pə́ːrpəs /

名 the reason for or aim of something being done — 目的

≒ goal

🔑 〈pur-（前に）+pose（置く）〉

ⓘ on purpose（故意に）という表現も覚えておこう。

例 The **purpose** of this experiment is to see how smart rats are.

この実験の目的は、ラットがどれだけ賢いかを確認することだ。

□□□ 0105

form
/ fɔ́ːrm /

名 formation 形成

名 ① a type of something — 形態

ⓘ 「スポーツでの動作の型」の意味の「フォーム」もこのform。

例 Swimming is a great **form** of exercise for people with weak joints.

水泳は関節の弱い人にとって優れた運動の形態だ。

② a document that has spaces for you to write your information — 用紙

例 Mark asked his parents to help him fill out his tax **forms**.

マークは両親に納税申告用紙に記入するのを手伝ってほしいと頼んだ。

動 to make something into a specific shape, usually with your hands — ～を作る、形成する

例 The girl **formed** the cookie dough into squares.

その女の子はクッキーの生地を正方形に成形した。

□□□ 0106

prepare

/ prɪpéər /

名 preparation 準備
形 preparatory 準備の

動 ① to get ready for something

(～の) 準備をする

ⓘ prepare (～を準備する) という他動詞の使い方とprepare for (～に備えて準備する) という自動詞の使い方の違いを押さえておこう。

〈pre-(前に)+pare(準備する)〉

例 The farmers spent months **preparing** for the harvest festival.

農家の人たちは数か月かけて収穫祭の準備をした。

② to make something that can be used

〈食事など〉を作る

例 His father **prepares** dinner on the weekends.

彼の父は週末に夕飯を作る。

□□□ 0107

share

/ ʃéər /

動 ① to use something together with other people

～を共有する、分かち合う

ⓘ 「～を (均等に) 分配する」という意味もある。また、「分け前」「市場占有率」のような名詞の意味もある。

例 The brothers **share** a bedroom.

その兄弟は、寝室を共同で使っている。

② to tell someone how you feel, what you think, etc.

〈意見など〉を (人に) 話す

例 The manager asked everyone to **share** their ideas for a new logo.

部長は皆に新ロゴのアイデアを出してほしいと言った。

□□□ 0108

customer
/ kʌ́stəmər /

名 **someone who buys something from a business**

（店などの）顧客

ⓘ パーティーなどに招かれた「客」はguest、医師・弁護士などの「客」はclient。

例 The staff at the coffee shop remember their regular **customers'** orders.

そのコーヒーショップのスタッフは、常連客の注文を覚えている。

□□□ 0109

control
/ kəntróul /

動 ① **to make someone or something do what you want**

～を支配する

ⓘ 過去形・過去分詞はcontrolled、現在分詞はcontrollingとlを2つ重ねる。

例 Nobody in the house could **control** their pet dog.

その家では誰も飼い犬に言うことを聞かせることができなかった。

② **to direct what something is doing or make it act in a certain way**

～を制御する

例 This toy airplane can be **controlled** by a remote.

このおもちゃの飛行機は、リモコンで操作できる。

名 **the ability to direct the actions of someone or something**

制御

例 After the surgery, Anna gained **control** of her arm again.

手術後、アナは再び腕を自由に動かせるようになった。

0109語

0110

culture

/ kʌ́ltʃər /

形 cultural 文化の

名 **all of the beliefs, customs, arts, and so on of a particular society, group, or time period**

文化

ⓘ 「文明」はcivilization。

〈cult（耕す）+-ure（名詞）〉

例 The woman studied Polynesian **culture** at university.

その女性は大学でポリネシアの文化を研究した。

0111

favorite

/ féɪvərət /

名 favor 好意、ひいき

形 **the most liked**

一番好きな、お気に入りの

ⓘ イギリス英語ではfavouriteとつづる。最上級の意味を含んでいるので、比較変化はしない。

例 Gerald's **favorite** color is yellow.

ジェラルドの一番好きな色は黄色だ。

0112

damage

/ dǽmɪdʒ /

動 **to harm or cause problems for something**

～に害を与える

ⓘ アクセントはdaの位置。maの発音に注意。

例 Many buildings were **damaged** in the earthquake.

多くの建物が地震で被害を受けた。

名 **harm that is done to something or someone**

損害、被害

ⓘ 数えられない名詞。

例 The **damage** caused by the floods took many months to fix.

洪水がもたらした被害は、修復するのに何か月もかかった。

0113

possible

/ pá:səbl /

名 possibility 可能性

形 ① **able to be done**

可能な

⇔ impossible

ⓘ 〈人＋be動詞＋possible〉の形にはならない。

例 It is **possible** to see Mt. Fuji from some places in Saitama in the winter.

冬には埼玉のいくつかの場所から富士山を見ることが可能だ。

② **able to happen or exist**

起こり得る、あり得る

例 It is **possible** that it will rain today.

今日は雨が降る可能性がある。

0114

effect

/ ɪfékt /

形 effective 効果的な
副 effectively 効果的に

名 **the change that results when something is done or happens**

効果；結果、影響

⇔ cause

〈ef- (外に) +fect (作る)〉

例 Hiking in the mountains had a calming **effect** on me.

山歩きは私の心を落ち着かせる効果があった。

0115

protect

/ prətékt /

名 protection 保護
形 protective 保護の

動 **to keep someone or something safe**

～を保護する、守る

≒ defend

〈pro- (前を) +tect (覆う)〉

例 She tried to **protect** her books from the rain as she ran inside the house.

彼女は家に駆け込みながら、本を雨から守ろうとした。

□□□ 0116

image

/ ímɪʤ /

名 ①**the idea or feelings that you have about someone or something**

印象、イメージ

ⓘ 発音・アクセントの位置に注意。

例 The actress is worried about what will happen to her **image** if she gets married.

その女優は、結婚したら自分のイメージがどうなるか心配している。

②**a picture that is made by a camera, artist, computer, etc.**

映像、画像

例 Black and white **images** from the war interest many people.

その戦争の白黒の画像は、多くの人々の関心を集めている。

□□□ 0117

raise

/ réɪz /

動 ①**to put something or someone in a higher place or position**

～を上げる

⇔ lower

ⓘ「上がる」はrise。

例 Students must **raise** their hand when they want to speak during class.

生徒たちは授業中、発言したいときには手を挙げなければならない。

②**to take care of children or animals and teach them how to do things**

～を育てる、飼育する

≒ grow, bring up

例 He was **raised** by his aunt and uncle.

彼はおばとおじに育てられた。

 0118

amount
/ əmáʊnt /

名 a quantity of something
量

ⓘ amountの「多い／少ない」はlarge/smallで表す。「数」はnumber。

🔑 〈a-（～に）+mount（山）〉

例 You wouldn't believe the **amount** of time it took to animate this movie.
この映画をアニメ化するのにどれだけ時間がかかったか、信じられないでしょう。

□□□ 0119

thought
/ θɔ́:t /

名 something that you think of in your mind
考え、思いつき

≒ idea, opinion

ⓘ ghは発音しない。thinkの過去形・過去分詞と同じつづり・発音。

例 After hearing about the fire, her first **thought** was about the children.
火事のことを聞いたとき、彼女が真っ先に考えたのは子どもたちのことだった。

□□□ 0120

public
/ pʌ́blɪk /

副 publicly 公に
名 publicity 周知；広告
動 publicize ～を公にする

形 allowed to be used by anyone (usually supported by the government)
公の、公共の

⇔ private

🔑 〈publ（人々）+-ic（形容詞）〉

例 **Public** restrooms in Japan are very clean compared to the ones in other countries.
日本の公衆トイレは、ほかの国のものに比べてとても清潔だ。

名 the people of a country, state, etc.
一般の人々、大衆

ⓘ ふつうthe publicの形で使う。

例 The government lost the support of the **public** because of their poor performance.
政府は乏しい成果のせいで大衆の支持を失った。

□□□ 0121

subject

/ sʌ́bʤekt /

形 subjective 主観的な

名 ① **what is being talked about**

主題、話題

ⓘ 文法の「主語」という意味もある。

〈sub-（下に）+ject（投げられたもの）〉

例 Claire didn't want to talk about sad things, so she changed the **subject**.

クレアは悲しいことについては話したくなかったので、話題を変えた。

② **someone or something that is studied in an experiment**

（実験などの）被験者

例 The **subjects** of the test had to sign some forms before it started.

そのテストの被験者たちは、始まる前にいくつかの書類に署名しなければならなかった。

形 **having a high chance of doing something or having something happen**

受けやすい

≒ prone

ⓘ be subject to（～の影響を受けやすい、～にかかりやすい）の形で押さえておこう。

例 Japan is **subject** to earthquakes.

日本は地震が起こりやすい。

□□□ 0122

track

/ trǽk /

動 **to follow someone or something and find them using what they have left behind**

～を追跡する、たどる

ⓘ 乗り物の「トラック」はtruckなので注意しよう。

例 The hunter had to **track** the bear for three kilometers before he found it.

そのハンターは、クマを見つけるまで3キロも追跡しなければならなかった。

0123

movement

/ múːvmənt /

動 move 動く

名 ① **the act of moving something or someone**

動き

〈move(動く)+-ment(名詞)〉

例 People who do yoga wear clothes that make **movement** easier.

ヨガをする人たちは動きを楽にする服を着る。

② **activities by a group of people who share the same goals or ideas, often political**

(政治的・社会的な)運動

ⓘ 健康のための「運動」はexercise。

例 He took a class in university on the civil rights **movement** in the United States.

彼は大学で、アメリカの公民権運動に関する授業を受けた。

0124

role

/ róʊl /

名 **the job that someone has within an activity or situation**

役割

例 Journalists play a major **role** in educating the public about the world.

ジャーナリストは一般の人々に世界のことを伝える上で大きな役割を果たしている。

0125

similar

/ símələr /

副 similarly 同様に
名 similarity 類似(点)

形 **almost the same as another person or thing**

似た

⇔ different

〈simil(似た)+-ar(形容詞)〉

ⓘ 「～に似た」と言うときにはsimilar toの形になる。

例 The color of their eyes is **similar**.

彼らの目の色は似ている。

□□□ 0126

condition

/ kəndíʃən /

形 conditional 条件つきの

名 ① **the state of something that exists**

状況、状態

ⓘ アクセントはdiの位置。

例 His bicycle was in perfect **condition** when he bought it.

彼の自転車は、買ったときは完全な状態だった。

② **something that has to be done for something to happen**

条件

例 In Japan, being over 20 years old is a **condition** for being allowed to drink alcohol.

日本では20歳以上であることが、飲酒を許可される条件だ。

□□□ 0127

research

/ ríːsəːrtʃ /

名 researcher 研究者

名 **something that is done to get information about something**

調査、研究

≒ study

〈re-（再び）+search（探す）〉

ⓘ アクセントはreの位置。ふつう数えられない名詞の扱い。「～を研究する」という動詞の意味もあるが、その場合の発音は[rɪsə́ːrtʃ]。

例 The young woman did a lot of **research** before deciding what university she wanted to go to.

その若い女性は、志望大学を決める前にたくさん調査をした。

□□□ 0128

fill

/ fíl /

動 **to add something to something else to make it full**

～を満たす

⇔ empty

例 The waiter **filled** her glass with wine after she ordered.

彼女が注文した後、ウエイターは彼女のグラスいっぱいにワインをついだ。

0129

perform

/ pərfɔ́ːrm /

名 performance 演技、演奏

動 ① to do something (that requires training or skill)

〈仕事など〉を行う

〈per-(完全に)+form(形作る)〉

例 Doctors have many roles that they must **perform**.

医師には担わなければならない役割がたくさんある。

② to entertain other people by singing, acting, playing music, etc.

演じる、演奏する

例 His favorite band will be **performing** at 5 o'clock.

彼のお気に入りのバンドは5時から演奏する。

0130

instead

/ ɪnstéd /

副 in place of another thing or person

その代わりに

ⓘ instead of（～の代わりに）という表現も覚えておこう。

例 She wanted to buy pizza, but she bought chicken nuggets **instead**.

彼女はピザを買おうと思っていたが、代わりにチキンナゲットを買った。

0131

serious

/ síəriəs /

副 seriously 深刻に、重く

形 being important or possibly dangerous

重大な、深刻な

≒ major, severe

⇔ minor

例 Smoking can cause **serious** health problems.

喫煙は深刻な健康問題を引き起こすことがある。

0132

address

/ ədrés /

名 **the written words and numbers that show the location of a person's home, workplace, etc.**

住所

ⓘ つづりに注意。dとsは2つずつ。

例 The **address** on the letter was wrong, so it was returned to the sender.

その手紙の住所は間違っていたので、送り主に戻された。

動 **to pay attention to and try to solve something (like a problem)**

〈問題など〉に取り組む

≒ treat, deal with, cope with

例 The teachers gathered together to **address** the bullying problem at the school.

教師たちは学校におけるいじめの問題に取り組むために集まった。

0133

create

/ kriéɪt /

名 creation 創造
形 creative 創造的な

動 **to make something new**

～を作り出す、創造する

例 The first computer was **created** in the 1930s.

最初のコンピュータは1930年代に作り出された。

0134

expensive

/ ɪkspénsɪv /

動 expend ～を費やす
名 expense 費用

形 **having a high price**

高価な

⇔ cheap, inexpensive

例 Tickets to see a Broadway show in New York can be very **expensive**.

ニューヨークでブロードウェイのショーを見るためのチケットはかなり高価になることがある。

□□□ 0135

project

/ 名 prá:ʤekt 動 prəʤékt /

名 projector 投影機

名 a planned piece of work that usually takes a long time

計画、プロジェクト

≒ plan

ⓘ 学校の「(自主) 研究課題」という意味もある。

例 The highway construction **project** will take two years to finish.

その幹線道路の建設計画は、完成するのに2年かかる。

動 to make something appear on a surface

～を投影する

例 The device used to **project** movies onto the screen at movie theaters has changed a lot over the years.

映画館のスクリーンに映画を映写するのに使われる機器は、長年にわたり大きく変化してきた。

□□□ 0136

rise

/ ráɪz /

動 to increase in number or level

上昇する、増加する

⇔ fall, decrease

ⓘ rise-rose-risenと活用する。「～を上げる」はraise。

例 The **rising** prices of food make buying healthy food difficult.

食品の価格が上がると、健康的な食品を買うのが難しくなる。

名 an increase in the number or level of something

上昇、増加

⇔ decrease

例 The **rise** in taxes this year helped fund a new community park.

今年の増税は、地域の新しい公園の資金調達に役立った。

□□□ 0137

allow

/ əláʊ /

動 **to give someone permission to do something, or to let something happen**

～を許す

≒ permit

ⓘ low（低い）の発音は[lóʊ]だが、allowのlowの部分は違う。

例 In Canada, people are not **allowed** to drink alcohol in public.

カナダでは、公共の場でアルコールを飲むことは許されていない。

□□□ 0138

process

/ prá:ses /

動 proceed 進行する

名 **the series of actions that produce a result**

過程

〈pro-（前に）+cess（行く）〉

例 The **process** of learning English is long but worth it.

英語を学ぶ過程は長いが、その価値はある。

□□□ 0139

remain

/ rɪméɪn /

名 remainder 残り（物）

動 **to not change or be changed**

（依然として）～のままである、残る

≒ stay

〈re-（元に）+main（留まる）〉

例 The location of the missing boy **remains** unknown.

行方不明の少年の居場所は、依然として不明のままだ。

名 **what is left behind after someone or something dies or something has been used**

残り、遺物

ⓘ ふつう複数形で使う。

例 The couple found the **remains** of a castle in the forest.

そのカップルは、森の中で城跡を見つけた。

 0140

taste

/ téɪst /

動 to have a specific flavor

～の（ような）味がする

ⓘ 後ろにlikeやofを伴う。taste good（おいしい）、taste salty（塩辛い）のように形容詞が続く使い方も重要。

例 They sell chips that **taste** like pizza, chicken, and cheese.

そのチップスはピザ味、チキン味、チーズ味が発売されている。

名 the flavor that you can sense when something is in your mouth

味

例 The woman doesn't like the **taste** of natto.

その女性は納豆の味が好きではない。

□□□ 0141

include

/ ɪnklúːd /

名 inclusion 包含
前 including ～を含めて

動 to have someone or something as part of a group

～を含む

≒ contain

⇔ exclude

〈in-（中に）+clude（閉じる）〉

例 Max wants to be **included** in the sleep study.

マックスは、その睡眠に関する研究に参加させてほしいと思っている。

□□□ 0142

active

/ ǽktɪv /

動 act 行動する
名 activity 活動

形 doing things that require energy and physical movement

活動的な

⇔ inactive

例 Continuing to be **active** when you get older keeps your mind and body healthy.

年をとってからも活動的であり続けることは、精神と肉体を健全に保つ。

□□□ 0143

offer

/ ɔ́(:)fər /

動 **to give someone a chance to accept something or say that you will do something**

～を提供する

ⓘ アクセントはoの位置。

〈of-（～に）+fer（運ぶ）〉

例 He was **offered** the chance to meet his favorite idol.

彼は大好きなアイドルに会うチャンスを与えられた。

名 **the act of giving someone a chance to accept something**

申し出

例 She refused an **offer** to become president of the company.

彼女はその会社の社長にならないかという申し出を断った。

□□□ 0144

sense

/ séns /

形 sensible 分別のある
形 sensitive 敏感な

名 **① an emotion that you feel and know you have**

感じ、感覚

ⓘ「意味」という意味もあり、in a sense（ある意味で）のように使う。洋服などの「センス」は英語ではtasteと言う。

例 After her pet dog died, she was filled with a **sense** of loss.

ペットの犬が死んだ後、彼女は喪失感でいっぱいだった。

② a way of thinking that is calm and reasonable

分別

例 Bob had the **sense** to leave the party before it got too late.

ボブは時間が遅くなりすぎる前にパーティーから帰る分別があった。

□□□ 0145

improve

/ ɪmprúːv /

名 improvement 改良、向上

動 to make something better, or to become better

～を向上させる；向上する

例 He **improved** his language skills by practicing every day.

彼は毎日練習することで、語学力を向上させた。

□□□ 0146

recently

/ ríːsntli /

形 recent 最近の

副 in a time that was not long ago

最近、ついこの間

≒ lately

ⓘ 過去形または現在完了形の動詞と共に使う。

例 George used to live in Kyoto, but he **recently** moved to Tokyo.

ジョージは京都に住んでいたが、最近東京に引っ越した。

□□□ 0147

quality

/ kwɑ́ːləti /

動 qualify ～に資格を与える

名 ① how good or bad an object is

質、品質

ⓘ a quality service（質の高いサービス）のように「良質の」という意味の形容詞としても使われる。「量」は quantity。

例 The company is known for the **quality** of their shoes.

その会社は品質のよい靴を作ることで知られている。

② something noticeable that someone or something has

性質

≒ character, nature

例 Her worst **quality** is that she gets angry easily.

彼女の一番悪い性質はすぐに怒ることだ。

□□□ 0148

major

/ méɪdʒər /

名 majority 大多数

形 **very important**

主要な、重大な

⇔ minor

ⓘ aの発音に注意。

例 There have been **major** developments in technology this year.

今年は非常に大きなテクノロジーの発展があった。

名 **the main topic you study at university**

専攻

例 She chose math as her **major** a few months after entering university.

彼女は大学に入った数か月後、専攻として数学を選んだ。

□□□ 0149

notice

/ nóʊtəs /

形 noticeable 目立つ、容易に気づく

動 **to become aware of something or someone**

～に気づく

≒ realize

ⓘ notice that...（…ということに気づく）の形も押さえておこう。
例：The boy didn't notice that his shirt was on backwards.
（その男の子はシャツが後ろ前になっているのに気づかなかった）

例 The boy **noticed** a ketchup stain on his shirt.

その男の子はシャツにケチャップの染みがあるのに気づいた。

名 **information that tells you about what will or should happen**

通知

例 The man got a **notice** in the mail to go collect his new passport.

その男性は新しいパスポートを取りに来るようにという通知を郵便で受け取った。

0150

gift

/ gíft /

形 gifted 天賦の才のある

名 ① **something that you give to a person or a group**

贈り物

≒ present

例 The woman went to the store to buy Christmas **gifts** for her family.

その女性は家族へのクリスマスプレゼントを買うためにその店に行った。

② **a natural skill for doing something**

（生まれつきの）才能

≒ talent

例 His daughter has a **gift** for playing the violin.

彼の娘はバイオリンを弾く才能がある。

0151

produce

/ prəd(j)úːs /

名 production 製造、生産
名 product 製品、生産物
名 producer 生産者

動 **to make something**

～を生産する、生み出す

〈pro-（前に）+duce（導く）〉

例 Many cars are **produced** in that prefecture.

多くの車がその県で生産されている。

0152

compare

/ kəmpéər /

名 comparison 比較
形 comparable 匹敵する、同等の

動 **to talk or think about what is similar or different between people or things**

～を比較する、比べる

i 「AをBと比較する」はcompare A with [to] Bと言う。

〈com-（共に）+pare（対等にする）〉

例 In the book club, we **compared** the writing styles of two different authors.

読書会で、私たちは異なる2人の作家の文体を比較した。

0152語

□□□ 0153

display

/ dɪspléɪ /

動 **to put something in a place where others can see it**

〜を展示する

≒ exhibit

🔑 〈dis-（否定）+play（たたむ）〉

ⓘ「（パソコンの）ディスプレー」もこのdisplay。

例 He **displays** all his trophies in the living room.

彼はリビングルームに自分のトロフィーのすべてを展示している。

名 **a group of objects set up together for a specific reason**

展示（品）

例 The library set up a **display** this month to showcase local authors.

その図書館では今月、地元の作家を紹介するための展示を設置した。

□□□ 0154

opinion

/ əpínjən /

名 **what you think about something**

意見

≒ thought, idea

例 His mother listened to everyone's **opinions** before choosing what to make for dinner.

彼の母親は、夕飯に何を作るか決める前に、みんなの意見を聞いた。

□□□ 0155

personal

/ pə́ːrsənəl /

名 person 人
副 personally 個人的には

形 **relating to an individual person or their private feelings**

個人的な

ⓘ「パソコン」はpersonal computerを短くした和製英語。PCという略語は英語でもよく使われる。

🔑 〈person（人）+-al（形容詞）〉

例 Some **personal** information is not allowed to be shared without permission.

個人情報には、許可なく共有できないものもある。

□□□ 0156

material
/ mətíəriəl /

名 ① **something that is used to make something else** — 材料、原料

ⓘ「物質の」という形容詞の意味もある。

例 The **materials** needed to make masks were sold out. — マスクを作るのに必要な材料は売り切れた。

② **information or ideas used in books, movies, etc.** — 題材、素材

例 The writer gets a lot of his **material** from reading history books. — その作家は歴史書を読むことから多くの題材を得ている。

□□□ 0157

adult
/ ədʌ́lt /

名 adulthood 大人であること、成人期

名 **a person or animal that has finished growing** — 大人、成人

⇔ child

例 Many **adults** like to watch movies made for children. — 多くの大人が子ども向けに作られた映画を見るのを好む。

形 **fully grown and finished developing** — 大人の、成人した

≒ grown-up

例 The university offers classes to **adult** learners on the weekend. — その大学では週末に成人学習者向けの授業を開講している。

□□□ 0158

introduce

/ ìntrəd(j)úːs /

名 introduction 紹介；導入
形 introductory 紹介の；入門の

動 ① **to tell your name or someone else's to another person**

～を紹介する

ⓘ introduce *oneself*で「自己紹介をする」という意味。

〈intro-（中に）+duce（導く）〉

例 She **introduced** herself to the class as Ms. Smith.

彼女はクラスの人たちにミズ・スミスですと自己紹介した。

② **to make something start or be available for the first time**

～を導入する

例 The company **introduced** a new and faster way to send money to family and friends.

その会社は、家族や友人により速く送金する新しい方法を導入した。

□□□ 0159

position

/ pəzíʃən /

名 ① **the job that you hold at an organization**

職

ⓘ「ポジション」はカタカナ語にもなっている。

〈posit（置く）+-ion（名詞）〉

例 You usually have to take a test to be hired for a translation **position**.

通常、翻訳者の職に雇われるには試験を受けなければならない。

② **the place where you are in relation to other things or people around you**

位置、場所

例 From his high **position** in the tree, the man could see the whole town.

その男性は木の高い位置から町全体を見渡すことができた。

0160

expect

/ ɪkspékt /

名 expectation 予期、予想

動 **to think that something is probably going to happen or someone is going to arrive**

～を予期する、予想する

〈ex- (外を) +pect (見る)〉

例 The price of her new computer was higher than she **expected** it to be.

彼女の新しいコンピュータの価格は、彼女が予想していたよりも高かった。

□□□ 0161

policy

/ pá:ləsi /

名 **official rules that say how things are to be done**

方針、政策

例 You should check the return **policy** before you buy expensive items online.

インターネットで高額商品を買う前には、返品条件を確認した方がよい。

□□□ 0162

rate

/ réɪt /

名 **the number of times something happens or is done within a period of time**

割合、率

i 「相場、レート」という意味もある。

例 The unemployment **rate** has gone down this year.

今年の失業率は低下した。

動 **to judge the quality, ability, or value of someone or something**

～を評価する

例 This application is highly **rated** by a lot of users.

このアプリは多くのユーザーから高評価を受けている。

□□□ 0163

class

/ klǽs /

名 ① **a meeting or course where students are taught something**

授業

ⓘ「教室」はclassではなく、classroom。

例 His university has several language **classes** available for students to take.

彼の大学には、学生が受講できる語学の授業がいくつかある。

② **a group of people who have a similar economic and social situation**

階級

例 The middle **class** makes up most of the country's population.

中流階級がその国の人口のほとんどを占めている。

□□□ 0164

contest

/ kɑ́:ntest /

名 contestant（競技会の）出場者

名 **a competition in which people try to win by doing something better than others**

競争、競技

ⓘ「審査員」はjudgeと言う。

〈con-(共に)+test(証言する)〉

例 The little boys had a **contest** to see who could stand on one foot for the longest.

男の子たちは誰が片足で一番長く立っていられるか競争した。

□□□ 0165

skill

/ skíl /

形 skilled 熟練した
形 skillful 上手な

名 **something that you can do because you practiced or trained**

技術

ⓘ「スキル」というカタカナ語にもなっている。

例 Millions of children in the world lack basic reading and writing **skills**.

基礎的な読み書きの技術を持たない子どもが世界には何百万人もいる。

□□□ 0166

disease

/ dɪzíːz /

名 **a sickness that a person or an animal has, especially one that cannot be made better easily**

病気

≒ illness

ⓘ seaseの発音に注意。

例 Chicken pox is a **disease** that many people get when they are children.

水ぼうそうは、多くの人が子どものときにかかる病気だ。

□□□ 0167

guess

/ gés /

動 **to think or say that something might be true although you are not sure**

〜だと推測する、思う

ⓘ Guess what!は「ねえ、聞いて聞いて!」という話の切り出しの言葉。

例 If you **guess** correctly how many beans are in the jar, you can win a prize.

ビンの中にいくつ豆が入っているか正確に言い当てたら、賞品がもらえる。

□□□ 0168

cost

/ kɔ́(ː)st /

形 costly 費用のかかる

名 **the amount of money needed to buy or pay for something**

費用

例 The **cost** of living in the city is higher than in the countryside.

都市部での生活にかかる費用は、田舎よりも高い。

動 **to be the price that needs to be paid**

〈お金〉がかかる

ⓘ cost-cost-costと活用する。

例 It **costs** 15 dollars to see the exhibition.

その展覧会を見るのに15ドルかかる。

□□□ 0169

term

/ tə́ːrm /

名 ① **a word or phrase that is used as the name of something specific**

用語

例 Doctors use a lot of **terms** that regular people cannot understand.

医師は一般人が理解できない用語をたくさん使う。

② **a period of time that has a decided length**

期間

例 The president of the United States can only lead the country for two **terms**.

アメリカ大統領は2期しか国の指導者を務めることができない。

□□□ 0170

society

/ səsáɪəti /

形 social 社会の

名 **a group of people that live together with shared laws and values**

社会

例 For **society** to work well, people need to be safe and healthy.

社会がうまく機能するためには、人々が安全で健康である必要がある。

□□□ 0171

wonder

/ wʌ́ndər /

形 wonderful 素晴らしい

動 **to be curious about something and think about it**

～だろうかと思う

ⓘ 「驚くべきこと［人］」という名詞の意味もある。wander（うろつき回る）と混同しないように注意。

例 I **wonder** when it is going to stop raining.

雨はいつやむのだろう。

□□□ 0172

match

/ mǽtʃ /

動 ① **to go well with something because of specific traits**

～と調和する、似合う

≒ fit

ⓘ 火をつける「マッチ」も同じつづり。

例 Her earrings **match** her dress perfectly.

彼女のイヤリングはワンピースと見事に合っている。

② **to agree with something based on available information**

〈情報などが〉～と一致する

例 The story the woman told the police didn't **match** the facts that they already knew.

その女性が警察に話した話は、警察がすでに知っていた事実と一致しなかった。

名 **a game that is played between people or teams**

試合

例 The school's volleyball team won their first **match**.

その学校のバレーボールチームは初戦に勝った。

□□□ 0173

court

/ kɔ́ːrt /

名 **the place where legal meetings about crimes are held, and the events of such meetings**

法廷、裁判所

ⓘ テニスなどの「コート」もこのcourt。「外套」の意味の「コート」はcoatなので混同しないように注意。

例 The people waited outside the **court** for the results of the trial.

人々は、裁判所の外でその裁判の結果を待った。

0174
single

/ síŋgl /

形 singular 単数の

形 ① **including only one person or thing**

たった1つ［1人］の

例 She only had a **single** egg left in the refrigerator.

彼女の冷蔵庫にはたった1つの卵しか残っていなかった。

② **not being in a relationship or married to someone**

独身の

例 This organization helps **single** parents look after their children.

この組織は、ひとり親が子どもの面倒を見るのを助けている。

0175
traffic

/ træfɪk /

名 **all the cars, trucks, or motorcycles that are driving in an area at a certain time**

交通、交通量

ⓘ 数えられない名詞。交通量の多い［少ない］はheavy [light]で表す。

例 There is more **traffic** than usual because there was an accident on the highway.

幹線道路で事故があったため、いつもよりも交通量が多くなっている。

0176
modern

/ mɑ́:dərn /

形 **relating to current time or a time in the recent past**

現代の

≒ contemporary

⇔ ancient

ⓘ アクセントはoの位置。

例 There are a large number of words in **modern** Japanese that nobody used 100 years ago.

現代の日本語には、100年前には誰も使っていなかった言葉が多数ある。

0177

surprise / sərpráɪz /

動 **to give someone a feeling caused by something unexpected or unusual**

～を驚かせる

ⓘ 「(人が) 驚く」と言う場合はbe surprisedの形になる。

〈sur- (上から) +prise (捕まえる)〉

例 He **surprised** his daughter with a new puppy for her birthday.

彼は娘の誕生日に新しい子犬を迎えて娘を驚かせた。

名 **the feeling that you get when something unexpected or unusual happens**

驚き

ⓘ surprise party (不意打ちパーティー) のような形容詞的な使い方もある。

例 The parents planned a trip to Disney World as a **surprise** for their children.

親たちは子どもたちを驚かせようと、ディズニーワールドへの旅行を計画した。

0178

flight / fláɪt /

動 fly 飛ぶ、飛行機で行く

名 **the trip you make on an airplane, or the airplane making the trip**

(飛行機の) 便、フライト

例 The **flight** from Tokyo to Sydney takes nine and a half hours.

東京発シドニー行きのフライトは9時間半かかる。

0179

pain / péɪn /

形 painful 痛い

名 **the feeling of something hurting (physically or emotionally)**

苦痛、痛み

ⓘ acheは体の特定の部位に感じる継続的な「痛み」。

例 After she fell down, the girl felt **pain** in her right foot.

その女の子は転んだ後、右足に痛みを感じた。

0180

comment

/ káːment /

名 **a spoken or written opinion about someone or something**

論評、コメント

≒ feedback

ⓘ アクセントはoの位置。

例 The author received many positive **comments** about her new book.

その著者は新刊書籍について多数の肯定的なコメントを受け取った。

動 **to say something about someone or something**

論評する、コメントする

例 The police officer wouldn't **comment** on the investigation.

警察官は捜査についてコメントしようとしなかった。

0181

various

/ véəriəs /

形 **several different or many different**

さまざまな

ⓘ ふつう名詞の前で使う。varは「変化する」を意味する語根で、vary（変化する）やvaried（さまざまな）、variety（多様性）なども同語源語。

例 **Various** types of ice cream are sold at that store.

その店ではさまざまな種類のアイスクリームが売られている。

0182

normal

/ nɔ́ːrml /

副 normally 通常は
名 normality 正常さ

形 **not unusual or strange**

普通の、標準的な

≒ common, ordinary, usual

⇔ abnormal

〈norm（物差し）+-al（形容詞）〉

例 Being sad sometimes is part of a **normal** and healthy life.

ときどき悲しくなることは、普通の健全な生活の一部だ。

0183

patient

/ péɪʃənt /

副 patiently 根気強く
名 patience 忍耐

名 **someone who receives medical care**

患者

ⓘ patieの発音に注意。

例 The room was full of **patients** waiting to see the doctor.

その部屋は医者の診療を待つ患者でいっぱいだった。

形 **able to stay calm when waiting for a long time, trying to solve problems, or talking with annoying people**

我慢強い

⇔ impatient

例 The best teachers are **patient** with their students.

最も優れた教師は生徒に対して我慢強いものだ。

0184

increase

/ 動 ɪnkríːs 名 ínkriːs /

副 increasingly だんだんと

動 **to get or make something bigger in size or number**

増える；～を増やす

≒ grow

⇔ decrease

例 The value of their house **increased** after they painted it.

彼らの家の価値は、家を塗装してから上がった。

名 **the act of getting or making something bigger in size or number**

増加

⇔ decrease

例 There has been an **increase** in reports of fires over the past few weeks.

ここ数週間、火事の報告件数が増加している。

0184語

□□□ 0185

copy

/ kάːpi /

動 **to make another version of something that is the same or almost the same as the original thing**

～をコピーする、写す

例 Money is made to be hard for criminals to **copy**.

お金は犯罪者が複製しにくいように作られている。

名 **one of many things that are the same and are sold or given to people, such as books or magazines**

（本などの）1部

例 Her newest book of poetry has sold over two million **copies**.

彼女の最新の詩集は、200万部以上売れている。

□□□ 0186

detail

/ díːteɪl /

形 detailed 詳細な

名 **information about something or someone that is specific or precise**

詳細

ⓘ in detail（詳細に）という表現も覚えておこう。

例 That book is full of historical **details** about the Ainu people.

その本には、アイヌ民族に関する詳しい歴史的記述が満載だ。

□□□ 0187

tax

/ tǽks /

名 taxation 課税

名 **money that people must pay to the government based on their income, property, purchases, etc.**

税金

例 The consumption **tax** on most items in Japan was raised to 10% in 2019.

日本ではほとんどの品物の消費税が2019年に10%に引き上げられた。

□□□ 0188

exercise

/ éksərsàɪz /

名 ① **an action that is done to practice and get better at doing something**

練習

≒ practice

ⓘ アクセントはexの位置。

例 The textbook has writing **exercises** at the end of every chapter to help students review the lessons.

生徒が課の復習をしやすいように、その教科書の各章末にはライティングの練習が載っている。

② **physical activity that you do to get stronger and stay healthy**

運動

≒ workout

例 Regular **exercise** is an important part of a healthy lifestyle.

定期的な運動は、健康的な生活習慣の一部として重要だ。

動 **to use an ability or right to do something**

〈能力〉を働かせる、〈権力など〉を行使する

例 The doctor **exercised** great caution when he checked the patient's throat.

その医師は、患者の喉を診察するときとても用心した。

□□□ 0189

collect

/ kəlékt /

名 collection 収蔵品；収集
形 collective 集団の

動 **to gather things and keep them together, sometimes as a hobby**

～を集める、収集する

ⓘ collector（コレクター）は「集める人」のこと。correct（～を訂正する）と混同しないように注意。

〈col-（共に）+lect（集める）〉

例 He has been **collecting** stamps since he was a child.

彼は子どもの頃から切手を集めている。

0189語

□□□ 0190

general

/ ʤénərəl /

副 generally 一般的に
動 generalize ～を一般化する

形 ① **of, relating to, or affecting most people, places, or things**

世間一般の、全般的な

ⓘ general hospital（総合病院）のような使い方もある。

例 There is a **general** shortage of labor in the country.

その国では全般的に労働力が不足している。

② **including the main or major parts of something and not specific details**

概略の、大ざっぱな

例 He had only a **general** idea of what he wanted to do during his trip in Europe.

彼はヨーロッパ旅行中に何をしたいか、大ざっぱにしか考えていなかった。

□□□ 0191

regular

/ régjələr /

副 regularly 規則的に
名 regularity 規則性

形 **happening often at the same time or in the same way**

定期的な、規則正しい

⇔ irregular

〈regul（物差し）+-ar（形容詞）〉

ⓘ 「常連の」「通常サイズの」という意味もある。

例 Gardening has become a **regular** part of her life since she moved to the countryside.

彼女が田舎に引っ越して以来、ガーデニングは定期的に行う生活の一部になった。

□□□ 0192

ability

/ əbíləti /

形 able 能力がある

名 **a skill that you have to do something**

能力

〈abl（できる）+-ity（状態）〉

例 A writer must have the **ability** to interest their readers.

物書きは読者の関心を引く能力を持っていなければならない。

0193

central

/ séntrəl /

名 center 中心
動 centralize 〜を中央に集める

形 ① being in the middle of a place

中心の、中央の

例 Aichi Prefecture is located in **central** Japan.

愛知県は日本の中部に位置している。

② most important or main

中心的な、主要な

≒ major

⇔ minor

例 The movie's **central** character is a nurse named Sue.

その映画の中心人物はスーという名前の看護師だ。

0194

environment

/ ɪnváɪərənmənt /

形 environmental 環境の、環境的な
副 environmentally 環境的に

名 the natural world and everything natural that is in it

環境

〈environ（取り囲まれた）+ -ment（名詞）〉

例 Plastic and other things made from oil are very bad for the **environment**.

プラスチックなど石油から作られたものは環境にとても悪い。

0195

excellent

/ éksələnt /

動 excel 秀でている
名 excellence 優秀さ

形 very good

優秀な、素晴らしい

≒ wonderful

〈ex-(外に)+cel(l)(そびえる)+ -ent（形容詞）〉

例 The soup your mother makes is **excellent**.

あなたのお母さんの作るスープは絶品です。

0196

tool

/ tú:l /

名 **something used to do something**

道具

ⓘ「ツール」はカタカナ語にもなっている。

例 The paint brush is an important **tool** for painters.

絵筆は画家にとって重要な道具だ。

0197

medical

/ médɪkl /

名 medicine 医学；医薬

形 **relating to the treatment of diseases, injuries, etc.**

医学の

〈med(i)(癒す)+-cal(形容詞)〉

例 High **medical** bills cause problems for many people in that country.

その国では高額な医療費が多くの人々に問題をもたらしている。

0198

complete

/ kəmplí:t /

副 completely 完全に
名 completion 完成

動 **to finish something**

～を完成させる

〈com-(完全に)+plete(満たす)〉

例 Jenny **completed** her essay after hours of work.

ジェニーは何時間も作業してエッセイを完成させた。

形 **including everything that is needed**

完全な、全部そろった

⇔ incomplete

ⓘ「完成した」という意味もある。

例 The child has a **complete** train set.

その子どもは電車の全セットを持っていた。

 0199

degree

/ dɪgríː /

名 ① **a level of something that can be compared to another level**

程度、度合い

ⓘ 温度や角度の「度」も表す。

例 That teacher has had a high **degree** of success in teaching her students about world history.

その教師は生徒たちに世界史を教えることにおいて高い度合いで成功してきた。

② **an official paper and title given to someone who has finished all the needed classes in a specific subject at a university**

学位

例 Greg finished his **degree** in computer science five years ago.

グレッグは5年前にコンピュータサイエンスで学位を修了した。

□□□ 0200

count

/ káʊnt /

動 ① **to add people or things together to figure out the total**

～を数える

ⓘ「～するもの」を意味する-erがついたのがcounter（カウンター；計数器）。

例 The man **counted** his money three times before giving it to the cashier.

その男性はレジ係に渡す前に3回お金を数えた。

② **to be important or have value**

重要である

例 Every vote **counts** in the elections for class president.

学級委員長を決める選挙では、一票一票が重要性を持つ。

章末ボキャブラリーチェック

次の語義が表す英単語を答えてください。

語義	解答	連番
❶ doing things that require energy and physical movement	active	0142
❷ of, relating to, or affecting most people, places, or things	general	0190
❸ a group of people that live together with shared laws and values	society	0170
❹ to get ready for something	prepare	0106
❺ the most liked	favorite	0111
❻ a skill that you have to do something	ability	0192
❼ having a high price	expensive	0134
❽ a person or animal that has finished growing	adult	0157
❾ to make another version of something that is the same or almost the same as the original thing	copy	0185
❿ to make something new	create	0133
⓫ money that people must pay to the government based on their income, property, purchases, etc.	tax	0187
⓬ the state of something that exists	condition	0126
⓭ the trip you make on an airplane, or the airplane making the trip	flight	0178
⓮ a planned piece of work that usually takes a long time	project	0135
⓯ something that you think of in your mind	thought	0119
⓰ how good or bad an object is	quality	0147
⓱ something used to do something	tool	0196
⓲ able to be done	possible	0113
⓳ to make something better, or to become better	improve	0145
⓴ to make someone or something do what you want	control	0109
㉑ to keep someone or something safe	protect	0115

語義	解答	連番
㉒ to make something	produce	0151
㉓ something that is used to make something else	material	0130
㉔ to finish something	complete	0198
㉕ relating to an individual person or their private feelings	personal	0155
㉖ a spoken or written opinion about someone or something	comment	0180
㉗ allowed to be used by anyone (usually supported by the government)	public	0120
㉘ several different or many different	various	0181
㉙ to follow someone or something and find them using what they have left behind	track	0122
㉚ to add something to something else to make it full	fill	0128
㉛ happening often at the same time or in the same way	regular	0191
㉜ to increase in number or level	rise	0136
㉝ a level of something that can be compared to another level	degree	0199
㉞ being important or possibly dangerous	serious	0131
㉟ official rules that say how things are to be done	policy	0161
㊱ to become aware of something or someone	notice	0149
㊲ the natural world and everything natural that is in it	environment	0194
㊳ the feeling of something hurting (physically or emotionally)	pain	0179
㊴ the job that someone has within an activity or situation	role	0124
㊵ an emotion that you feel and know you have	sense	0144
㊶ something that you give to a person or a group	gift	0150
㊷ a type of something	form	0105
㊸ to be curious about something and think about it	wonder	0171
㊹ a sickness that a person or an animal has, especially one that cannot be made better easily	disease	0166

語義	解答	連番
㊺ all the cars, trucks, or motorcycles that are driving in an area at a certain time	traffic	0175
㊻ an action that is done to practice and get better at doing something	exercise	0188
㊼ to add people or things together to figure out the total	count	0200
㊽ the idea or feelings that you have about someone or something	image	0116
㊾ to gather things and keep them together, sometimes as a hobby	collect	0189
㊿ to get or make something bigger in size or number	increase	0184
51 not unusual or strange	normal	0182
52 very good	excellent	0195
53 to go well with something because of specific traits	match	0172
54 to do something (that requires training or skill)	perform	0129
55 information about something or someone that is specific or precise	detail	0186
56 a number that represents a particular amount	figure	0103
57 the reason for or aim of something being done	purpose	0104
58 something that you can do because you practiced or trained	skill	0165
59 the change that results when something is done or happens	effect	0114
60 the place where legal meetings about crimes are held, and the events of such meetings	court	0173
61 in a time that was not long ago	recently	0146
62 to think or say that something might be true although you are not sure	guess	0167
63 including only one person or thing	single	0174
64 to give someone a chance to accept something or say that you will do something	offer	0143
65 what you think about something	opinion	0154
66 relating to current time or a time in the recent past	modern	0176

語義	解答	連番
67 to have someone or something as part of a group	include	0141
68 the act of moving something or someone	movement	0123
69 to put something or someone in a higher place or position	raise	0117
70 all of the beliefs, customs, arts, and so on of a particular society, group, or time period	culture	0110
71 being in the middle of a place	central	0193
72 almost the same as another person or thing	similar	0125
73 very important	major	0148
74 relating to the treatment of diseases, injuries, etc.	medical	0197
75 to put a part of your body, such as your hand, on someone or something	touch	0102
76 to harm or cause problems for something	damage	0112
77 to give someone permission to do something, or to let something happen	allow	0137
78 what is being talked about	subject	0121
79 to have a specific flavor	taste	0140
80 the amount of money needed to buy or pay for something	cost	0168
81 a word or phrase that is used as the name of something specific	term	0169
82 a meeting or course where students are taught something	class	0163
83 to put something in a place where others can see it	display	0153
84 someone who receives medical care	patient	0183
85 someone who buys something from a business	customer	0108
86 the job that you hold at an organization	position	0159
87 a competition in which people try to win by doing something better than others	contest	0164
88 to not change or be changed	remain	0139
89 the written words and numbers that show the location of a person's home, workplace, etc.	address	0132

語義	解答	連番
⑳ to talk or think about what is similar or different between people or things	compare	0152
㉑ the series of actions that produce a result	process	0138
㉒ to use something together with other people	share	0107
㉓ a quantity of something	amount	0118
㉔ something that is done to get information about something	research	0127
㉕ the number of times something happens or is done within a period of time	rate	0162
㉖ to think that something is probably going to happen or someone is going to arrive	expect	0160
㉗ in place of another thing or person	instead	0130
㉘ to tell your name or someone else's to another person	introduce	0158
㉙ to give someone a feeling caused by something unexpected or unusual	surprise	0177
⑩⓪ involving the whole world	global	0101

Stage 3

Practice makes perfect.
継続は力なり。

□□□ 0201

custom

/ kʌ́stəm /

形 customary 習慣的な

名 **a common or traditional action or behavior that is done by the people in a particular group or place**

慣習

ⓘ customsと複数形で「税関」も意味する。

例 It is the **custom** in India for brides to wear red on their wedding day.

結婚式の日に花嫁が赤い服を身につけるのはインドの慣習だ。

□□□ 0202

tie

/ táɪ /

動 **to wrap something around itself so that it stays in place or attached to something else**

〈ひもなど〉を結ぶ、結びつける

ⓘ 現在分詞はtying。「ネクタイ」もtieと言う。

例 They **tied** a rope around the tree, then tried to pull it out.

彼らは木にロープを結びつけ、そして引き抜こうとした。

□□□ 0203

hurt

/ hə́ːrt /

動 ① **to injure or cause pain to yourself, someone else, or a part of your body**

～を傷つける、痛める

ⓘ hurt-hurt-hurtと活用する。

例 Betty **hurt** her back carrying the groceries to the car.

ベティーは車に食料品を運んでいて背中を痛めた。

② **to be the origin or cause of pain**

痛む

例 His teeth **hurt** whenever he eats cold food.

彼は冷たい食べ物を食べるといつも歯が痛む。

0204

fair

/ féər /

名 **a large event where things are sold or information is provided**

博覧会

例 A book **fair** is held at the school every spring.

その学校では毎年春にブックフェアが開かれる。

形 **treating people equally**

公平な

⇔ unfair

例 Not being allowed to do something because you are a girl is not **fair**.

女の子だからという理由で何かをさせてもらえないのは、公平ではない。

0205

reduce

/ rɪd(j)úːs /

名 reduction 削減

動 **to make something smaller in size, number, etc.**

～を減らす

≒ decrease

⇔ increase

〈re- (元へ) +duce (導く)〉

例 The family **reduced** the amount of money they spent by eating out less.

その家族は、外食を減らすことで使うお金の量を減らした。

0206

method

/ méθəd /

形 methodical 秩序立った

名 **the way something is done**

方法

≒ approach

例 There are many **methods** that can be used to learn a new language.

新しい言語を学ぶのに使える方法はたくさんある。

□□□ 0207

fat

/ fǽt /

㊊ fatty 脂肪の多い

形 having a lot of extra flesh on your body

太った

⇔ thin

ⓘ 直接的でぶしつけな語なので、他人についてはoverweight（肥満の）などを使うのが無難。

例 The vet told the man he had let his dog get too **fat**.

獣医は男性に犬を太らせすぎだと言った。

名 the thing on the body of people and animals that keeps them warm and is where extra energy is stored

脂肪

例 You must watch what you eat and exercise regularly to burn **fat**.

脂肪を燃やすには、食べるものに注意して定期的に運動しなければならない。

□□□ 0208

object

/ 名 ɑ́:bʤɪkt 動 əbʤékt /

名 objection 反対
形 objective 客観的な

名 something that you can see and touch but is not living

もの、物体

ⓘ UFOはUnidentified Flying Object（未確認飛行物体）の略。

〈ob-（～に対して）+ject（投げる）〉

例 The man likes to collect **objects** that are small and yellow.

その男性は小さくて黄色いものを集めるのが好きだ。

動 to not agree with someone or something

反対する

≒ disagree

例 The children **objected** loudly when their mother told them it was time for bed.

寝る時間だと母親が言うと、子どもたちは大声で異議を唱えた。

□□□ 0209

force

/ fɔ́ːrs /

動 **to make someone or something do something even though they do not want to do it**

無理に～させる

例 The people in the factory were **forced** to work 15 hours per day.

その工場の人々は1日15時間労働を強制されていた。

名 ① **the power or physical strength of something or someone**

力

例 Scientists use various tools to measure the **force** of the wind during storms.

科学者たちは、嵐の間、風力を計測するためにさまざまな道具を使う。

② **a group of soldiers meant to fight in a war**

軍隊

i 「集団、一団」の意味もあり、labor force（全従業員）のように使う。

例 The woman belongs to the Air **Force**.

その女性は空軍に所属している。

□□□ 0210

provide

/ prəváɪd /

接 provided ～でさえあれば

動 **to give or do something that is wanted or needed by others**

～を提供する、供給する

i 〈provide A for B〉〈provide B with A〉（AをBに供給する）いずれの構文も重要。

〈pro-（前もって）+vide（見る）〉

例 The city **provides** translation services to foreign residents.

その市は、外国人の住民向けに翻訳サービスを提供している。

0210語

0211

direction

/ dərékʃən /

動 direct ～に指図する

名 ① **the way that something or someone is moving or facing**

方向

〈di-（離れて）+rect（真っすぐな）+-ion（名詞）〉

例 You can see far in all **directions** from the top of the mountain.

その山の頂上からはどの方向でも遠くを見渡せる。

② **something that tells someone what to do or how to do something**

指示、説明

≒ instruction

例 There are **directions** on the back of the package showing how to cook the noodles.

パッケージの裏に麺の調理法を示す指示がある。

0212

likely

/ láɪkli /

名 likelihood 可能性

形 **《likely to *do*》 showing that something will probably happen or be done**

～しそうだ

⇔ unlikely

例 School is **likely to** be canceled tomorrow if it snows a lot tonight.

今夜たくさん雪が降ったら、明日は学校が休校になりそうだ。

0213

community

/ kəmjúːnəti /

名 **a group of people who live in the same area or share interests or beliefs**

地域社会、共同体

〈commun(共通の)+-ity(名詞)〉

例 The **community** holds a small beer festival every year.

その地域では、毎年小さなビール祭りを開いている。

□□□ 0214

suffer
/ sʌ́fər /

動 ① **to feel pain or deal with illness or injury** — 苦しむ、患う

ⓘ suffer from（〜に苦しむ、〜を患う）の形で押さえておこう。

🔑〈suf-（下で）+fer（耐える）〉

例 Her grandfather **suffers** from skin cancer.
彼女の祖父は皮膚がんを患っている。

② **to experience something that makes you feel bad** — 〈嫌なこと〉を経験する

例 They **suffered** the loss of their parents when they were very young.
彼らはとても幼いときに両親を亡くした。

□□□ 0215

grade
/ gréɪd /

名 ① **a number or letter that shows how well someone did on a test or in a class** — 成績

ⓘ「成績表、通信簿」はアメリカ英語ではreport card、イギリス英語ではreportと言う。

例 Harry has the best **grades** in the class.
ハリーはクラスで最高の成績を取っている。

② **one of the levels of study in a school completed by students of a similar age** — 学年

ⓘ アメリカ英語の用法。イギリス英語ではyearを使う。
例：She is in year seven.

例 She is in the seventh **grade**.
彼女は7年生だ。

0216

announce

/ ənáʊns /

名 announcement 発表

動 **to tell people about something officially or publicly**

〜を発表する

〈an-(〜に)+nounce(伝える)〉

例 The marriage of the prince was **announced** on the news.

王子の結婚はニュースで発表された。

0217

plastic

/ plǽstɪk /

名 **a light, strong substance that can be made into many things and is used in many products**

プラスチック、ビニール

ⓘ「レジ袋」はplastic bagと言う。

例 Old toys were made out of wood or metal, not **plastic**.

古いおもちゃはプラスチックではなく、木や金属から作られていた。

0218

nation

/ néɪʃən /

形 national 国家の
名 nationality 国籍

名 ① **a large area that has its own government**

国、国家

≒ state

ⓘ「国連」はthe United Nationsと言う。

例 Many **nations** in Europe are part of the European Union.

ヨーロッパの多くの国が欧州連合に加盟している。

② **the people that live in a country**

国民

ⓘ ふつうthe nationの形で使う。

例 The **nation** celebrated the end of the war.

国民は戦争の終結を祝った。

0219

thirsty

/ θə́ːrsti /

名 thirst のどの渇き

形 **having a dry feeling in your mouth or throat because you need something to drink**

のどが渇いた

ⓘ「(～を) 渇望した」という比喩的な意味もある。

例 She was really **thirsty** after finishing her workout.

彼女は運動を終えた後とてものどが渇いていた。

0220

private

/ práɪvət /

副 privately 密かに、個人的に
名 privacy プライバシー

形 **meant to be used by one person or group and not for the public**

個人的な、私用の

ⓘ vateの発音に注意。アクセントはpriの位置。

例 The singer owns a **private** beach in the Caribbean.

その歌手はカリブ海に私用のビーチを所有している。

0221

fix

/ fíks /

動 ① **to repair something that has been broken**

～を修理する

≒ mend

例 They took their car to the mechanic to get it **fixed**.

彼らは車を修理してもらうために、修理工のところへ持っていった。

② **to attach something to another thing so that it will not move**

～を固定する

例 They **fixed** the bookshelf to the wall so that it wouldn't fall over in an earthquake.

彼らは、地震で倒れないように、本棚を壁に固定した。

□□□ 0222

asleep

/ əslíːp /

形 **being in a state of sleep**

眠って

⇔ awake

ⓘ be asleep（眠っている）、fall asleep（眠りに落ちる）のように動詞の後ろで使う。

例 The cat is **asleep** in the laundry basket.

その猫は洗濯かごの中で眠っている。

□□□ 0223

earn

/ ə́ːrn /

動 **to get something, especially money, because of something that you have done, such as a job**

～を得る、稼ぐ

ⓘ He earned the promotion.（彼は昇進を手に入れた）のような使い方もある。

例 That woman **earns** a very large salary.

その女性はとても高い給料を稼いでいる。

□□□ 0224

shoot

/ ʃúːt /

名 shot 発射、発砲

動 ① **to make something come out of a weapon and move toward something**

～を撃つ

ⓘ shoot-shot-shotと活用する。「（ゴールに）シュートする」という意味もあるが、名詞の「シュート」はshotと言う。

例 The hunter **shot** the bear before it could hurt him

漁師はクマが彼を傷つける前にクマを撃った。

② **to film or take pictures of something**

～を撮影する

例 A lot of movies are **shot** in Toronto instead of New York because it is cheaper.

その方が安いので、多くの映画がニューヨークではなくトロントで撮影されている。

□□□ 0225

medicine

/ médəsn /

形 medical 医学の

名 **something that you eat or drink to help deal with a sickness**

薬

≒ drug, medication

ⓘ 「薬を飲む」はtake medicineで、drink medicineではない。「医学」という意味もある。

例 He has to take **medicine** every morning and every night.

彼は毎日朝と晩に薬を飲まなければならない。

□□□ 0226

describe

/ dɪskráɪb /

名 description 描写

動 **to tell someone what something is like**

～を描写する

〈de-（下に）+scribe（書く）〉

例 He **described** his future plans in perfect detail.

彼は将来の計画を完全に細かいところまで描写した。

□□□ 0227

lay

/ léɪ /

動 ① **to gently put someone or something down on a surface**

～を置く、横たえる

ⓘ lay-laid-laidと活用する。「横たわる」はlie。

例 She **laid** her book on the table and looked out the window.

彼女はテーブルに本を置いて、窓の外を眺めた。

② **to produce and push an egg out of the body**

〈卵〉を産む

例 That type of chicken only **lays** brown eggs.

その種類のニワトリは茶色い卵しか産まない。

0227語

□□□ 0228

circle

/ sə́ːrkl /

形 circular 円形の

名 **a shape that is (perfectly) round**

円、円周

ⓘ 「～に丸をつける」という意味の動詞もある。「同好会、サークル」はclubと言う。

〈circ (円) +-le (指小辞)〉

例 The little girl drew a **circle** in the sand with a stick.

その小さな女の子は棒で砂に円を描いた。

□□□ 0229

government

/ gʌ́vərnmənt /

動 govern ～を統治する
名 governmental 政府の

名 **the organization that makes choices for and controls a country, state, etc.**

政府

ⓘ nを入れ忘れないように注意。

例 The **government** moved quickly to save the economy.

政府は経済を救済するために迅速に動いた。

□□□ 0230

capital

/ kǽpətl /

名 ① **the city in which the government's main offices are located**

首都

ⓘ アメリカなどの州の「州都」にも使う。

〈capit (頭の) +-al (形容詞)〉

例 Tokyo is the **capital** of Japan.

東京は日本の首都だ。

② **the money that is used to start or run a business, or the money, property, and so on that a person or business owns**

資本

例 Sadly, the woman didn't have enough **capital** to start her own business.

残念ながら、その女性は自分の事業を立ち上げるのに十分な資本がなかった。

□□□ 0231

hunger

/ hʌ́ŋgər /

形 hungry 空腹の

名 **the feeling in your stomach that you get when you need to eat**

空腹

ⓘ hanger（ハンガー、吊るすもの）と混同しないように注意。

例 His **hunger** was not satisfied even after he ate lunch.

彼の空腹は昼食を食べた後も満たされなかった。

□□□ 0232

flat

/ flǽt /

動 flatten ～を平らにする

形 **having no bumps and a level surface**

平らな

≒ even

ⓘ have a flat tire（パンクする）という表現も覚えておこう。

例 A large and **flat** area is needed to put up a swimming pool.

プールを設置するには広くて平らな場所が必要だ。

□□□ 0233

separate

/ 動 sépərèɪt 形 sépərət /

副 separately 別々に
名 separation 分離

動 **to divide people or things to keep them away from each other**

～を分離する

⇔ mix

ⓘ アクセントはseの位置。

〈se-（離れて）+par（準備する）+-ate（動・形）〉

例 You must **separate** the egg white from the yolk to make this recipe.

この料理を作るには卵の白身と黄身を分けなければならない。

0233語

形 **not kept together**

別々の

≒ different

例 The university is made up of seven **separate** buildings.

その大学は7棟の別々の建物から成っている。

□□□ 0234

audience

/ ɔ́:diəns /

名 **the people who gather to watch or listen to something**

観客、聴衆

ⓘ「たくさんの観客」は many audience ではなく large audience と言う。

🔑〈audi（聞く）+-ence（名詞）〉

例 The **audience** was quiet while they waited for the play to start.

聴衆は公演が始まるのを待っている間、静かだった。

□□□ 0235

deal

/ dí:l /

名 dealer 販売店、ディーラー

名 **an agreement between multiple people or groups that benefits all of them in some way**

取引

ⓘ deal with（～を扱う）という動詞の表現も覚えておこう。

例 She made a **deal** with her husband that he would cook dinner every weekend.

彼女は夫との間で、週末は彼が夕飯を作ると取り決めた。

□□□ 0236

approach

/ əpróutʃ /

動 **to move toward or get closer to someone or something**

～に近づく

ⓘ 他動詞であることに注意。

🔑〈ap-（～に）+proach（近く）〉

例 The cat **approached** the dog from behind and bit his tail.

猫は後ろから犬に近づき、そのしっぽをかんだ。

名 **a way of doing something**

（問題などへの）取り組み方

例 A more direct **approach** is needed to solve this problem.

この問題を解決するためには、より直接的な取り組みが必要だ。

□□□ 0237

spirit

/ spírət /

形 spiritual 精神の

名 ① **the non-physical part of a person that is believed to give them life, energy, and power**

精神

ⓘ spirは「息」を意味する語根で、aspire（～を熱望する）、expire（期限が切れる、息を引き取る）、perspire（汗をかく）なども同語源語。

例 Some religions believe that a **spirit** can be reborn into many different bodies.

霊魂は多くの異なる肉体の中に生まれ変わることができると考える宗教もある。

② **the feeling that someone has about something**

気分、機嫌

例 Learning that the concert was canceled put the girl in low **spirits**.

コンサートが中止されたと知り、その女の子は意気消沈した。

□□□ 0238

exactly

/ ɪgzǽktli /

形 exact 正確な

副 **used to show that something is completely accurate**

正確に、ちょうど

例 The piece of wood was **exactly** 50 centimeters long.

その木片は長さがちょうど50センチだった。

□□□ 0239

range

/ réɪnʤ /

名 **the upper and lower limits of something**

範囲、幅

例 The orchestra has many members in the 20 to 30 age **range**.

そのオーケストラには20歳から30歳の年齢層のメンバーがたくさんいる。

0240

bright

/ bráɪt /

副 brightly 明るく
名 brightness 明るさ

形 ① being full of and making a lot of light 明るい

⇔ dark

例 A **bright** and sunny day is perfect for going for a walk.
明るい晴れた日は散歩に行くのにぴったりだ。

② able to learn things quickly 利口な

≒ intelligent, smart, clever

例 Going to the store during a typhoon isn't very **bright**.
台風のさなかにその店に行くというのはあまり利口ではない。

0241

unique

/ ju(:)ní:k /

形 different from everything or everyone else 独特の、特有の

≒ special, particular

⇔ common

〈uni（一つ）+-que（形容詞）〉

ⓘ「ユニークな」というカタカナ語にもなっているが「面白い」という意味はない。

例 The pattern on a leopard's fur is **unique**.
ヒョウの毛皮の模様は独特だ。

0242

thick

/ θík /

形 having a large area between the top and bottom or front and back of something 厚い

⇔ thin

例 Burt likes pizza with a **thick** crust.
バートは厚いクラストのピザが好きだ。

□□□ 0243

accept

/ əksépt /

名 acceptance 受け取り
形 acceptable 受け入れられる

動 **to take something that is being given to you**

〜を受け入れる

⇔ reject, refuse, decline

〈ac-（〜に）+cept（受ける）〉

例 Tina decided to **accept** the job offer she got from the company.

ティナはその会社からもらった内定を受けることに決めた。

□□□ 0244

suit

/ súːt /

形 suitable 適した

動 **to match the needs or style of someone or something**

〜に適する

≒ fit

i 「(衣服の) スーツ」「訴訟」という名詞の意味も重要。

例 Her job as an actress doesn't **suit** her personality at all.

女優の仕事は彼女の性格にまったく合っていない。

□□□ 0245

manage

/ mǽnɪʤ /

名 management 経営
名 manager 経営者、管理者

動 **① to control what happens in a business or other group**

〜を運営する、監督する

i man(u)は「手」を表す語根で、manufacture（製作）、manuscript（原稿）なども同語源語。

例 He has **managed** the baseball team for over 10 years.

彼は10年以上その野球チームの監督を務めている。

②《manage to *do*》to be able to do what you need to do with limited resources

何とか〜する

例 Even though they had no heat, the couple **managed to** make it through the winter.

暖房が何もなかったにもかかわらず、その夫婦は冬を何とかしのいだ。

0245語

□□□ 0246

item

/ áɪtəm /

名 ① **one object or part of an object**

品、商品

≒ goods

ⓘ「アイテム」はカタカナ語にもなっている。

例 This store has a wide range of **items** for sale.

この店は幅広い品物を販売している。

② **one part of the news or one piece of information**

記事

≒ article

例 There was an **item** in the newspaper yesterday about the robbery.

昨日の新聞にはその強盗事件についての記事があった。

□□□ 0247

company

/ kʌ́mpəni /

名 companion 同伴者

名 **the state or condition of being with another person or animal and not alone**

同伴、付き合い

ⓘ「会社」という意味もあるが、具体的な会社名の一部として使われる場合はCo.と略されることもある。

〈com-（共に）+pany（パンを食べる人）〉

例 Alice's dog kept her **company** while her husband was on his business trip.

アリスの犬は、彼女の夫が出張に行っている間、彼女と一緒にいた。

□□□ 0248

gentle

/ ʤéntl /

副 gently やさしく、親切に

形 **being kind and quiet**

温厚な、やさしい

例 The dog was always very **gentle** with the baby.

その犬はいつでもその赤ん坊にとてもやさしかった。

□□□ 0249

rent

/ rént /

形 rental 賃貸用の

動 ① to pay money to be able to use something that belongs to someone else

～を賃借りする

例 They were able to **rent** their apartment for cheap because it was a bit old.

そのアパートは少し古かったので、彼らは安く借りることができた。

② to let someone use something if they give you money for it

～を賃貸しする

例 The couple **rented** their spare bedroom to a college student last year.

その夫婦は昨年、空いている寝室を大学生に賃貸しした。

名 the money that is paid to use a property that you do not own

賃貸料、家賃

例 They pay their **rent** on the first of every month.

彼らは賃貸料を毎月1日に支払っている。

□□□ 0250

positive

/ pá:zətɪv /

副 positively 肯定的に、積極的に

形 thinking about things that are good

肯定的な、積極的な

≒ optimistic

⇔ negative, pessimistic

i 「有益な、ためになる」という意味もある。例：Learning a second language was a positive experience for Tom.（第2言語を学ぶことは、トムにとってためになる経験だった）

例 On the **positive** side, losing his job gave him more time to spend with his family.

肯定的に考えると、彼は仕事を失ったことで家族と過ごす時間が増えた。

0250語

□□□ 0251

charge
/ tʃá:rdʒ /

動 **to ask a customer to pay money for something they received**

～を請求する、課す

ⓘ「請求書」はbill。

例 That lawyer **charges** 60 dollars per hour for his work.

その弁護士は自分の業務1時間につき60ドルを請求する。

名 **the money that is paid or requested for a service**

料金

例 Businesses pay a monthly **charge** to use the project management software.

企業はプロジェクト管理ソフトを使うのに月々の料金を支払っている。

□□□ 0252

particular
/ pərtíkjələr /

副 particularly 特に、とりわけ

形 **referring to a specific person or thing instead of someone or something else**

特定の

ⓘ アクセントはtiの位置。in particular（特に）という表現も覚えておこう。

例 In this region, most rain falls during a **particular** time of year.

この地域では、1年の特定の時期に雨の大半が降る。

□□□ 0253

situation
/ sìtʃuéɪʃən /

形 situated 位置している

名 **all of the facts, conditions, and events affecting someone or something**

状況

ⓘ「シチュエーション」というカタカナ語にもなっている。「（特定のものの）状況」はconditionと言う。

例 His **situation** has improved since he found a new job.

新しい仕事を見つけてから、彼の状況は上向いた。

□□□ 0254

measure

/ méʒər /

名 measurement 測定

動 **to find out how big or small something is**

～を測定する

ⓘ major（主要な）と混同しないように注意。

例 The girl **measured** the milk before adding it to the bowl.

その女の子は牛乳をボウルに加える前に計量した。

名 **something that is planned or done to achieve a desirable result**

対策、手段

≒ means

ⓘ ふつう複数形で使う。

例 The city took various **measures** to strengthen the dam.

その市はダムを強化するためにさまざまな対策を講じた。

□□□ 0255

basic

/ béɪsɪk /

副 basically 基本的には
名 base 基礎、ベース

形 **being the simplest part of something**

基礎的な

⇔ advanced

〈bas（低い）+-ic（形容詞）〉

例 Only **basic** writing skills are taught in this class.

このクラスでは、基本的なライティングスキルだけを教えている。

□□□ 0256

nearly

/ níərli /

副 **not completely**

ほとんど、もう少しで

≒ almost

例 The children were **nearly** late for school because they overslept.

子どもたちは寝過ごしてしまったため、もう少しで学校に遅れるところだった。

□□□ 0257

worth

/ wə́ːrθ /

形 worthy 価値のある

前 **used to show the value that something has**

～に値する、～の価値がある

ⓘ 後ろに動詞がくるときは〈worth *doing*〉の形になる。

例 The works of that painter are **worth** millions of dollars.

その画家の作品は数百万ドルの価値がある。

□□□ 0258

yard

/ jάːrd /

名 **the area outside of your house that you own**

庭

≒ garden

ⓘ 長さの単位（ヤード）の意味もある。

例 They wanted to buy a house with a large **yard** for their children to play in.

彼らは、子どもたちが遊べる広い庭のある家を買いたかった。

□□□ 0259

site

/ sáɪt /

名 ① **a place where something is, was, or will be built**

用地

ⓘ sight（視力）と同音。

例 The construction **site** is protected by a guard at night.

その建設地は夜間、警備員によって警備されている。

② **a place on the Internet where content can be found**

（インターネット上の）サイト

例 The woman included a URL to her personal **site** on her business cards.

その女性は名刺に自分の個人ウェブサイトのURLを載せていた。

□□□ 0260

media

/ mí:diə /

名 **all of the sources of information that is provided to the public, such as television and newspapers**

メディア、媒体

ⓘ meの発音に注意。元々はmedium（中くらい、中間）の複数形。ふつうthe mediaの形で使う。

例 Bad things get the attention of the **media** more easily than good things.

よいことよりも悪いことの方がメディアの注目を集めやすい。

□□□ 0261

clothes

/ klóʊz /

名 **the things you wear on your body to cover it**

服

≒ clothing

ⓘ 漠然と「衣服」を表す語で、複数扱い。close（～を閉める）と同音。

例 Gary likes to wear bright yellow **clothes**.

ゲリーは明るい黄色の服を着るのが好きだ。

□□□ 0262

express

/ ıksprés /

名 expression 表現

動 **to share your thoughts or feelings by speaking or writing**

〈考え・気持ちなど〉を表す

〈ex-(外に)+press(押し出す)〉

例 She **expressed** an interest in buying the car.

彼女はその車を買うことについて関心を示した。

形 **moving quickly and without many stops**

急行の

例 The **express** train is almost always more crowded than the local train.

急行電車は、ほとんどいつも各駅停車の電車よりも混んでいる。

□□□ 0263

fashion

/ fǽʃən /

形 fashionable 流行の

名 ① the way of dressing that is popular at a certain time among certain people

流行、ファッション

≒ trend

例 Platform shoes were in **fashion** in the 1990's.

厚底靴は1990年代に流行した。

② a specific way of acting

方法

≒ manner

例 The fans were asked to line up in an orderly **fashion**.

ファンたちは整然と並んでほしいと言われた。

□□□ 0264

connect

/ kənékt /

名 connection つながり、関連

動 to join two or more things together

〜をつなぐ

i 〈connect A with [to] B〉(AとBをつなぐ)の形で押さえておこう。

例 The village is **connected** to the city by a single road.

その村は市へ1本の道でつながっている。

□□□ 0265

shy

/ ʃáɪ /

副 shyly 恥ずかしそうに
名 shyness 内気さ

形 feeling nervous about talking to and meeting other people, especially people that you do not know

内気な、恥ずかしがりの

i 「おとなしい」はquiet。

例 She is **shy**, so she had trouble making friends at her new school.

彼女は内気なので、新しい学校で友だちを作るのに苦労した。

□□□ 0266

stick

/ stɪ́k /

名 sticker ステッカー
形 sticky 粘着性の

動 to be on something or someone and not come off easily

くっつく

ⓘ stick-stuck-stuckと活用する。get stuck in traffic（交通渋滞に捕まる）という表現も覚えておこう。

例 The baby has rice **stuck** to his fingers.

その赤ちゃんは指にごはんがくっついている。

名 a long and thin object that is used for something

棒

例 Using a walking **stick** can help hikers keep their balance.

つえを使うと、ハイカーはバランスを保ちやすくなる。

□□□ 0267

staff

/ stǽf /

名 people who work for an organization or business

職員、スタッフ

ⓘ 集合的に「スタッフ」を表す。「スタッフ一人」を表すときには a staff memberと言う。

例 The entire **staff** was given a large bonus at the end of the year for their hard work.

熱心な仕事ぶりに対し、年末に全職員に多額のボーナスが支給された。

□□□ 0268

prevent

/ prɪvént /

名 prevention 防止
形 preventive 予防の

動 to keep something from happening

～を防ぐ、妨げる

ⓘ 〈prevent A from *doing*〉（Aが～しないようにする）の形で押さえておこう。

〈pre-（前に）+vent（来る）〉

例 Washing your hands helps **prevent** you from getting sick.

手を洗うことは、病気を防ぐのに役立つ。

0268語

□□□ 0269

marry

/ mǽri /

名 marriage 結婚
形 married 既婚の

動 to become the husband or wife of someone by law

～と結婚する

ⓘ marry withとしないように注意。get married（結婚する）という表現も覚えておこう。例：Her parents got married 20 years ago.（彼女の両親は20年前に結婚した）

例 He didn't have the courage to ask Meg to **marry** him.

彼にはメグに結婚を申し込む勇気がなかった。

□□□ 0270

solve

/ sɑ́ːlv /

名 solution 解決

動 to figure out the answer to a problem

～を解く、解決する

例 Ben likes to **solve** math problems.

ベンは数学の問題を解くのが好きだ。

□□□ 0271

official

/ əfíʃəl /

副 officially 公式に

形 being done in a public and often formal way

公式の

⇔ unofficial

ⓘ アクセントはfiの位置。

例 The **official** opening of the new train station was held on Saturday.

新しい駅の公式の開業式が土曜日に執り行われた。

名 a person who works in an important position in an organization or government

（組織の）職員；公務員

例 A city **official** secretly shared information with a journalist.

市の公務員がジャーナリストに情報をこっそり教えた。

□□□ 0272

treat

/ triːt /

㊔ treatment 治療

動 ① **to think about, deal with, or act toward someone or something in a particular way**

～を扱う

例 His grandmother **treats** everyone with kindness and respect.

彼の祖母は誰に対してもやさしさと敬意をもって接する。

② **to help someone or something with a medical problem**

～を治療する

≒ cure

例 The woman had to get her cat **treated** for fleas.

その女性は飼い猫にノミの治療を受けさせなければならなかった。

③ **to pay for something for someone else**

～におごる、ごちそうする

ⓘ「おごり、ごちそう」という名詞の意味もある。ハロウィンのときに子どもが言うTrick or treat.（お菓子をくれないといたずらするぞ）はこの意味の使い方。

例 Her father **treated** her to an expensive dinner.

彼女の父は彼女に高級なディナーをごちそうした。

□□□ 0273

depend

/ dɪpénd /

形 dependent 依存した
名 dependence 依存

動 **to need the help or support of someone or something**

頼る、依存する

ⓘ depend on [upon]（～に頼る）の形で押さえておこう。

〈de-（下へ）+pend（ぶら下がる）〉

例 She **depends** on her parents to help look after her kids.

彼女は両親に頼って自分の子どもたちの面倒を見るのを助けてもらっている。

□□□ 0274

issue

/ íʃuː /

名 ① **a problem or important thing that people are talking or thinking about**

問題

例 **Issues** of public health are always talked about during elections.

公衆衛生の問題は選挙中にいつも議論される。

② **one of a regular series of newspapers, magazines, etc. that is published at a particular time**

（新聞の）版、（雑誌の）号

例 The newest **issue** of that magazine was published last week.

その雑誌の最新号は先週刊行された。

動 **to officially give something to someone**

～を出す、発行する

例 The bank **issued** the woman a new credit card after she lost hers.

その女性がクレジットカードを紛失した後、銀行は彼女に新しいカードを発行した。

□□□ 0275

discuss

/ dɪskʌ́s /

名 discussion 話し合い

動 **to talk about something with other people**

～について話し合う

ⓘ 他動詞である点に注意。

〈dis-（離れて）+cuss（振る）〉

例 Vicky doesn't **discuss** politics with her family.

ヴィッキーは家族と政治について話し合わない。

0276

rather

/ rǽðər /

副 ① instead of something or someone else

むしろ

ⓘ 〈rather A than B〉（BよりむしろA）、would rather *do*（むしろ～したい）の形で押さえておこう。

例 He would **rather** buy organic vegetables than regular ones.

彼は普通の野菜より、むしろ有機栽培の野菜が買いたい。

② to a certain degree

かなり

≒ quite, pretty

例 It was **rather** hot last summer.

去年の夏はかなり暑かった。

0277

deliver

/ dɪlívər /

名 delivery 配達、デリバリー

動 ① to take something somewhere for someone

～を配達する

〈de-（～から）+liver（自由にする）〉

例 Her new TV was **delivered** this morning.

彼女の新しいテレビは今朝届けられた。

② to say something to a group of people in an official or public way

〈スピーチなど〉をする

≒ address

例 The emperor **delivered** a speech to the whole country.

皇帝は国全体に向けて演説をした。

□□□ 0278

army

/ ɑ́ːrmi /

名 **a large group of soldiers that are trained to fight on land**

軍、陸軍

ⓘ 「海軍」はnavy、「空軍」はair forceと言う。

〈arm（武装した）+y（もの）〉

例 The young woman decided to join the **army** after finishing high school.

その若い女性は、高校を卒業したら軍隊に入ることに決めた。

□□□ 0279

industry

/ índəstri /

形 industrial 産業の
動 industrialize ～を産業化する

名 **the act of making things with machines and in factories**

工業、産業

ⓘ アクセントはiの位置。

例 **Industry** was promoted in the area to grow the population.

人口を増やすため、その地域では工業が促進された。

□□□ 0280

original

/ əríʤənl /

名 origin 源、起源
副 originally 元々
名 originality 独創性

形 ① **being the first to be made or exist**

元の、本来の

ⓘ ふつう名詞の前で使う。

例 The **original** TV show was more popular than the remake.

元のテレビ番組はリメイク版よりも人気があった。

② **different from other things**

独創的な

≒ creative, inventive, unique

例 That boat has a very **original** design.

あのボートはとても独創的なデザインだ。

□□□ 0281

trade

/ tréɪd /

名 trader 商人、貿易業者

名 **the act of buying, selling, or exchanging things or services**

取引、貿易

例 **Trade** has stopped between the two countries because of a disagreement.

意見の相違のため、両国間の貿易は止まっている。

動 **to give something to someone so that they will give you something in return**

～を取引する、交換する

例 The boys **traded** Pokémon cards.

その男の子たちはポケモンのカードを交換した。

□□□ 0282

impact

/ ímpækt /

名 ① **a powerful effect or influence that something has on someone or something else**

影響

〈im-（反対に）+pact（固定する）〉

例 That book had a huge **impact** on the man's way of thinking.

その本はその男性の考え方に大きな影響を与えた。

② **the force that is released when one thing hits another thing**

衝撃

例 The glass broke on **impact** with the counter.

グラスはカウンターにぶつかった衝撃で割れた。

□□□ 0283

mention

/ ménʃən /

動 **to briefly talk or write about someone or something**

～に言及する

≒ refer to

〈ment(思い出す)+-ion(こと)〉

ⓘ 他動詞である点に注意。

例 That event was **mentioned** on TV this morning.

そのイベントは今朝テレビで言及された。

□□□ 0284

immediately

/ ɪmíːdiətli /

形 immediate 即座の

副 **without any delay**

すぐに、ただちに

≒ instantly

〈im- (否定) +mediate (介在する) +-ly (副詞)〉

例 The reason why the child was crying was not **immediately** clear.

その子が泣いていた理由はすぐにはわからなかった。

□□□ 0285

edge

/ éʤ /

名 **① the part of something where it starts or ends**

端、へり

ⓘ スキーやスケートの「エッジ」もこのedge。

例 The **edge** of the paper was torn.

その紙の端は破れていた。

② the part of something, such as a sword or knife, that cuts

刃

例 The **edge** of the knife was too dull to cut the meat.

そのナイフの刃はあまりにも切れ味が鈍っていて肉が切れなかった。

□□□ 0286

meaning

/ míːnɪŋ /

動 mean ～を意味する

名 **the idea that a word, phrase, etc. represents**

意味

例 The **meaning** of words can change over time.

言葉の意味は時間を経るうちに変わることがある。

□□□ 0287

knowledge

/ náːlɪʤ /

動 know ～を知っている
形 knowledgeable 精通している

名 **information or understanding of something that you have learned**

知識

ⓘ knowの発音に注意。

例 He gained **knowledge** of French by taking lessons.

彼はレッスンを受けてフランス語の知識を得た。

□□□ 0288

repeat

/ rɪpíːt /

名 repetition 繰り返し
副 repeatedly 繰り返して、何度も

動 ① **to do something again**

～を繰り返す

〈re-（再び）+peat（求める）〉

例 By studying history, we can avoid **repeating** the mistakes of the past.

歴史を学ぶことによって、われわれは過去の過ちを繰り返すことを避けることができる。

② **to say something after having already said it**

（～を）繰り返して言う

例 She couldn't hear him well, so she asked him to **repeat** the question.

彼の言うことがよく聞こえなかったので、彼女は質問をもう一度言ってほしいと頼んだ。

□□□ 0289

fail

/ féɪl /

名 failure 失敗、落第

動 ① **to do something and have it not succeed**

～に失敗する

例 The girl **failed** her exam because she didn't study.

その女の子は勉強しなかったので試験で失敗した。

② **《fail to *do*》 to not do something that you were supposed to do**

～しない、できない

例 The man **failed to** get to his interview on time.

その男性は時間通りに面接に行くことができなかった。

□□□ 0290

hurry

/ hə́ːri /

動 **to do something quickly**

急ぐ

ⓘ「急ぐこと」という名詞の意味もあり、in a hurry（急いで）は重要。

例 The teacher **hurried** through the explanation of the formula.

教師はその公式について急ぎ足で説明した。

□□□ 0291

average

/ ǽvərɪʤ /

形 **ordinary or usual**

平均的な、標準的な

≒ common

ⓘ アクセントは語頭のaの位置。「平均」という名詞の意味もある。on average で「平均すると」という意味。

例 The **average** dog lives 10 to 13 years.

平均的な犬は10年から13年生きる。

0292

realize

/ ríːəlàɪz /

形 real 本当の
名 realization 認識；実現

動 ① to gain awareness of something

〜を悟る、〜に気づく

≒ notice

〈real（現実）+-ize（動詞）〉

ⓘ アクセントはreの位置。イギリス英語ではrealiseともつづる。〈realize (that)...〉（…ということに気づく）の形で押さえておこう。

例 She **realized** she had forgotten her lunch when she got to school.

彼女は学校に着いたとき、弁当を忘れたことに気づいた。

② to make something happen or become real

〜を実現する

例 The couple **realized** their dream of owning a home.

その夫婦はマイホームを持つという夢をかなえた。

0293

conversation

/ kɑ̀ːnvərséɪʃən /

形 conversational 会話体の

名 the act of talking with someone or a group of people

会話

例 He had a **conversation** with his parents about what university he wanted to go to.

彼はどの大学に行きたいか、両親と話をした。

0294

responsible

/ rɪspɑ́ːnsəbl /

名 responsibility 責任

形 being expected to do or in charge of doing a particular job or task

責任のある

ⓘ be responsible for（〜に責任を負っている）の形で押さえておこう。「信頼できる」という意味もある。例：She is a responsible young woman, so she is allowed to borrow the family car.（彼女は信頼のおける若い女性で、家族の車を借りるのを許されている）

〈respons（答える）+-ible（できる）〉

例 Susie is **responsible** for looking after the family dog.

スージーは家の犬の世話をする責任を負っている。

□□□ 0295

consider

/ kənsídər /

名 consideration 熟考
形 considerable かなりの
形 considerate 思いやりのある

動 ① to think about something so that you can make a decision about it

～を考慮する

ⓘ アクセントはsiの位置。

例 She **considered** changing jobs to get more free time but decided not to.

彼女はもっと自由な時間を持てるように転職することを考えたが、そうしないことにした。

② to think about something or someone in a specific way

～だと見なす

例 The Beatles are **considered** to be one of the best bands of all time.

ビートルズは史上最高のバンドの一つだと見なされている。

□□□ 0296

path

/ pǽθ /

名 a track that is made by people or made naturally when people or animals walk somewhere a lot

道、小道

≒ way

例 There are several **paths** that lead to the top of the mountain.

その山の頂上へつながっている道がいくつかある。

□□□ 0297

strength

/ stréŋkθ /

形 strong 強い
動 strengthen ～を強化する、補強する

名 the state of being strong physically

強さ

⇔ weakness

例 Bonnie goes to the gym every week to improve the **strength** of her body.

ボニーは体の強さを鍛えるために、毎週ジムに通っている。

□□□ 0298

prove

/ prúːv /

名 proof 証拠

動 ① **to show others that something is right or real using logic**

～を証明する

ⓘ oの発音に注意。

例 There are scientists who are trying to **prove** that aliens are real.

異星人が現実のものだと証明しようとしている科学者たちがいる。

② **to turn out to be**

わかる、判明する

例 The new drug didn't **prove** to work as well as doctors thought it would.

新薬は医師たちが思ったほど効き目がないことがわかった。

□□□ 0299

technology

/ tekná:lədʒi /

形 technological 科学技術の

名 **the use of science to create new things or solve problems in new ways**

（科学）技術

ⓘ「テクノロジー」はカタカナ語にもなっている。くだけた場面ではよくtechと略される。

〈techno（技術）+logy（学）〉

例 Many companies are now using **technology** to save money.

現在、多くの企業がコストを削減するために科学技術を活用している。

□□□ 0300

opportunity

/ àːpərt(j)úːnəti /

形 opportunistic 機会をうかがう、日和見主義の

名 **a time or situation that allows for something to be done or happen**

機会

≒ chance, occasion

例 There are a lot of job **opportunities** in big cities.

都会には仕事を得る機会がたくさんある。

0300語

章末ボキャブラリーチェック

次の語義が表す英単語を答えてください。

語義	解答	連番
❶ to take something somewhere for someone	deliver	0277
❷ the things you wear on your body to cover it	clothes	0261
❸ having a lot of extra flesh on your body	fat	0207
❹ to get something, especially money, because of something that you have done, such as a job	earn	0223
❺ something that you eat or drink to help deal with a sickness	medicine	0225
❻ to find out how big or small something is	measure	0254
❼ having a dry feeling in your mouth or throat because you need something to drink	thirsty	0219
❽《------ to *do*》showing that something will probably happen or be done	likely	0212
❾ the part of something where it starts or ends	edge	0285
❿ to become the husband or wife of someone by law	marry	0269
⓫ the act of talking with someone or a group of people	conversation	0293
⓬ the area outside of your house that you own	yard	0258
⓭ the act of making things with machines and in factories	industry	0279
⓮ to take something that is being given to you	accept	0243
⓯ having no bumps and a level surface	flat	0232
⓰ to make something come out of a weapon and move toward something	shoot	0224
⓱ to pay money to be able to use something that belongs to someone else	rent	0249
⓲ to think about something so that you can make a decision about it	consider	0295
⓳ a time or situation that allows for something to be done or happen	opportunity	0300

語義	解答	連番
⑳ to injure or cause pain to yourself, someone else, or a part of your body	hurt	0203
㉑ one object or part of an object	item	0246
㉒ the upper and lower limits of something	range	0239
㉓ a shape that is (perfectly) round	circle	0228
㉔ being in a state of sleep	asleep	0222
㉕ to join two or more things together	connect	0264
㉖ being the simplest part of something	basic	0255
㉗ the way that something or someone is moving or facing	direction	0211
㉘ a powerful effect or influence that something has on someone or something else	impact	0282
㉙ being expected to do or in charge of doing a particular job or task	responsible	0294
㉚ to talk about something with other people	discuss	0275
㉛ a large event where things are sold or information is provided	fair	0204
㉜ to be on something or someone and not come off easily	stick	0266
㉝ a common or traditional action or behavior that is done by the people in a particular group or place	custom	0201
㉞ the idea that a word, phrase, etc. represents	meaning	0286
㉟ a problem or important thing that people are talking or thinking about	issue	0274
㊱ referring to a specific person or thing instead of someone or something else	particular	0252
㊲ to think about, deal with, or act toward someone or something in a particular way	treat	0272
㊳ to figure out the answer to a problem	solve	0270
㊴ ordinary or usual	average	0291
㊵ a large group of soldiers that are trained to fight on land	army	0278

語義	解答	連番
㊶ a number or letter that shows how well someone did on a test or in a class	grade	0215
㊷ to give or do something that is wanted or needed by others	provide	0210
㊸ being full of and making a lot of light	bright	0240
㊹ to divide people or things to keep them away from each other	separate	0233
㊺ the non-physical part of a person that is believed to give them life, energy, and power	spirit	0237
㊻ feeling nervous about talking to and meeting other people, especially people that you do not know	shy	0265
㊼ the organization that makes choices for and controls a country, state, etc.	government	0229
㊽ to tell someone what something is like	describe	0226
㊾ being done in a public and often formal way	official	0271
㊿ all of the sources of information that is provided to the public, such as television and newspapers	media	0260
51 having a large area between the top and bottom or front and back of something	thick	0242
52 something that you can see and touch but is not living	object	0208
53 to do something and have it not succeed	fail	0289
54 a group of people who live in the same area or share interests or beliefs	community	0213
55 a place where something is, was, or will be built	site	0259
56 not completely	nearly	0256
57 to make something smaller in size, number, etc.	reduce	0205
58 to control what happens in a business or other group	manage	0245
59 to share your thoughts or feelings by speaking or writing	express	0262
60 to feel pain or deal with illness or injury	suffer	0214
61 being the first to be made or exist	original	0280

語義	解答	連番
(62) the state of being strong physically	strength	0297
(63) to match the needs or style of someone or something	suit	0211
(64) to keep something from happening	prevent	0268
(65) to gently put someone or something down on a surface	lay	0227
(66) all of the facts, conditions, and events affecting someone or something	situation	0253
(67) the way of dressing that is popular at a certain time among certain people	fashion	0263
(68) people who work for an organization or business	staff	0267
(69) being kind and quiet	gentle	0248
(70) to briefly talk or write about someone or something	mention	0283
(71) the way something is done	method	0206
(72) the feeling in your stomach that you get when you need to eat	hunger	0231
(73) to show others that something is right or real using logic	prove	0298
(74) to move toward or get closer to someone or something	approach	0236
(75) used to show the value that something has	worth	0257
(76) meant to be used by one person or group and not for the public	private	0220
(77) different from everything or everyone else	unique	0241
(78) a light, strong substance that can be made into many things and is used in many products	plastic	0217
(79) a large area that has its own government	nation	0218
(80) to do something again	repeat	0288
(81) used to show that something is completely accurate	exactly	0238
(82) the state or condition of being with another person or animal and not alone	company	0247

語義	解答	連番
⑧③ the city in which the government's main offices are located	capital	0230
⑧④ the use of science to create new things or solve problems in new ways	technology	0299
⑧⑤ the act of buying, selling, or exchanging things or services	trade	0281
⑧⑥ to repair something that has been broken	fix	0221
⑧⑦ thinking about things that are good	positive	0250
⑧⑧ to need the help or support of someone or something	depend	0273
⑧⑨ to gain awareness of something	realize	0292
⑨⓪ the people who gather to watch or listen to something	audience	0234
⑨① information or understanding of something that you have learned	knowledge	0287
⑨② to do something quickly	hurry	0290
⑨③ instead of something or someone else	rather	0276
⑨④ to tell people about something officially or publicly	announce	0216
⑨⑤ a track that is made by people or made naturally when people or animals walk somewhere a lot	path	0296
⑨⑥ without any delay	immediately	0284
⑨⑦ to ask a customer to pay money for something they received	charge	0251
⑨⑧ to make someone or something do something even though they do not want to do it	force	0209
⑨⑨ to wrap something around itself so that it stays in place or attached to something	tie	0202
⑩⓪ an agreement between multiple people or groups that benefits all of them in some way	deal	0235

Stage 4

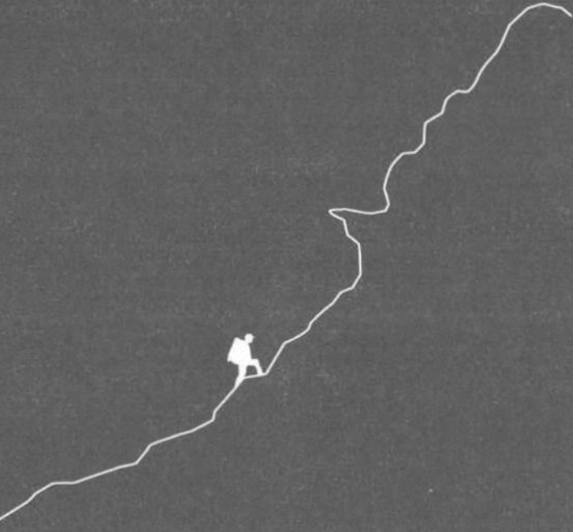

Slow and steady wins the race.
急がば回れ。

□□□ 0301

limit

/ límət /

形 limited 限られた
名 limitation 制限

動 to only allow something to be a certain size or amount

～を制限する

例 Hospital visits are **limited** to family members only.

病院へのお見舞いは家族だけに限られている。

名 the highest or lowest size or amount of something that is allowed

制限

例 The reading section of the exam has a two-hour time **limit**.

試験のリーディングセクションは2時間の時間制限がある。

□□□ 0302

select

/ səlékt /

名 selection 選択
形 selective 慎重に選ぶ

動 to choose someone or something from a group of people or things

～を選ぶ

〈se-（離れて）+lect（選ぶ）〉

例 Only five people will be **selected** to attend the conference this year.

5人だけが今年の会議の参加者に選ばれる。

□□□ 0303

series

/ síəri:z /

形 serial 連続して起きる

名 a number of things that happen or are arranged one after the other

連続、シリーズ

ⓘ アクセントはseの位置。

例 The city holds an outdoor movie **series** every summer.

その市では、毎年夏に映画の屋外上映会シリーズを開催している。

□□□ 0304

lie
/ láɪ /

動 ① to be or put yourself in a flat position
横たわる

ⓘ lie-lay-lainと活用する。同じつづりで「嘘；嘘をつく」という意味の語もあるが、その場合の活用はlie-lied-lied。「～を横たえる」はlay。

例 She found her dog **lying** asleep under the table.
彼女は飼い犬がテーブルの下で横になって寝ているのを見つけた。

② to exist or be found in a particular place
ある

例 For the company, the problem **lies** in not having enough money to hire new workers.
その会社の問題は、新たに社員を雇うだけの資金がないという点にある。

□□□ 0305

cell
/ sél /

形 cellular 細胞の

名 the smallest living part of a plant or animal
細胞

ⓘ sell（～を売る）と同音。cell phone（携帯電話）という表現も覚えておこう。

例 The human body is made up of around 37 trillion **cells**.
人体は約37兆個の細胞でできている。

0306語

□□□ 0306

quarter
/ kwɔ́ːrtər /

形 quarterly 年4回の

名 one of four equal parts of something
4分の1

ⓘ「四半期」「15分」という意味もある。「半分」はhalf、「3分の1」はone thirdと言う。

例 The four of us each had a **quarter** of the cake.
私たち4人はそれぞれケーキを4分の1食べた。

□□□ 0307

require

/ rɪkwáɪər /

名 requirement 要件
形 required 必須の

動 ① to need something

～を必要とする

〈re-（再び）+quire（求める）〉

例 Raising a child **requires** a lot of effort and patience.

子育てはかなりの努力と忍耐を必要とする。

② to make someone do something because of a law, rule, etc.

～を要求する

≒ demand

例 Tourists in Japan are **required** to carry their passports with them at all times.

日本にいる旅行者はいつでもパスポートを持ち歩くよう求められている。

□□□ 0308

burn

/ bə́ːrn /

動 to light something on fire, or to be on fire

～を燃やす；燃える

ⓘ -er（～するもの）のついたburnerは（バーナー、燃焼装置）。

例 The family **burned** the fallen leaves in their backyard.

その家族は裏庭で落ち葉を燃やした。

□□□ 0309

agent

/ éɪdʒənt /

名 a person who does business and other actions for another person

代理業者

ⓘ 映画などでは「スパイ、諜報員」の意味でも使われる。agency（代理店）は、業務や場所に重点のある語。

例 She hired a literary **agent** to help get her book published.

彼女は自著の出版を助けてもらうために著作権代理業者を雇った。

□□□ 0310

security

/ sɪkjʊ́ərəti /

形 secure 安全な

名 ① **the state of being protected or safe from something dangerous**

安全

≒ safety

例 There were strong **security** measures put in place at the concert.

そのコンサートでは強力な安全対策が実施されていた。

② **what is done to make people or places safe**

警備

例 After 9/11, **security** at airports became stricter.

9.11の後、空港での警備はより厳しくなった。

□□□ 0311

enemy

/ énəmi /

名 **someone who is against you**

敵

ⓘ スポーツの対戦相手はopponent。

〈en-（否定）+emy（友達）〉

例 He wasn't a kind man and had many **enemies** because of it.

彼は親切な男ではなく、そのせいでたくさん敵がいた。

□□□ 0312

gather

/ gǽðər /

名 gathering 集まり

動 **to come together to form a group, or to collect things or people and put them together**

集まる；～を集める

例 The children **gathered** together to play a game of baseball.

子どもたちは野球の試合をするために集まった。

0312語

□□□ 0313

huge

/ hjúːʤ /

形 **very big in size, amount, or degree**

巨大な

≒ grand

⇔ tiny

例 Most stores have **huge** sales at the end of the year.

ほとんどの店では年末に莫大な売上がある。

□□□ 0314

platform

/ plǽtfɔ̀ːrm /

名 **a raised surface that is higher than the ground and that people stand on when performing or speaking**

演壇、ステージ

ⓘ「(コンピュータの) プラットフォーム」「(駅の) プラットフォーム」の意味もある。

〈plat (平らな) +form (形)〉

例 The audience cheered when the presidential candidate stepped up onto the **platform**.

大統領の候補者が演壇に上がると聴衆は喝采を送った。

□□□ 0315

attend

/ əténd /

名 attendance 出席
名 attention 注目
形 attentive 注意深い

動 ① **to go to an event or meeting**

～に出席する、参加する

ⓘ「～を世話する」「注意を向ける」という意味もある。

〈at- (～に) +tend (伸ばす)〉

例 The professor **attends** several events about artificial intelligence every year.

その教授は毎年、人工知能に関するいくつかのイベントに参加する。

② **to go to a school or another type of organization regularly**

〈学校など〉に通う

例 His mother **attends** night classes after she finishes work.

彼の母は仕事が終わった後、夜のクラスに通っている。

0316

search

/ sə́ːrtʃ /

動 **to try to find someone or something**

（～を）探す

ⓘ search for（～を探す）の形で押さえておこう。

例 The police used dogs to **search** for the lost little boy.

警察は行方不明の男の子を探すために犬を使った。

名 **the act of trying to find someone or something (that has been lost)**

捜索、探査

例 The company began their **search** for new engineers last week.

その会社は先週、新しいエンジニア探しを始めた。

0317

balance

/ bǽləns /

名 **a state in which multiple things have or exist in equal or proper amounts**

均衡、バランス

ⓘ アクセントはbaの位置。strike a balance（バランスをとる、両立させる）という表現も覚えておこう。

例 It is important to maintain a **balance** between your family life and your work life.

家庭生活と仕事との間のバランスを維持することは重要だ。

0318

professor

/ prəfésər /

名 **a (high-ranking) teacher at a college or university**

教授

ⓘ「准教授」はassociate professorと言う。

例 Dr. Hawthorn works as a biology **professor** at the nearby university.

ホーソーン博士は近くの大学で生物学の教授として働いている。

0319

challenge / tʃǽlɪndʒ /

形 challenging (困難だが)やりがいのある

名 **a problem or task that is not easy to do**

難題、課題

ⓘ アクセントはchaの位置。

例 After getting past the **challenge** of entrance exams, she could relax.

入学試験という難題を乗り越えて、彼女はリラックスできた。

動 **to say that something is not true or legal**

～に異議を唱える

≒ dispute

ⓘ「物事に取り組んでみる」という意味の、カタカナ語の「～にチャレンジする」は英語ではtryと言う。

例 Many people have **challenged** the information that was written in that newspaper.

多くの人々がその新聞に書かれた情報に異議を唱えている。

0320

interview / íntərvjùː /

名 ① **a meeting that is held with a person who is applying for a position at an organization**

面接

ⓘ「面接官」はinterviewer、「面接を受ける人」はintervieweeと言う。

〈inter-(間に)+view(見る)〉

例 The woman wasn't late for her **interview**, but she forgot her résumé in the taxi.

その女性は面接には遅れなかったが、履歴書をタクシーに忘れてきてしまった。

② **a meeting where a reporter is asking someone else questions to use in an article**

インタビュー

例 That singer never agrees to do **interviews** with reporters.

その歌手は記者のインタビューを受けることに決して同意しない。

□□□ 0321

gain

/ géɪn /

動 ① **to get something that you want or something that is valuable**

～を得る、獲得する

≒ obtain

例 She **gained** a lot of customer service experience working in her parents' shop.

彼女は両親の店で働くことで、豊富な顧客対応の経験を得た。

② **to (gradually) get more of something**

（次第に）増える

例 This band has been **gaining** in popularity since they sang the song for that movie.

このバンドは、その映画の主題歌を歌って以来、人気を高めている。

名 **money that is earned through an activity**

利益

例 The economic **gains** for the company were large.

その会社の経済的利益は大きかった。

□□□ 0322

generation

/ ʤènəréɪʃən /

動 generate ～を生み出す

名 **people who are grouped together because they were born around the same time**

世代、同世代の人々

ⓘ「世代間の断絶、ジェネレーションギャップ」はgeneration gapと言う。

例 The **generation** of people born after World War II in the United States is called "baby boomers."

第二次世界大戦後にアメリカで生まれた世代の人々は「ベビーブーマー」と呼ばれる。

□□□ 0323

option

/ ɑ́:pʃən /

動 opt 選ぶ
形 optional 任意の

名 **something you can choose**

選択肢

≒ choice

例 There are three different dessert **options** available at the diner.

その料理店ではデザートの選択肢が3種類ある。

□□□ 0324

contain

/ kəntéɪn /

名 content 内容、中身

動 **to have something as a part**

～を含む

≒ include

〈con-（共に）+tain（保つ）〉

i 「～するもの」を意味する-erのついたcontainer（容器、コンテナ）はカタカナ語にもなっている。

例 Foods that **contain** a high amount of sugar are bad for your health.

多量の砂糖を含む食品は健康に悪い。

□□□ 0325

press

/ prés /

名 pressure 押すこと、圧力
形 pressing 緊急の

名 **newspapers, magazines, and other media organizations**

新聞、報道機関

i printing press（印刷機）から派生した意味。

例 The freedom of the **press** is in danger in many countries.

報道の自由は多くの国々で危機にさらされている。

動 **to push something (often without stopping)**

～を押す

例 The doctor told the man to **press** the button whenever he could hear the sound.

医師はその男性に、音が聞こえたときはいつでもボタンを押すように言った。

□□□ 0326

citizen

/ sítəzn /

名 ① **someone who lives in a particular place** 市民、住民

ⓘ cit/civは「市民」を意味する語根で、city（都市）、civil（市民の）、civilization（文明）なども同語源語。citizenship（市民権）という語も覚えておこう。

例 The **citizens** of that city are known for their kindness. その市の市民は親切なことで知られている。

② **someone who legally belongs to a country** 国民

例 Even if you live in Japan, if you are not a **citizen**, you aren't allowed to vote. 日本に住んでいても、国民でない限り、投票することはできない。

□□□ 0327

bill

/ bíl /

名 ① **something that says how much you have to pay for something you bought** 請求書

ⓘ a five-dollar bill（5ドル紙幣）のように「紙幣」の意味でも使われる。

例 The gas **bill** comes in the mail once per month. ガス代の請求書は月に1回郵便で届く。

② **the written information about a possible law that is being suggested** 法案

例 The **bill** was not supported by most of the politicians and didn't become a law. その法案は政治家のほとんどが賛成せず、法律にはならなかった。

□□□ 0328

accident

/ ǽksɪdənt /

形 accidental 偶然の

名 a sudden event that was not planned and that causes something bad to happen

事故

ⓘ by accident（偶然に）という表現も覚えておこう。

〈ac-（〜に）+cid（起こる）+-ent（名詞）〉

例 The roads were icy that morning, and there were a large number of car **accidents**.

その日の朝は道が凍っていて、多数の車両事故があった。

□□□ 0329

exist

/ ɪgzíst /

形 existing 現在の
名 existence 存在

動 to be real

存在する

〈ex-（外に）+ist（立たせる）〉

例 Many people research whether life **exists** on other planets.

ほかの惑星に生命が存在するのか、多くの人々が調査している。

□□□ 0330

risk

/ rísk /

形 risky 危険な

名 the chance that something bad will happen

危険（性）

例 There is always a **risk** of getting badly sunburned when you go outside in the summer.

夏に屋外へ行くときはいつもひどい日焼けをするリスクがある。

動 to do something that could have a bad result

〜を危険にさらす

例 The people **risked** everything they had to move to a new country.

その人々は新しい国に移り住むために、持っていたあらゆるものを危険にさらした。

0331

request

/ rɪkwést /

名 an act of asking someone to do or give something in a formal or polite way

依頼、要請

〈re-（再び）+quest（求める）〉

例 Her manager accepted her **request** for time off work.

部長は休暇を取りたいという彼女の要請を受け入れた。

動 to ask someone to do or give something in a formal or polite way

～を依頼する、要請する

≒ require

例 Everyone was **requested** to wear formal clothing to the party.

そのパーティーには誰もがフォーマルな服装を身につけるよう求められた。

0332

access

/ ǽkses /

形 accessible 利用できる、入手できる

名 ① the ability to enter, go near, or use something or talk with someone

利用する権利、入手できること

〈ac-（～に）+cess（行く）〉

例 The journalist couldn't get **access** to the information she needed to write the article.

そのジャーナリストは記事を書くのに必要な情報を入手できなかった。

② a way that people can get near someone or something or get to a place

（場所などへの）接近

例 The wheelchair **access** at many train stations in Tokyo is still not good.

東京の多くの駅における、車いすの使いやすさはまだ不十分だ。

□□□ 0333

fee

/ fíː /

名 ① **money that must be paid to use or do something**

料金、手数料

ⓘ 運賃はfare。

例 The admission **fee** to the concert is 50 dollars.

そのコンサートの入場料は50ドルだ。

② **money that you must pay for work done by others (especially doctors and lawyers)**

(医者・弁護士などへの)報酬

例 There are a lot of people in that country who cannot pay hospital **fees**.

その国には入院費を払えない人たちがたくさんいる。

□□□ 0334

relate

/ rɪléɪt /

名 relation 関係、関連
名 relationship 間柄

動 **to show or make a connection between different things**

～を関係づける

ⓘ 〈relate A to B〉(AをBに関連づける)の形で押さえておこう。

例 His stomachache was **related** to the ice cream he ate for lunch.

彼の腹痛は、昼食に食べたアイスクリームに関係していた。

□□□ 0335

seldom

/ séldəm /

副 **almost never**

めったに～ない

ⓘ ふつう一般動詞の前、be動詞の後ろに置く。

例 His mother **seldom** wears make-up.

彼の母はめったに化粧をしない。

□□□ 0336

trust

/ trʌ́st /

形 trustworthy 信頼できる

動 **to believe in someone or something and their ability to be good and reliable**

〜を信用する、信頼する

例 You shouldn't **trust** all of the information you read online.

オンライン上で目にする情報すべてを信用するべきではない。

名 **the belief in the goodness or reliability of someone or something**

信用

例 Police officers must have **trust** in their partners if they want to work well together.

警察官たちは、一緒にうまく仕事をしたければ、仕事仲間を信頼しなければならない。

□□□ 0337

handle

/ hǽndl /

動 **to deal with someone or something**

〜を扱う

≒ treat, cope with

例 The call center **handles** over 700 calls per day.

そのコールセンターでは1日に700件以上の電話に対応している。

名 **a part of something that is made so that it can be held by your hand**

取っ手

ⓘ 自動車の「ハンドル」は(steering) wheel、自転車、オートバイなどの「ハンドル」はhandlebarと言う。

例 It was so cold that the door **handle** froze.

とても寒かったので、ドアの持ち手が凍っていた。

0338

aware

/ əwéər /

名 awareness 自覚

形 **knowing or realizing something**

気づいている、認識している

⇔ unaware

〈a-(～に)+ware(用心して)〉

ⓘ be aware of（～に気づいている）の形で押さえておこう。

例 She wasn't **aware** of how hard it was to make good pizza until she tried to make it herself.

彼女は自分でピザを作ってみるまで、おいしいピザを作るのがどれだけ大変か知らなかった。

0339

structure

/ strʌ́ktʃər /

形 structural 構造（上）の

名 **the way that something is organized or built**

構造、構成

ⓘ「構造物、建造物」という意味もある。

〈struct(建てる)+ure(結果)〉

例 In biology class, students are taught about the **structure** of flowers.

生物学の授業で、生徒たちは花の構造について教わる。

0340

lack

/ lǽk /

名 **the state of not having enough of something**

不足

例 The musical was canceled because of a **lack** of ticket sales.

そのミュージカルは、チケットの販売数が足りなかったため、中止された。

動 **to not have enough of something**

～を欠いている

例 The organization **lacked** enough skilled workers and went out of business.

その組織は、熟練した労働者が足りず、事業が続けられなくなった。

0341

correct

/ kərékt /

副 correctly 正しく
名 correction 訂正

形 **true or agreeing with the facts**

正しい、正確な

⇔ incorrect

ⓘ collect（～を集める）と混同しないように注意。

〈cor-（完全に）+rect（まっすぐな）〉

例 You must get more **correct** answers than wrong answers to pass the test.

試験に合格するには、誤った解答よりも多く正しい解答をしなければならない。

動 **to fix something that was wrong so that it is accurate**

〈誤りなど〉を訂正する

例 She had to **correct** the mistakes in her application before she could submit it.

彼女は申込書を提出する前に誤りを訂正しなければならなかった。

0342

destroy

/ dɪstrɔ́ɪ /

名 destruction 破壊

動 **to damage something so much that it does not exist anymore**

～を破壊する

⇔ construct

ⓘ アクセントはroyの位置。

〈de-（否定）+story（積み上げる）〉

例 Many important buildings were **destroyed** in the hurricane.

そのハリケーンでたくさんの重要な建物が破壊された。

0343

adventure

/ ədvéntʃər /

形 adventurous 冒険的な

名 **a fun and sometimes dangerous experience**

冒険

例 The man went on a one-week **adventure** in the forest.

その男性は森の中へ1週間の冒険に出かけた。

0343語

0344

career
/ kəríər /

名 ① **the length of time spent at a (type of) job** 経歴、キャリア

ⓘ アクセントはreerの位置。

例 Her **career** as an editor lasted 30 years.
彼女の編集者としての経歴は30年続いた。

② **a (type of) job that someone does for a long time** 職業

例 Her son wants to have a **career** in music when he grows up.
彼女の息子は大人になったら音楽関係の職業に就きたいと思っている。

0345

demand
/ dımǽnd /

動 **to strongly say that something must be done or given to you** ～を要求する

ⓘ「～を要する、必要とする」という意味もある。例：Her job demands a very strict dress code.（彼女の仕事は、非常に厳しい服装規定を求める）

〈de-(強意)+mand(命令する)〉

例 She **demanded** a refund for the broken laptop that she purchased.
彼女は購入したノートPCが故障していたので、返金を要求した。

名 **the need or desire to buy goods and services from someone or an organization** 需要

ⓘ supply and demand（需要と供給）という表現も覚えておこう。日本語と順序が逆になる。

例 There was high **demand** for portable radios before the typhoon.
台風前、携帯用ラジオの需要が高まった。

□□□ 0346

duty

/ d(j)úːti /

名 **something that you do because it is your job to do it**

義務

ⓘ dutiesと複数形で「関税」という意味もある。

〈du（負う）+-ty（名詞）〉

例 She has a variety of **duties** as a secretary.

彼女には秘書として多種多様な業務がある。

□□□ 0347

respect

/ rɪspékt /

形 respectful 丁重な

動 **to have a very good opinion of someone or something because of their good qualities**

～を尊敬する、尊重する

〈re-（後ろを）+spect（見る）〉

例 The man was **respected** by everyone in the neighborhood.

その男性は近所の皆に尊敬されていた。

名 ① **a very good opinion of someone or something because of their good qualities**

尊敬

例 She has a lot of **respect** for her grandparents.

彼女は祖父母をとても尊敬している。

② **a way of thinking about something**

点、項目

ⓘ with respect to（～に関して）、in this respect（この点で）という表現も覚えておこう。

例 In many **respects**, lions are no different from house cats.

多くの点で、ライオンは家猫とまったく変わらない。

0347語

□□□ 0348

judge
/ ʤʌ́ʤ /

名 judgment 判断

動 **to have an opinion about someone or something after thinking about it for a while**

～を判断する

ⓘ 名詞形のjudgmentはイギリス英語ではjudgementとつづる。

例 If you always **judge** food by how it looks, you might miss out on something delicious.

食べ物をいつも見た目で判断しているなら、おいしいものを見逃しているかもしれない。

名 **a person who makes decisions in a court**

裁判官

ⓘ 「審判、審査員」という意味もある。

例 That woman has been a federal court **judge** for many years.

その女性は長年、連邦裁判所の裁判官を務めている。

□□□ 0349

bear
/ béər /

動 ① **to accept or endure something that is usually not easy**

～に耐える

≒ stand

ⓘ bear-bore-born(e)と活用する。同じつづりで「クマ」という意味の名詞もある。

例 The summer weather in Tokyo is too hot to **bear**.

東京の夏の気候は、暑すぎて耐えられない。

② **to give birth to a child**

～を産む

ⓘ とても堅い言い方だが、be born（生まれる）はごく普通の表現。

例 The woman **bore** two daughters.

その女性は2人の娘を産んだ。

□□□ 0350

review

/ rɪvjúː /

動 **to check something again after you have already studied or looked at it**

～を再検討する、見直す

〈re-（再び）+view（見る）〉

例 He **reviewed** his answers one more time before handing in his test.

彼はテストを提出する前にもう1回答えを見直した。

名 **something that someone writes to share their opinion about something with other people**

批評、レビュー

例 The new movie got a lot of great **reviews** after it was released.

その新作映画は公開された後、素晴らしいレビューがたくさん寄せられた。

□□□ 0351

scan

/ skǽn /

名 scanner スキャナー

動 **to use a machine to copy something into a digital format**

～をスキャンする

例 The police officer **scanned** the woman's ID to keep it on record.

警察官は記録を残すためにその女性の身分証明書をスキャンした。

0352語

□□□ 0352

device

/ dɪváɪs /

動 devise ～を考案する

名 **something that is made to do a specific thing**

装置

例 The shop sells phones, speakers, and other electronic **devices**.

その店では電話、スピーカー、その他の電子機器を販売している。

□□□ 0353

loss

/ lɔ́(ː)s /

動 lose ～を失う

名 ① **failure to keep something**

喪失

例 The Lehman shock caused the **loss** of many jobs.

リーマンショックは多くの失業を引き起こした。

② **money that is lost by a business or organization**

損失

例 That company suffered large **losses** after their product didn't sell well.

その会社は製品があまり売れず、大きな損失をこうむった。

□□□ 0354

wheel

/ wíːl /

名 ① **one of the round things under something (such as a car or bicycle) that let it roll and move**

車輪

ⓘ wheel（車輪）のついたchair（いす）がwheelchair（車いす）。

例 The **wheels** on the bottom of the suitcase made it easier to move.

底についている車輪のおかげで、スーツケースは動かしやすかった。

② **the object inside a vehicle that lets you change the direction you are moving in**

（車の）ハンドル

ⓘ steering wheelとも言う。

例 The first time behind the **wheel**, he was very nervous.

彼は初めて車のハンドルの前に座り、とても緊張していた。

□□□ 0355

exchange

/ ɪkstʃéɪndʒ /

動 to give something to someone and also receive something from them

～を交換する

ⓘ exchange greetings（挨拶を交わす）のように、もの以外にも使う。「交換」という名詞の意味もあり、exchange student で「交換留学生」。

〈ex-(外に)+change(換える)〉

例 Everyone **exchanged** business cards before the start of the meeting.

会議が始まる前に、誰もが名刺を交換した。

□□□ 0356

waste

/ wéɪst /

形 wasteful 無駄の多い

動 to use something poorly or use more of it than needed

～を無駄にする

ⓘ waist（腰、ウエスト）と同音。

例 The people were asked not to **waste** water on baths during the drought.

渇水の間、人々は風呂の水を無駄にしないように求められた。

名 ① an action that causes the unnecessary loss of something

無駄、浪費

例 The store was closed, so walking there was a **waste** of time.

その店は閉まっていたので、そこへ歩いていったのは時間の無駄だった。

② the unwanted things that are left after something has been finished

廃棄物、ごみ

例 The couple decided to decrease their household **waste** by buying food in bulk.

その夫婦は、食品をまとめ買いすることで、家から出る廃棄物を減らすことに決めた。

□□□ 0357

economic

/ èkənɑ́:mɪk /

名 economy 経済
形 economical 経済的な、無駄のない

形 relating to the systems that involve producing, buying, and selling things or services

経済の、経済に関する

例 The **economic** growth of the town has been slowing down for many years.

その町の経済成長は長年鈍化している。

□□□ 0358

prefer

/ prɪfə́:r /

名 preference 好み
形 preferable 好ましい
形 preferential 優遇の

動 to like someone or something more than another person or thing

～の方を好む

ⓘ アクセントはferの位置。〈prefer A to B〉(BよりAの方が好きだ) の形で押さえておこう。

〈pre- (前に) +fer (運ぶ)〉

例 She **prefers** milk chocolate to dark chocolate.

彼女はダークチョコレートよりもミルクチョコレートの方が好きだ。

□□□ 0359

spot

/ spɑ́:t /

動 to see someone or something that is not easy to see or find

～を見つける、～に気づく

例 She **spotted** a mistake in the book she was reading.

彼女は読んでいた本に誤植を見つけた。

名 a particular space or area

場所、地点

≒ place

例 He found a **spot** under a tree to take a nap.

彼は木の下に昼寝をする場所を見つけた。

□□□ 0360

spread

/ spréd /

動 ① to get larger or move into more places

広まる

ⓘ spread-spread-spreadと活用する。

例 The fire **spread** to the neighbor's house before being put out.

火事は消し止められる前に隣の家に広がった。

② to put something over a large area

～を広げる

例 They **spread** the blanket across the grass.

彼らは芝生の上に毛布を広げた。

□□□ 0361

statement

/ stéɪtmənt /

動 state ～を明確に述べる

名 something that you say or write about something in a formal or official situation

発言

〈state(述べる)+-ment(名詞)〉

例 The police took a **statement** from the man who saw the car accident.

警察は車両事故を目撃した男性から供述を取った。

□□□ 0362

avoid

/ əvɔ́ɪd /

名 avoidance 回避

動 to keep away from someone or something

～を避ける

ⓘ 後ろに動詞がくるときにはing形になる。

〈a-(離れて)+void(空にする)〉

例 The man **avoids** large groups because they make him uncomfortable.

その男性は大人数の集団を避けている。大人数でいると、居心地が悪くなるためだ。

0362語

□□□ 0363

function

/ fʌ́ŋkʃən /

形 functional 機能的な

名 **the purpose for which something exists or is used**

機能、働き

例 The **function** of a pen is to write information on paper.

ペンの機能は、紙の上に情報を書くことだ。

動 **to work or operate**

作動する、働く

例 Her car wasn't **functioning** well, so she took it to a mechanic.

彼女の車は正常に動いていなかったので、修理工に持っていった。

□□□ 0364

temperature

/ témpərətʃər /

名 **the measurement that shows how hot or cold something is**

気温、温度

ⓘ Celsius(摂氏)とFahrenheit(華氏)も覚えておこう。20℃はtwenty degrees Celsiusと読む。

例 The large **temperature** changes last week made him sick.

先週は気温の変化が大きかったため、彼は体調を崩した。

□□□ 0365

former

/ fɔ́ːrmər /

形 **showing what someone or something was before**

前の、以前の

≒ previous

ⓘ the latter（後者）に対するthe former（前者）という使い方も覚えておこう。

例 Her **former** teacher retired this year.

彼女の前の先生は今年退職した。

0366

benefit

/ bénəfɪt /

形 beneficial 有益な

名 **something that is good or helpful**

利益、利点

≒ advantage

⇔ disadvantage

〈bene（よい）+fit（行い）〉

例 There are many **benefits** to learning a new language when you are young.

若いうちに新しい言語を学ぶことの利点はたくさんある。

動 ① **to be useful to someone or something**

～のためになる

≒ help, aid

例 The new tax rules only **benefit** large businesses.

新しい税制は大企業のためにしかならない。

② **to be helped**

利益を得る

例 He **benefited** from going to bed early the day before the race.

彼はレースの前日に早く寝ることで恩恵を得た。

□□□ 0367

brand

/ brǽnd /

名 **a group of products that are all made by one company and share that company's name**

銘柄、ブランド

ⓘ 高級品を意味する「ブランドもの」はname brandと言う。

例 Expensive **brands** are sold for less money at outlet malls.

高級ブランドがアウトレットモールではより安い値段で販売されている。

□□□ 0368

extra

/ ékstrə /

形 **more than what is usual, or more than what is needed**

余分の、追加の

例 It costs 100 yen more to add **extra** cheese to a pizza.

ピザにチーズの増量を追加するにはもう100円かかる。

□□□ 0369

blow

/ blóʊ /

名 **a sudden event that causes trouble, damage, disappointment, etc.**

（精神的な）打撃、衝撃

ⓘ 同じつづりで、「〈風が〉吹く」「息を吹きかける」という意味の動詞もある。この動詞のblowは、blow-blew-blownと活用する。

例 Losing the match was a major **blow** to the boxer's pride.

敗戦はそのボクサーのプライドを粉々に打ち砕いた。

□□□ 0370

release

/ rɪlíːs /

動 ① **to let something freely enter somewhere or something else**

～を放つ

ⓘ 元々「ゆるめる」という意味で、そこから「解放する」→「放つ、公表する、発売する」になった。「放出」という名詞の意味もある。

〈re-（再び）+lease（ゆるめる）〉

例 Oil was **released** into the ocean when the boat crashed.

船が衝突し、海に原油が放出された。

② **to give access to something to people**

～を発表する、発売する

≒ launch

例 Cameron's favorite band **released** a new album last month.

キャメロンのお気に入りのバンドが、先月新しいアルバムを発表した。

 0371

flow

/ flóʊ /

動 **to move without stopping and at a steady speed**

流れる

ⓘ「流れ」という名詞の意味もある。flood（洪水）、fluent（流暢な）、fluid（流動体）などと同語源語。

例 This river **flows** from the top of the mountain.

この川はその山の頂上から流れている。

□□□ 0372

symbol

/ símbəl /

形 symbolic 象徴的な
動 symbolize ～を象徴する

名 **something that represents something else**

象徴

ⓘ「シンボル」はカタカナ語にもなっている。

例 White is a **symbol** of cleanliness and purity in many cultures.

白は多くの文化において清潔さや純粋さの象徴だ。

□□□ 0373

beat

/ bíːt /

動 ① **to hit something over and over again**

～を（何度も）打つ

ⓘ beat-beat-beatenと活用する。音楽の「ビート」もこのbeat。

例 At the end of the song, he **beat** the drums faster and faster.

その曲の最後で、彼はドラムを打つ手をどんどん速めた。

② **to win against someone in a game or contest**

～を負かす

≒ defeat

例 His school was **beaten** at the baseball game.

彼の学校は野球の試合で負けた。

0373語

□□□ 0374

progress

/ 名 prá:gres 動 prəgrés /

名 progression 前進
形 progressive 進歩的な

名 **the process of something getting better as time passes**

進歩

ⓘ make progress（〈物事が〉進展する）という表現も覚えておこう。

〈pro-（前に）+gress（行く）〉

例 The **progress** of science in the past 100 years is impressive.

過去100年間における科学の進歩は印象的だ。

動 **to develop or get better as time passes**

〈物事が〉前進する

例 Preparations for the festival have been **progressing** well.

祭りの準備は順調に進んでいる。

□□□ 0375

physical

/ fízɪkl /

副 physically 身体的に；物理的に
名 physics 物理学

形 ① **relating to the body of someone or something**

身体の

⇔ mental, spiritual

例 **Physical** education classes are taught at most schools.

体育の授業はほとんどの学校で行われている。

② **being in a form that can be seen or touched**

物理的な

≒ material, tangible

例 No one was able to find any **physical** proof that the boy had been there.

その男の子がそこにいたという物理的な証拠を誰も見つけることはできなかった。

 0376

scale

/ skéɪl /

名 **the size or level of something**

規模

ⓘ「はしご」が語源で、ascend（登る）やescalator（エスカレーター）なども同語源語。同じつづりで「はかり」「うろこ」という意味の名詞もある。

例 The large **scale** of the music festival means it will take a long time to organize.

その音楽祭の規模の大きさから、準備に長い時間がかかることがわかる。

□□□ 0377

feed

/ fíːd /

動 **to give food to someone or something**

～に食べ物を与える

ⓘ feed-fed-fedと活用する。

例 Anna liked to help **feed** her younger brother when he was a baby.

アナは弟が赤ちゃんだったとき、弟に食事をあげるのを手伝うのが好きだった。

□□□ 0378

fear

/ fíər /

形 fearful 恐れて

名 **the feeling of being afraid**

恐れ、恐怖

ⓘ 〈for fear of A/that...〉（A／…することを恐れて）という表現も覚えておこう。

例 After years of effort, she finally overcame her **fear** of insects.

長年努力した後、彼女はついに昆虫に対する恐怖を克服した。

動 **to be afraid of something or someone**

～を恐れる

例 The little boy **fears** swimming in the ocean.

その小さな男の子は海で泳ぐことを恐れている。

0378語

□□□ 0379

vehicle

/ víːəkl /

名 **a machine, such as a car, that is used to move around people or things**

乗り物、車

ⓘ ehの発音に注意。hは発音しない。

〈vehi（運ぶ）+-cle（指小辞）〉

例 The picture of the stolen **vehicle** was shown on the news.

盗まれた車の写真がニュースで映し出された。

□□□ 0380

surface

/ sə́ːrfəs /

名 **the outside layer of something**

表面

ⓘ faceの発音に注意。

〈sur-（～の上）+face（顔）〉

例 The astronauts collected rocks from the **surface** of the Moon.

宇宙飛行士たちは月の表面から岩石を採集した。

□□□ 0381

maintain

/ meɪntéɪn /

名 maintenance メンテナンス、保守

動 ① **to make something continue to exist without changing**

～を維持する；～を整備する

〈main（手）+tain（保つ）〉

例 The man **maintains** a healthy weight through diet and exercise.

その男性は、食事と運動で健康的な体重を維持している。

② **to continue to say that something is true**

…と主張する

例 Grace **maintains** that her grandfather makes the best pie in town.

グレイスは、自分の祖父が焼くパイが町で一番おいしいと主張している。

□□□ 0382

hang

/ hǽŋ /

動 ① **to attach something to another thing in a way that it does not have any support from the bottom**

〜を掛ける、つるす

ⓘ hang-hung-hungと活用する。服の「ハンガー」はhanger。

例 She **hung** her favorite painting on the wall of her new apartment.

彼女は、大好きな絵を新しいアパートの壁に掛けた。

② **to attach to another thing in a way that it does not have any support from the bottom**

ぶら下がる

例 All of her dresses are **hanging** in the closet.

彼女のドレスはすべてクローゼットに掛かっている。

□□□ 0383

assist

/ əsíst /

名 assistance 支援、補助

動 **to help someone do something**

〜を助ける

ⓘ「assistする人」がassistant（助手、アシスタント）。

〈as-（そばに）+sist（立つ）〉

例 The nurse **assisted** the doctor during the exam.

その看護師は検査の間、医師を手伝った。

□□□ 0384

birth

/ bə́:rθ /

名 **the time when a baby leaves its mother's body and enters the world**

誕生；出産

⇔ death

ⓘ give birth to（〜を生む）という表現も覚えておこう。

例 She was lucky enough to be at the hospital for the **birth** of her niece.

彼女は運よく、姪の誕生時に病院に居合わせることができた。

0384語

□□□ 0385

publish

/ pʌ́blɪʃ /

名 publishing 出版
名 publisher 出版社

動 ① **to make something ready to be sold or shared, such as a book, magazine, etc.**

～を出版する

〈publ (公) +-ish (～にする)〉

例 That author's book has been **published** in 25 different languages.

その著者の本は、25か国語で出版されている。

② **to share information with a large group or the public**

～を発表する

例 The scientist became famous when he **published** his cancer research.

その科学者はがん研究を発表して有名になった。

□□□ 0386

document

/ dɑ́:kjəmənt /

名 documentary 記録映画

名 **a paper, usually official, that has information about something or proves something to someone**

書類

〈doc(u)(教える)+-ment(名詞)〉

例 You have to give many **documents** to immigration to renew your visa.

ビザを更新するには、出入国管理当局へたくさんの書類を提出しなければならない。

□□□ 0387

political

/ pəlítɪkl /

名 politics 政治
名 politician 政治家

形 **relating to the actions and policies of a government**

政治の

i アクセントはliの位置。

例 That country's **political** system doesn't work well.

その国の政治制度はうまく機能していない。

□□□ 0388

direct

/ dərékt /

副 directly 直接(に)
名 direction 方向；指示

動 ① **to tell someone to do something**

～に指示する、指図する

〈di- (離れて) +rect (まっすぐな)〉

例 The manager **directed** the staff to move the flowers out of the room.

部長はスタッフに花を部屋の外へ動かすように指示した。

② **to make someone or something move in a certain way**

～を向ける

例 He **directed** his flashlight in the direction that he heard the sound.

彼は音が聞こえた方向に懐中電灯を向けた。

形 **having no other people, things, actions, etc. in between**

直接の

⇔ indirect

例 She is one of the few people who have **direct** access to the prime minister.

彼女は首相に直接会うことができる数少ない人の一人だ。

□□□ 0389

celebrate

/ séləbrèɪt /

名 celebration 祝賀
名 celebrity 有名人

動 **to do something special and fun because of something important or a holiday**

～を祝う

ⓘ アクセントはceの位置。

例 She **celebrated** her birthday by having a large BBQ with the family.

彼女は家族と盛大なバーベキューをして誕生日を祝った。

□□□ 0390

link

/ líŋk /

名 linkage つながり、連鎖

動 **to join or connect things or places together**

～を結びつける、関連づける

ⓘ インターネットの「リンク（をはる）」もこのlink。スケートなどの「リンク」はrinkなので注意。

例 An underwater tunnel **links** the Shinkansen network to Hokkaido.

海底トンネルが新幹線網を北海道と結んでいる。

名 **something connecting things or people together**

関連、結びつき

≒ relation

例 There is a clear **link** between lack of exercise and poor health.

運動不足と不健康には明確な関連がある。

□□□ 0391

willing

/ wílıŋ /

形 **not refusing to do something**

いとわない

ⓘ 〈be willing to *do*〉（～することをいとわない）の形で押さえておこう。

例 Ned has always been **willing** to try interesting food from different countries.

ネッドはいつでも、いろいろな国の面白い食べ物を試してみることをいとわない。

□□□ 0392

income

/ ínkʌm /

名 **the money you get from working, investing, etc.**

収入

≒ revenue, earnings

⇔ expense, spending

〈in-（中に）+come（入ってくるもの）〉

例 The **income** of a famous lawyer is usually very high.

有名弁護士の収入はたいていとても高い。

0393

manner

/ mǽnər /

名 ① **the way that something is done or happens**

方法、やり方

≒ fashion

〈man(n)（手）+-er（行為）〉

例 Sitting in that **manner** is bad for your back.

そんなふうに座ると、背中に悪いですよ。

② **how you act around and treat other people**

礼儀、マナー

ⓘ 複数形で使う。

例 It's bad **manners** to eat with your elbows on the table in many countries.

多くの国で、テーブルにひじをついて食事をすることはマナーが悪いとされる。

0394

attempt

/ ətémpt /

名 **the act of trying to do something**

試み

ⓘ 〈attempt to *do*〉（～する試み）の形で押さえておこう。

〈at-（～に）+tempt（試みる）〉

例 His **attempt** to get around the world in 80 days failed.

80日間で世界一周するという彼の試みは失敗した。

動 **to try to do something**

～を試みる

ⓘ 〈attempt to *do*〉（～しようとする）の形で押さえておこう。

例 Fiona **attempted** to swim across the river for charity last summer.

フィオナは去年の夏、慈善活動のため川を泳いで渡ることに挑戦した。

0394語

□□□ 0395

achieve

/ ətʃíːv /

名 achievement 業績、偉業

動 to work hard and get or reach something because of it

〈目的など〉を達成する

〈a-(～に)+chieve(頭、頂点)〉

例 She **achieved** the highest grades in the school because of how much she studied.

彼女は猛勉強のおかげで、学校で最高の成績を収めた。

□□□ 0396

knee

/ níː /

動 kneel ひざまずく

名 the joint that connects your lower leg and your upper leg together

ひざ

i kは発音しない。「ひじ」はelbow。

例 If you're not careful, lifting heavy objects can damage your **knees**.

注意しないと、重いものを持ち上げるとひざを傷めることがある。

□□□ 0397

represent

/ rèprɪzént /

名 representation 表現；代表(すること)

名 representative 代表者

動 ① to be a symbol of someone or something

～を表す

i アクセントはseの位置。

例 Many people think that the eagle **represents** the United States.

ワシはアメリカを表すと多くの人々が思っている。

② to do something or speak for someone

～を代表する

例 The poet's agent **represented** her at the meeting.

その詩人の代理人は、彼女の代わりに会議に出席した。

0398

equal

/ íːkwəl /

副 equally 平等に、等しく
名 equality 平等

形 **being the same in number or quality**

等しい

ⓘ 発音に注意。アクセントはeの位置。数学の「イコール（＝）」はこのequal。「平等な」という意味も重要。

〈equ（等しい）+-al（形容詞）〉

例 The profits of a smaller company are not usually **equal** to the profits of a larger company.

小さい企業の利益はたいてい、大企業の利益と同等ではない。

0399

affect

/ əfékt /

動 **to cause a change in someone or something**

～に影響する

≒ impact, influence

〈af-（～に）+fect（する）〉

ⓘ effect（効果）と混同しないように注意。

例 The movie **affected** the way she viewed the world.

その映画は、彼女の世界の見方に影響を与えた。

0400

firm

/ fə́ːrm /

名 **a business, especially one that sells a service, such as legal or business support**

会社、企業

≒ company

ⓘ farm（農場）と混同しないように注意。

例 She got her first job at a law **firm** when she was 28 years old.

彼女は28歳のとき、法律事務所で初めての仕事を得た。

形 **fairly hard**

堅めの

例 I sleep better on a **firm** mattress.

私は堅めのマットレス方がよく眠れる。

章末ボキャブラリーチェック

次の語義が表す英単語を答えてください。

語義	解答	連番
❶ the length of time spent at a (type of) job	career	0344
❷ someone who lives in a particular place	citizen	0326
❸ newspapers, magazines, and other media organizations	press	0325
❹ the ability to enter, go near, or use something or talk with someone	access	0332
❺ money that must be paid to use or do something	fee	0333
❻ to check something again after you have already studied or looked at it	review	0350
❼ the smallest living part of a plant or animal	cell	0305
❽ to have a very good opinion of someone or something because of their good qualities	respect	0347
❾ the outside layer of something	surface	0380
❿ relating to the actions and policies of a government	political	0387
⓫ almost never	seldom	0335
⓬ the size or level of something	scale	0376
⓭ to work hard and get or reach something because of it	achieve	0395
⓮ a meeting that is held with a person who is applying for a position at an organization	interview	0320
⓯ to move without stopping and at a steady speed	flow	0371
⓰ to come together to form a group, or to collect things or people and put them together	gather	0312
⓱ to help someone do something	assist	0383
⓲ the way that something is organized or built	structure	0339
⓳ a fun and sometimes dangerous experience	adventure	0343
⓴ to give food to someone or something	feed	0377
㉑ to make something continue to exist without changing	maintain	0381

語義	解答	連番
㉒ a person who does business and other actions for another person	agent	0309
㉓ very big in size, amount, or degree	huge	0313
㉔ to accept or endure something that is usually not easy	bear	0349
㉕ to be real	exist	0329
㉖ a paper, usually official, that has information about something or proves something to someone	document	0386
㉗ to get something that you want or something that is valuable	gain	0321
㉘ someone who is against you	enemy	0311
㉙ something that is good or helpful	benefit	0366
㉚ to have an opinion about someone or something after thinking about it for a while	judge	0348
㉛ the process of something getting better as time passes	progress	0374
㉜ to light something on fire, or to be on fire	burn	0308
㉝ a raised surface that is higher than the ground and that people stand on when performing or speaking	platform	0314
㉞ the feeling of being afraid	fear	0378
㉟ a business, especially one that sells a service, such as legal or business support	firm	0400
㊱ to show or make a connection between different things	relate	0334
㊲ a problem or task that is not easy to do	challenge	0319
㊳ to only allow something to be a certain size or amount	limit	0301
㊴ failure to keep something	loss	0353
㊵ knowing or realizing something	aware	0338
㊶ to use a machine to copy something into a digital format	scan	0351
㊷ to be a symbol of someone or something	represent	0397

語義	解答	連番
㊸ to see someone or something that is not easy to see or find	spot	0359
㊹ not refusing to do something	willing	0391
㊺ the way that something is done or happens	manner	0393
㊻ something you can choose	option	0323
㊼ something that you do because it is your job to do it	duty	0346
㊽ to strongly say that something must be done or given to you	demand	0345
㊾ being the same in number or quality	equal	0398
㊿ to try to find someone or something	search	0316
51 to go to an event or meeting	attend	0315
52 to like someone or something more than another person or thing	prefer	0358
53 to do something special and fun because of something important or a holiday	celebrate	0389
54 relating to the systems that involve producing, buying, and selling things or services	economic	0357
55 a (high-ranking) teacher at a college or university	professor	0318
56 the measurement that shows how hot or cold something is	temperature	0364
57 a machine, such as a car, that is used to move around people or things	vehicle	0379
58 to need something	require	0307
59 to choose someone or something from a group of people or things	select	0302
60 something that is made to do a specific thing	device	0352
61 the money you get from working, investing, etc.	income	0392
62 the state of being protected or safe from something dangerous	security	0310
63 a group of products that are all made by one company and share that company's name	brand	0367

語義	解答	連番
(64) people who are grouped together because they were born around the same time	generation	0322
(65) to make something ready to be sold or shared, such as a book, magazine, etc.	publish	0385
(66) to keep away from someone or something	avoid	0362
(67) to deal with someone or something	handle	0337
(68) the chance that something bad will happen	risk	0330
(69) a sudden event that was not planned and that causes something bad to happen	accident	0328
(70) to have something as a part	contain	0324
(71) the time when a baby leaves its mother's body and enters the world	birth	0384
(72) the joint that connects your lower leg and your upper leg together	knee	0396
(73) to let something freely enter somewhere or something else	release	0370
(74) to cause a change in someone or something	affect	0399
(75) to be or put yourself in a flat position	lie	0304
(76) true or agreeing with the facts	correct	0341
(77) to hit something over and over again	beat	0373
(78) to get larger or move into more places	spread	0360
(79) the round things under something (such as a car or bicycle) that let it roll and move	wheel	0354
(80) to use something poorly or use more of it than needed	waste	0356
(81) to believe in someone or something and their ability to be good and reliable	trust	0336
(82) showing what someone or something was before	former	0365
(83) to join or connect things or places together	link	0390
(84) something that says how much you have to pay for something you bought	bill	0327
(85) to tell someone to do something	direct	0388

語義	解答	連番
86 a sudden event that causes trouble, damage, disappointment, etc.	blow	0369
87 the act of trying to do something	attempt	0394
88 to give something to someone and also receive something from them	exchange	0355
89 to damage something so much that it does not exist anymore	destroy	0342
90 a state in which multiple things have or exist in equal or proper amounts	balance	0317
91 something that represents something else	symbol	0372
92 to attach something to another thing in a way that it does not have any support from the bottom	hang	0382
93 an act of asking someone to do or give something in a formal or polite way	request	0331
94 the purpose for which something exists or is used	function	0363
95 something that you say or write about something in a formal or official situation	statement	0361
96 the state of not having enough of something	lack	0340
97 more than what is usual, or more than what is needed	extra	0368
98 a number of things that happen or are arranged one after the other	series	0303
99 relating to the body of someone or something	physical	0375
100 one of four equal parts of something	quarter	0306

Stage 5

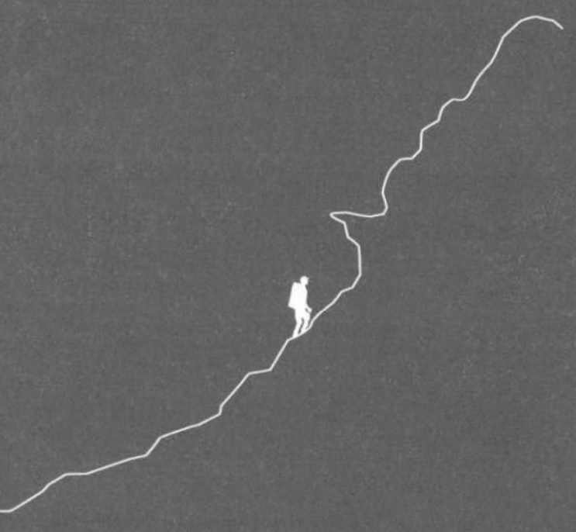

Never put off till tomorrow what you can do today.
今日できることを明日まで延ばすな。

□□□ 0401

soldier

/ sóʊldʒər /

名 **a member of the military or an army**

軍人、兵士

ⓘ dierの発音に注意。

例 There were a lot of **soldiers** in town for the parade.

そのパレードのために町にはたくさん兵士がいた。

□□□ 0402

steal

/ stíːl /

動 **to take something that does not belong to you or that you are not allowed to have without asking permission**

～を盗む

ⓘ steal-stole-stolenと活用する。steel（鋼鉄、スチール）と同音。

例 The little girl **stole** some toy cars from her cousin.

その小さな女の子はいとこからおもちゃの車をいくつか盗んだ。

□□□ 0403

hide

/ háɪd /

動 **① to put something where it cannot be easily seen or found**

～を隠す

≒ conceal

ⓘ hide-hid-hiddenと活用する。

例 He **hid** his comic books under his bed.

彼は漫画本をベッドの下に隠した。

② to go or stay somewhere you hope you will not be seen or found

隠れる

例 Molly **hid** behind a big tree during the game of hide-and-seek.

モリーは隠れんぼのゲームの間、大きな木の陰に隠れた。

□□□ 0404

population

/ pὰ:pjəléɪʃən /

動 populate ～を住まわせる
形 populous 人口の多い

名 **the number of people who live somewhere**

人口

ⓘ 人間だけでなく、動物の「総数、個体数」の意味でも使う。

〈popul（人）+-ation（名詞）〉

例 The **population** of the Greater Tokyo Area is bigger than that of all of Canada.

首都圏の人口は、カナダ全体の人口よりも多い。

□□□ 0405

joke

/ ʤóʊk /

副 jokingly 冗談で、ふざけて

動 **to say something funny to make people laugh**

冗談を言う

例 The girl is always **joking** in class and getting in trouble with her teacher.

その女の子はいつも授業中に冗談を言って、担任の教師ともめている。

□□□ 0406

admit

/ ədmít /

名 admission（入場）許可

動 ① **to say or accept that something is true, even though you do not want to**

～を認める、～に同意する

〈ad-(～に)+mit(送り入れる)〉

例 It is sometimes hard to **admit** your mistakes.

自分の誤りを認めるのは時として難しい。

② **to let someone enter somewhere**

（場所などに）～を入れる、通す

例 The woman was **admitted** to the hospital to give birth this morning.

出産のため、その女性は今朝病院に入院した。

0407

individual

/ ìndəvíʤuəl /

副 individually 個々に

形 ① **connected to or made for one person**

個人の

〈in-(否定)+dividu(分ける)+-al(形容詞)〉

例 The teacher tried to meet the **individual** needs of all of her students.

その教師は生徒たち全員の個人的なニーズに応えようとした。

② **considered separately from any group**

個々の

例 Each **individual** member of the band was interviewed for the TV show.

そのバンドの個々のメンバーそれぞれがテレビ番組でインタビューを受けた。

名 **a person who is seen as being separate from any group**

個人

例 You can join the marathon as part of a group or as an **individual**.

団体の一員としても個人としてもそのマラソン大会に参加できる。

0408

advantage

/ ədvǽntɪʤ /

形 advantageous 有利な

名 **something that helps someone or something have a higher chance of succeeding at something**

利点、メリット

≒ benefit

⇔ disadvantage

〈advant(前にある)+-age(状態)〉

ⓘ take advantage of(～を利用する)という表現も覚えておこう。

例 The other team had an **advantage** over us because they got more time to practice.

相手チームの方が練習時間があったので、私たちより有利だった。

0409

length

/ léŋkθ /

形 long 長い

名 **how long something is**

長さ

ⓘ width（幅）、depth（深さ、奥行き）もあわせて覚えておこう。

例 The **length** of this string is 30 centimeters.

このひもの長さは30センチだ。

□□□ 0410

smooth

/ smúːð /

副 smoothly なめらかに；順調に

形 **having a soft and flat surface, without any rough areas or holes**

（表面が）滑らかな

ⓘ thの発音に注意。「順調な」という意味もある。

例 Babies have very **smooth** skin.

赤ちゃんはとても滑らかな肌をしている。

□□□ 0411

occasion

/ əkéɪʒən /

形 occasional 時たまの
副 occasionally たまに

名 ① **an event or time during which something special happens**

（特別な）出来事

〈oc-（～に）+cas（落ちる）+-ion（名詞）〉

例 They only use the porcelain dishes on special **occasions**.

彼らは特別なときにしかその磁器の皿を使わない。

② **a suitable time for something to be done**

機会

≒ chance, opportunity

例 Performance reviews are an **occasion** for employees to talk about problems in the company.

勤務評価は従業員が会社での問題について話す機会だ。

□□□ 0412

familiar
/ fəmíljər /

名 familiarity よく知っていること
動 familiarize ～を慣れさせる

形 ① **often seen, heard, or experienced by many people**

よく知られた

ⓘ アクセントは mi の位置。

例 Quite a few foods that are **familiar** to Japanese people are not available overseas.

日本人にはよく知られた食べ物の多くが海外では手に入らない。

② **having (a lot of) knowledge about something**

よく知っている、詳しい

ⓘ be familiar with（～に詳しい）の形で押さえておこう。

例 She wasn't **familiar** with her new neighborhood and got lost.

彼女は引っ越してきたばかりの近所に詳しくなく、迷子になった。

□□□ 0413

replace
/ rɪpléɪs /

名 replacement 取り換え；代替品

動 ① **to put a new person or thing in the place or position of what was there before**

～を取り換える

≒ substitute

〈re-(元の場所に)+place(置く)〉

例 The couple decided to **replace** their refrigerator because it was very old.

その夫婦は、冷蔵庫がとても古くなったので、買い換えることに決めた。

② **to be used instead of something**

～に取って代わる

例 CDs have been **replaced** by digital music in many countries.

CDは多くの国々でデジタル配信の音楽に取って代わられている。

0414

shrine

/ ʃráɪn /

名 **a place where people go to worship because it is connected to a holy person or event**

神社、聖堂

ⓘ「明治神宮」はMeiji Shrineと言う。「寺」はtemple、「教会」はchurch。

例 There are many famous **shrines** in Kyoto.

京都には多くの有名な神社がある。

0415

intend

/ ɪnténd /

名 intention 意図
形 intentional 故意の

動 **to plan or want to do something**

～を意図する

ⓘ〈intend to *do*〉(～しようと思う)の形で押さえておこう。

〈in- (中に) +tend (向ける)〉

例 Zack **intends** to live in China for the rest of his life.

ザックは残りの人生を中国で暮らすつもりだ。

0416

native

/ néɪtɪv /

形 ① **connected to the place a person was born or spent their childhood**

生まれた土地の、母語の

例 He is a **native** speaker of English, but he can also speak German and Spanish.

彼は英語母語話者だが、ドイツ語とスペイン語も話すことができる。

② **relating to groups of people who were living somewhere when a different group of people, especially Europeans, came to that place**

先住民の

例 The **native** people of that island all got sick when the Europeans arrived in the 1700s.

1700年代にヨーロッパ人がやってくると、その島の先住民は皆、病気になった。

□□□ 0417

aim

/ éɪm /

名 **something you want to achieve**

目的、目標

≒ goal, purpose

例 Her **aim** is to be a best-selling author.

彼女の目標はベストセラー作家になることだ。

動 **to have or try to achieve a specific goal or purpose**

目指す

例 He **aims** to be the best soccer player in the country someday.

彼はいつか全国一のサッカー選手になることを目指している。

□□□ 0418

profit

/ prá:fət /

形 profitable 利益になる、もうかる

名 **the money that is made in a business or investment after all the costs involved have been paid**

利益

ⓘ make a profit（利益を上げる）という表現も覚えておこう。

〈pro-（前に）+fit（進む）〉

例 The **profits** of the company dropped after the scandal.

不祥事の後、その会社の利益は低下した。

□□□ 0419

client

/ kláɪənt /

名 **a person who is paying a professional or an organization for a service**

顧客、依頼人

ⓘ 商店の「客」はcustomer、招待された「客」やホテルなどの「宿泊客」はguestと言う。

例 The lawyer stopped accepting new **clients** because she was too busy.

その弁護士は忙しくなりすぎたので、新しい依頼人の受付を停止した。

□□□ 0420

military

/ mílətèri /

形 **relating to soldiers and armed forces** — 軍の

ⓘ the militaryで「軍、軍隊」という名詞の意味もある。

〈milit (兵士) +-ary (形容詞)〉

例 There is a **military** base in Tara's hometown.

タラの故郷には軍事基地がある。

□□□ 0421

refer

/ rɪfə́ːr /

名 reference 参照

動 ①《refer to》**to (briefly) talk or write about someone or something** — ～に言及する

ⓘ アクセントはferの位置。「～を（…と）言う、呼ぶ」という意味もある。例：Nova Scotia, Canada is referred to as "Canada's Ocean Playground." (カナダのノヴァスコシア州は「カナダの海の遊び場」と呼ばれる)

〈re- (元に) +fer (運ぶ)〉

例 In an interview, you shouldn't **refer to** problems you've had with previous employers.

面接では前の雇用者とのトラブルには触れない方がいい。

②《refer to》**to have a direct connection or relationship to another thing** — ～を表す、示す

例 The term "domestic fowl" **refers to** birds that live with humans, like chickens.

「家禽類」という言葉は、ニワトリのように人間と一緒に暮らしている鳥を指している。

③《refer to》**to look at or in something to find information** — ～を参照する

例 The company asks all customers to **refer to** their website for more information.

その会社は、さらなる情報はウェブサイトを参照するよう全顧客に求めている。

□□□ 0422

fit

/ fit /

動 **to match the size and shape needed (for something or someone)**

(～に) 合う、適合する

≒ suit

ⓘ fit-fitted/fit-fitted/fitと活用する。「適した」「健康な」という形容詞の意味もある。

例 Wearing shoes that don't **fit** well can hurt your feet.

合わない靴を履いていると足を痛めることがある。

□□□ 0423

proper

/ prá:pər /

副 properly 適切に

形 **right for a purpose or situation**

適切な

≒ appropriate

例 Without the **proper** training, you cannot become a doctor.

適切な訓練なしに、医者になることはできない。

□□□ 0424

influence

/ ínfluəns /

形 influential 影響力の強い

名 **the power to change the way people think or behave, or the way something is done**

影響

≒ impact

〈in-(中に)+fluence(流れ込むこと)〉

ⓘ アクセントはinの位置。

例 Our parents have a lot of **influence** over us when we are children.

両親は、私たちが子どもの頃に私たちに多くの影響を及ぼす。

動 **to affect someone or something indirectly or make them change**

～に影響を与える

≒ impact

例 The birth of his daughter **influenced** him to quit smoking.

娘の誕生に影響されて、彼はタバコをやめた。

0425

expert

/ ékspəːrt /

名 expertise 専門知識

名 **a person who knows a lot about something specific or has trained to have a special skill**

専門家

ⓘ アクセントはexの位置。

例 His father is an **expert** on wine.

彼の父親はワインの専門家だ。

0426

tiny

/ táɪni /

形 **very small**

ごく小さい

⇔ huge, grand

例 She grew up in a **tiny** town with only three restaurants.

彼女はレストランが3つしかないとても小さな町で育った。

0427

belong

/ bɪlɔ́(ː)ŋ /

名 belongings 所有物

動 ①《belong to》**to be a member of something**

～に所属している

〈be-(まったく)+long(適切な)〉

例 Victor **belongs to** the curling club.

ヴィクターはカーリング部に所属している。

②《belong to》**to be owned by a person or an organization**

～の所有物である

ⓘ belongingsで「所有物」という意味。

例 That building **belongs to** the city.

その建物は市の所有物である。

□□□ 0428

previous

/ príːviəs /

副 previously 以前、前に

形 **existing or happening before**

前の、以前の

≒ former

〈pre-（前に）+vi（道）+-ous（形容詞）〉

例 This job doesn't require **previous** work experience.

この仕事は以前の職務経験を必要としない。

□□□ 0429

article

/ ɑ́ːrtɪkl /

名 **a piece of writing that talks about something in a magazine, newspaper, or online**

記事

≒ item

ⓘ 文法用語の「冠詞」という意味もある。

例 There was an interesting **article** about the Inuit people in that magazine last month.

先月、その雑誌にイヌイットの人々について面白い記事が載っていた。

□□□ 0430

senior

/ síːnjər /

形 ① **having a higher rank than someone in the same position**

（役職などが）上位の

⇔ junior

例 After many years of hard work, she became the **senior** editor of a famous magazine.

長年熱心に働いた後、彼女は有名な雑誌の上級編集者になった。

② **older in age than someone else**

年長の

⇔ junior

例 His sister is 10 years **senior** to him.

彼の姉は彼よりも10歳年上だ。

□□□ 0431

current

/ kə́ːrənt /

副 currently 現在
名 currency 通貨；流通

形 ① **happening or existing in the present time**

現在の

〈cur(r)(走る)+-ent(形容詞)〉

例 **Current** ideas about education are more liberal than they used to be.

教育に関する現在の考え方は、かつてよりもリベラルだ。

② **used or accepted by the majority of people**

広く流通している

例 Over time, certain words stop being **current**.

時間を経るにつれて、使われなくなる言葉もある。

□□□ 0432

female

/ fíːmeɪl /

形 **belonging to the sex that can give birth or make eggs**

女性の、雌の

⇔ male

ⓘ feminine（女性の、女性らしい）、feminist（フェミニスト）なども同語源語。

例 Male birds usually have brighter feathers than **female** birds.

雄の鳥は、たいてい雌の鳥よりも明るい色の羽をしている。

□□□ 0433

technique

/ tekníːk /

形 technical 工業技術の

名 **a way to do something that requires special knowledge or skill**

技術、テクニック

ⓘ アクセントはniの位置。niの発音にも注意。

例 He has spent many years learning the **techniques** to dye kimono.

彼は長年、着物を染色する技術を学んでいる。

□□□ 0434

struggle

/ strʌ́gl /

動 **to try very hard to do something that is not easy**

奮闘する、努力する

ⓘ 〈struggle to *do*〉（～しようと努力する）の形で押さえておこう。

例 She has always **struggled** to do well in math class.

彼女はいつも数学の授業でよい成果を出そうと努力している。

名 **a long time spent trying to do something that is not easy**

奮闘

例 The **struggle** for civil rights is still ongoing for many people.

公民権を獲得するための奮闘は、多くの人々にとって今でも続いている。

□□□ 0435

tend

/ ténd /

名 tendency 傾向

動 **to be likely to happen or be done, or to happen or be done often**

傾向がある

ⓘ 〈tend to *do*〉（～する傾向がある）の形で押さえておこう。

例 The cat **tends** to nap right after eating breakfast.

その猫は朝ごはんを食べるとすぐにうたた寝をする傾向がある。

□□□ 0436

except

/ ɪksépt /

名 exception 例外
形 exceptional 例外的な；並外れた

前 **not including someone or something**

～を除いて、～以外は

ⓘ except for（～を除いて）という表現も重要。

〈ex-（外に）+cept（取り出された）〉

例 The little girl likes all vegetables **except** zucchini.

その小さな女の子は、ズッキーニ以外は野菜が全部好きだ。

□□□ 0437

sight

/ sáɪt /

名 ① **the act of seeing someone or something**

見ること

ⓘ site（用地）、cite（～を引用する）と同音。

例 The **sight** of cute puppies makes her grandmother smile.

かわいい子犬を見ると、彼女の祖母は笑顔になる。

② **a place within an area that is famous or interesting**

名所、観光地

ⓘ ふつう複数形で使う。

例 The couple took a bus tour to see all the **sights** of Paris.

そのカップルはバスツアーを利用して、パリの名所すべてを見てまわった。

③ **the sense that lets animals and people see with their eyes**

視覚、視力

例 Thanks to the surgery, she regained **sight** in both eyes.

手術のおかげで彼女は両眼の視力を取り戻した。

□□□ 0438

commercial

/ kəmə́ːrʃəl /

副 commercially 商業的に
名 commerce 商業活動

形 **related to the buying and selling of goods and services**

商業的な、営利的な

〈com-（共に）+merc（商う）+ -ial（形容詞）〉

例 **Commercial** flights started to become popular after World War II.

商用旅客機の飛行は第二次世界大戦以降、一般的になり始めた。

0439

habit

/ hǽbət /

形 habitual 常習的な；習慣的な

名 **something that you do regularly**

習慣、癖

ⓘ 主に個人の習慣を指す。社会的な「慣習」はcustomと言う。

例 She has a bad **habit** of biting her fingernails when she is nervous.

彼女には、緊張すると爪をかむ悪い癖がある。

0440

committee

/ kəmíti /

動 commit ～を委ねる

名 **a group of people who are chosen to make decisions about something**

委員会

〈committ(任せる)＋-ee(人)〉

例 A special **committee** was set up to look into the matter.

その件を調査するための特別委員会が設置された。

0441

terrible

/ térəbl /

副 terribly ひどく

形 ① **showing how bad something is**

(程度が) ひどい

≒ severe

例 Nancy gets **terrible** headaches from the lights in the cafeteria.

ナンシーはカフェテリアの照明が原因でひどい頭痛になる。

② **being of very bad quality**

(質が) ひどい

⇔ excellent

例 Her nephew is a **terrible** driver.

彼女の甥は運転がひどく下手だ。

0442

source
/ sɔ́ːrs /

名 **a place, person, or thing from which you get something needed or wanted**

源

ⓘ 調味料の「ソース」はsauce。

例 His main **source** of protein is tofu.

彼の主なタンパク源は豆腐だ。

□□□ 0443

supply
/ səplάɪ /

名 supplier 供給者

動 **to provide something that is needed for someone or something**

～を供給する

⇔ demand

〈sup-（下に）+ply（満たす）〉

例 The actors were **supplied** with lunch after they finished filming.

俳優たちは撮影が終わってから昼食を支給された。

名 ① **the amount of something that is available for use**

供給

⇔ demand

例 There are many countries that don't have enough **supply** of fresh water.

真水の供給が十分にない国はたくさんある。

② **the things you need to do something**

必需品

ⓘ 複数形で使う。

例 If you live in Japan, you should always have emergency earthquake **supplies** ready.

日本に住んでいるなら、急な地震に備えた必需品を常に用意しておいた方がいい。

0444

electricity

/ ɪlèktrísəti /

形 electric 電動の
形 electrical 電気の
形 electronic 電子工学の

名 **a type of energy that provides the power needed to use lights, devices, and so on**

電気、電力

ⓘ アクセントはriの位置。

例 That wind farm generates enough **electricity** for the whole town.

あの風力発電所では町全体に十分な電力を発電している。

0445

seed

/ síːd /

名 **a small object produced by a plant from which a new plant can grow**

種

例 Some flower **seeds** are very big, and others are very small.

とても大きな花の種もあれば、とても小さいものもある。

0446

mark

/ máːrk /

形 marked 顕著な
副 markedly 著しく

名 **a symbol written or printed that is used as a sign for something else**

印

例 He put a **mark** on the paper every time he drank a glass of water.

水を1杯飲むたびに、彼は紙に印をつけた。

動 **to occur at, indicate, or celebrate a particular time or event**

〈時期・出来事〉を示す、記念する

例 The fall of the Berlin Wall **marked** the beginning of a new era of German history.

ベルリンの壁崩壊はドイツ史の新時代の始まりを画した。

□□□ 0447

version

/ vǝ́ːrʒǝn /

名 **a form of something that is slightly different from other forms of the same thing**

版、バージョン

≒ edition

〈vers(回転する)+-ion(名詞)〉

例 The band put out a remixed **version** of their best-selling song.

そのバンドはヒット曲のリミックス版を出した。

□□□ 0448

essential

/ ɪsénʃǝl /

名 essence 本質

形 **extremely important and needed**

重要な、不可欠の

≒ critical, indispensable, vital

例 It is **essential** to arrive on time for job interviews.

仕事の採用面接では時間通りに到着することが不可欠だ。

□□□ 0449

examine

/ ɪgzǽmǝn /

名 examination 試験

動 ① **to look at something carefully to find out more about it**

〜を調べる、調査する

例 He **examined** the toy car to find out which part was broken.

彼はそのおもちゃの車を調べて、どの部分が壊れているのか見つけようとした。

② **to test and look over someone or something to see if they are sick or injured**

〜を診察する

例 Viola has to get her eyes **examined** every year.

ヴァイオラは毎年目の診察を受けなければならない。

0450

narrow

/ nǽroʊ /

副 narrowly かろうじて

形 **long and not wide**

（幅が）狭い

ⓘ「（面積が）狭い」と言う場合はsmallを使う。

例 The road was too **narrow** for the fire engine to enter.

その道路は狭すぎて消防車が入れなかった。

0451

district

/ dístrɪkt /

名 **an area that has a special purpose or characteristic**

地区、区域

〈di-（離れて）+strict（引く）〉

例 Shibuya is one of the main shopping **districts** of Tokyo.

渋谷は東京の主要なショッピング街の一つだ。

0452

strike

/ stráɪk /

形 striking 著しい
副 strikingly 著しく

動 **① to hit someone or something hard**

～にぶつかる、衝突する

ⓘ strike-struck-struckと活用する。原義は「打つ、打撃を加える」。野球の「ストライク」、好条件を求める「ストライキ」は共にこのstrike。

例 The Titanic **struck** an iceberg off the coast of Newfoundland.

タイタニック号はニューファンドランド島沖で氷山にぶつかった。

② to make someone suddenly act or feel a certain way

〈驚き・恐怖などが〉～を不意に襲う

ⓘ〈be struck＋形容詞〉（急に～になる）の形で押さえておこう。

例 Mandy was **struck** speechless when she saw her husband in a suit for the first time.

マンディは、スーツを着た夫を初めて見たとき、思わず言葉を失った。

□□□ 0453

tradition

/ trədíʃən /

形 traditional 伝統的な、従来の
副 traditionally 伝統的に

名 **a way of thinking or doing things that has been done by a particular group of people for a long time**

伝統

〈trad (引き渡す) +-(it)ion (名詞)〉

例 It is a **tradition** in this town to have a festival when the apple blossoms bloom.

リンゴの花が咲くと祭りを開くのがこの町の伝統だ。

□□□ 0454

concern

/ kənsə́ːrn /

形 concerned 心配して
前 concerning ～について

動 ① **to make someone feel worried**

～を心配させる

≒ worry

〈con- (完全に) +cern (ふるいにかける)〉

例 His poor health **concerns** his mother.

母親は彼が病弱なのを気にかけている。

② **to be about someone or something**

～に関わる

例 The book she wrote **concerns** human rights.

彼女が書いた本は人権に関するものだ。

名 **a feeling of worry, especially one that is shared by many people**

懸案事項、懸念

例 There was a lot of **concern** in the community about the construction of the factory.

工場の建設については地域内で多大な懸念があった。

□□□ 0455

tear

/ téər /

動 **to pull or cut something so that it is in different parts**

〜を引き裂く

ⓘ tear-tore-tornと活用する。同じつづりで「涙」という意味の名詞もあるが、発音は[tíər]。

例 He **tore** the letter into pieces because he was angry.

彼は怒っていたので手紙をびりびりに破いた。

□□□ 0456

hire

/ háɪər /

動 **to give a job to someone and pay them to do work**

〜を雇う

≒ employ

例 She was **hired** by a car magazine when she was in college.

彼女は大学に通っていたときに、車の雑誌に雇われた。

□□□ 0457

award

/ əwɔ́ːrd /

名 **something that is given to someone or something because they did well at something**

賞

≒ prize

ⓘ arの発音に注意。

例 That actress has won **awards** for most of her movies.

その女優は、出演した映画のほとんどで賞を獲得している。

動 **to give someone or something a prize or reward for doing something good**

〜に〈賞〉を与える

例 He was **awarded** a trophy for winning the race.

彼はレースに勝ってトロフィーを授与された。

□□□ 0458

communicate

/ kəmjúːnəkèɪt /

名 communication コミュニケーション
形 communicative 伝達の

動 to get someone to understand what you are thinking or feeling

意思疎通する

ⓘ アクセントはmuの位置。

例 People **communicate** with their words and their body language.

人々は言葉とジェスチャーで意思疎通する。

□□□ 0459

crew

/ krúː /

名 the group of people who work on a ship, airplane, or train

乗組員

例 The cabin **crew** serve food to passengers on long flights.

客室乗務員は、長距離のフライトでは乗客に食事を提供する。

□□□ 0460

fund

/ fʌ́nd /

名 an amount of money that is used for a specific thing

基金、資金

ⓘ 複数形で「財源、所持金」という意味も表す。

例 They created a library **fund** to help the library buy new books and computers.

彼らは、その図書館が新しい本とコンピュータを買うのを支援するための図書館基金を創設した。

動 to give money for something

〜に資金を供給する

例 Google helped **fund** the new business project in his town.

グーグルは、彼の町の新しいビジネスプロジェクトに資金提供するのを助けた。

□□□ 0461

respond

/ rɪspɑ́ːnd /

名 response 反応
形 responsive 反応する

動 **to do something because something has happened or been done**

反応する

〈re-（〜に対して）+spond（約束する）〉

例 The firefighters **responded** to the fire quickly and saved the house.

消防士たちはすぐに火事に対応し、その家を守った。

□□□ 0462

graduate

/ grǽʤuèɪt /

名 graduation 卒業

動 **to finish studies at a school or college**

卒業する

i graduate school（大学院）という表現も覚えておこう。

〈gradu（学位）+-ate（取る）〉

例 She **graduated** from elementary school over 10 years ago.

彼女は10年以上前に小学校を卒業した。

□□□ 0463

occur

/ əkə́ːr /

名 occurrence 出来事

動 ① **to happen**

（偶然に）起こる、生じる

i アクセントはcurの位置。

〈oc-（〜に）+cur（走る）〉

例 A solar eclipse **occurs** approximately every 18 months.

日食は約18か月ごとに起こる。

② **to come into your mind**

〈考えなどが〉浮かぶ

例 It just **occurred** to me that there is an easier way to do this.

私は、これをするのにもっと簡単な方法があると思いついた。

0464

trick

/ trík /

形 tricky 油断のならない、扱いづらい

名 **an action that someone does to entertain people**

芸当、手品

ⓘ「秘訣、こつ」という意味や、「～をだます」という動詞の意味もある。

例 The student likes to do card **tricks** in front of the class.

その生徒は、クラスの前でカードの手品をするのが好きだ。

□□□ 0465

inform

/ ɪnfɔ́ːrm /

名 information 情報
形 informed 情報通の

動 **to tell someone something, especially in an official way**

〈人〉に知らせる

ⓘ 〈inform A of B〉（AにBのことを知らせる）の形も押さえておこう。

〈in-(中に)+form(形を与える)〉

例 The nurse came to the waiting room to **inform** him that his wife had given birth to a baby girl.

看護師が待合室にやってきて、彼の妻が女の赤ちゃんを産んだと彼に知らせた。

□□□ 0466

sort

/ sɔ́ːrt /

名 **a type of person or thing**

種類

≒ kind

例 There are many **sorts** of animals at this aquarium.

この水族館には多くの種類の動物がいる。

動 **to divide different people or things and put them in a specific order**

～を分類する

例 Gail **sorts** the books on her bookshelf by color.

ゲイルは本棚の本を色で分類している。

□□□ 0467

load

/ lóʊd /

動 **to put an amount of something into or onto something**

(車・船などに)〈荷〉を積む

例 You can see people **load** goods onto the ships at the port.

港では人々が船に荷物を積むのが見られる。

名 **an amount of something that is carried or put into or onto something**

積み荷

例 The truck was weighed down by the heavy **load**.

トラックは重い積み荷で車体が沈み込んでいた。

□□□ 0468

crime

/ kráɪm /

名 criminal 犯罪者

名 **an action that is against the law and that you can be punished for doing**

犯罪

ⓘ criminalは「犯罪の」の意味でも使う重要語。宗教・道徳上の「罪」はsinと言う。

例 Murder is a very serious **crime**.

殺人は非常に重大な犯罪だ。

□□□ 0469

advise

/ ədváɪz /

名 advice 忠告
名 adviser 忠告者
形 advisory 助言する、諮問の

動 **to give someone your opinion about what should be done**

〜に忠告する

ⓘ 〈advise A to *do*〉(Aに〜するよう忠告する)の形で押さえておこう。

〈ad- (〜に) +vise (見る)〉

例 His doctor **advised** him to drink less coffee.

医師はコーヒーを飲むのを減らすよう彼に忠告した。

□□□ 0470

guard / gáːrd /

名 **a person who has the job of watching over or protecting someone or something** 警備員

ⓘ「ガードマン」は和製英語。英語ではguardだけでよい。

例 The security **guards'** job is to protect the museum's priceless collection of art. 警備員たちの仕事は、その美術館のかけがえのない美術コレクションを守ることだ。

動 **to protect someone or something from something dangerous** (害・危険から)～を守る、保護する

例 Two police officers **guarded** the entrance to the building. 2人の警察官が建物の入り口を警備していた。

□□□ 0471

therefore / ðéərfɔ̀ːr /

副 **for that reason** それゆえ、従って

≒ so, thus

例 You are sick and **therefore** won't be able to go to school today. あなたは体調がよくないのだから、今日は学校へ行くことができません。

□□□ 0472

independent / ìndɪpéndənt /

副 independently 独立して、自力で
名 independence 独立、自立

形 **not needing the help or support of other people or organizations** 独立した

⇔ dependent

〈in- (否定) +dependent (頼っている)〉

ⓘ 後ろにはof [from] がくることが多い。

例 She has been **independent** from her parents since she was 18 years old. 彼女は18歳のときから親元を離れて独立している。

0472語

□□□ 0473

instruction

/ ɪnstrʌ́kʃən /

動 instruct ～に指示する；～を指導する

名 ① **a statement or guide that says how to do something**

指示；指示書

ⓘ「instructする人」をinstructor（インストラクター、指導者）と言う。

〈in-（上に）+struct（建てる）+-ion（名詞）〉

例 He followed the **instructions** on the website to build his own bookshelf.

彼は自分だけの本棚を作るために、そのウェブサイトにあった作り方に従った。

② **the action of teaching someone about something or how to do something**

指導

例 The woman offers **instruction** in Japanese calligraphy every Wednesday.

その女性は毎週水曜日に書道の指導をしている。

□□□ 0474

height

/ háɪt /

形 high 高い
動 heighten ～を高める、強める

名 **how tall or short something is**

高さ

ⓘ eiのつづりに注意。

例 Her **height** is listed on her license.

彼女の身長は免許証に記載されている。

□□□ 0475

secretary

/ sékrətèri /

名 **a person who organizes records and other documents in an office as their job**

秘書、事務員

〈secret（秘密）+-ary（扱う人）〉

例 The school **secretary** is an old man with big glasses.

その学校の事務員は、大きな眼鏡をかけた高齢の男性だ。

□□□ 0476

identify

/ aɪdéntəfàɪ /

名 identification 識別
形 identifiable 識別できる

動 ① **to recognize someone or something for who or what they are**

～を特定する

〈ident(同じ)+-ify(～にする)〉

例 It was hard to **identify** her suitcase at the airport.

空港で彼女のスーツケースを特定するのは難しかった。

② **to think something is the same as something else**

～を（…と）見なす、同一視する

i identify with（～に共感［共鳴］する）という表現も覚えておこう。例：Millions of teenage girls identified with the main character of the novel.（何百万人もの十代の少女がその小説の主人公に共感した）

例 Many **identify** being thin with being healthy, but that isn't always true.

多くの人が痩せているのは健康な証しだと考えているが、それは必ずしも正しくない。

□□□ 0477

indeed

/ ɪndíːd /

副 **without any doubt**

本当に、確かに

≒ surely, certainly

例 This is a very expensive book **indeed**.

これは確かに大変高価な本だ。

□□□ 0478

climate

/ kláɪmət /

形 climatic 気候の

名 **the weather that is usual in a place or region**

気候

i mateの発音に注意。特定の日の「天気、天候」はweather。

例 Tokyo has a subtropical **climate**.

東京は亜熱帯気候だ。

□□□ 0479

unit

/ júːnɪt /

名 ① **a single thing, person, or group that is complete by itself but also is a part of something larger**

単位

ⓘ unは「1」を意味する語根で、unify（～を統一する）、unique（独特の）、unity（単一）などと同語源語。

例 Armies are divided into many smaller **units**.

軍隊は多くの小さい単位に分けられている。

② **a machine or a part of a machine that does a specific thing**

装置、（機械の）部品

例 Many people install air-conditioning **units** in the summer.

多くの人々が夏に空調装置を取りつける。

□□□ 0480

stuff

/ stʌ́f /

名 **an object or objects that you do not need to clearly name**

もの

ⓘ staff（職員、スタッフ）と混同しないように注意。

例 They sold all of their **stuff** at the market last weekend.

彼らは先週末に市場で自分たちのものを全部売った。

動 **to fill something so much that nothing else will fit in it**

～に詰める

例 She **stuffed** her bag full of snacks before going to her friend's house.

彼女は友人の家に行く前に、かばんいっぱいにお菓子を詰め込んだ。

□□□ 0481

instrument

/ ínstrəmənt /

形 instrumental 重要な；楽器の

名 ① a tool that is used to do something specific

器具

〈in-（上に）+stru（建てる）+ -ment（名詞）〉

例 Surgical **instruments** must be carefully cleaned to keep patients safe.

手術用の器具は患者の安全を守るため、入念に洗浄されなければならない。

② something that is used to make music

楽器

ⓘ musical instrumentとも言う。

例 Her favorite musical **instrument** is the clarinet.

彼女のお気に入りの楽器はクラリネットだ。

□□□ 0482

focus

/ fóukəs /

形 focal 焦点の

動 to concentrate on something specific

集中する

ⓘ focus on（～に集中する）の形で押さえておこう。

例 The cicadas were so loud that he couldn't **focus** on writing his essay.

セミの声がうるさくて、彼はエッセイを書くのに集中できなかった。

名 something that is being talked about or studied and that people are paying attention to

焦点

例 The **focus** of this study is on how much pet cats like their owners.

この研究の焦点は、ペットの猫がどれだけ飼い主を好んでいるかにある。

□□□ 0483

discount

/ dískaʊnt /

名 **an amount that is taken off the usual price of something**

割引

ⓘ「安売り、セール」はsale。

〈dis-(否定)+count(数える)〉

例 There was a large **discount** on all the items in the store after New Year's.

元日の後にその店では全商品の大幅な割引があった。

□□□ 0484

solid

/ sá:ləd /

動 solidify ～を凝固させる

形 **hard and not in the form of a gas or liquid**

固体の

例 After getting her wisdom teeth removed, she couldn't eat **solid** food for a few days.

親知らずを抜いてから、彼女は数日間固形物が食べられなかった。

□□□ 0485

advance

/ ədvǽns /

形 advanced 上級の
名 advancement 前進

動 **to make progress over time**

進歩する

≒ improve

例 Our understanding of the universe has **advanced** greatly over the past 100 years.

私たちの宇宙に関する理解は、過去100年間で大きく進歩した。

名 **the progress or improvement of something over time**

進歩

ⓘ in advance (前もって) という表現も覚えておこう。

例 **Advances** in medicine have made it possible to lessen the symptoms of some allergies.

医学の進歩のおかげで、いくつかのアレルギーは症状が軽減された。

0486

element

/ éləmənt /

形 elementary 初級の；元素の

名 **a specific part of something**

要素

ⓘ「元素」の意味もある。

例 There is always an **element** of risk in going scuba diving.

スキューバダイビングをすることには常にリスクの要素がある。

0487

grand

/ grǽnd /

形 **very large, or including a lot of people or things**

大きな、重大な

≒ huge

⇔ tiny

ⓘ grand piano（グランドピアノ）、grand slam（グランドスラム）などのgrand。

例 That country has a **grand** plan to send people to Mars.

その国には人を火星に送る壮大な計画がある。

0488

coin

/ kɔ́ɪn /

名 **a small, flat, and usually round piece of metal that is used as money**

硬貨

例 Some countries in the European Union have their own **coin** designs.

欧州連合の中には独自の硬貨のデザインを有する国もある。

動 **to make a new word or saying that other people start to use**

〈新語など〉を作る

例 Shakespeare **coined** many words that are still used in English today.

シェイクスピアは、現在の英語でも使われている多くの言葉を作った。

0489

author

/ ɔ́ːθər /

名 **a person who has written something**

著者、作家

〈auth (増やす) +-or (人)〉

例 She wrote a blog post about her favorite **authors**.

彼女はお気に入りの作家についてブログに記事を書いた。

0490

negative

/ négətɪv /

副 negatively 否定的に

形 **thinking about things that are not good**

否定的な、消極的な

⇔ positive

〈negat (否定する) +-ive (形容詞)〉

例 He had a **negative** attitude about the building design when he first saw it.

彼はその建物の設計を初めて見たとき、否定的な態度を取った。

0491

regard

/ rɪgáːrd /

前 regarding ～に関して、～について

動 **to think of someone or something in a particular way**

～を（…と）見なす

i 〈regard A as B〉(AをBと見なす) の形で押さえておこう。

例 He is **regarded** as an expert in the medical field.

彼は医学分野の専門家と見なされている。

名 **the act of caring or worrying about someone or something**

考慮、配慮

i with regard to（～に関して）という表現も覚えておこう。

例 She has little **regard** for her health, so she often gets sick.

彼女は自分の健康にほとんど配慮していないので、よく体調を崩す。

0492

refuse

/ rɪfjúːz /

名 refusal 拒否

動 to say or show that you will not do something that someone wants you to do

（～を）拒否する、断る

⇔ accept

〈re-（元に）+fuse（注ぐ）〉

例 She **refused** to help her brother with his science project.

彼女は弟の理科の課題を手伝うのを断った。

0493

permit

/ pərmít /

名 permission 許可

動 to let something happen or let someone do something

～を許す

〈per-（通って）+mit（送る）〉

例 Dogs are not **permitted** in this park without a leash.

犬はリードなしでこの公園に入ることが許されていない。

0494

ideal

/ aɪdíːəl /

副 ideally 理想的に
動 idealize ～を理想化する

形 right for the situation or person

理想的な

例 It was the **ideal** environment for learning a language because she was living with native speakers.

彼女はネイティブスピーカーたちと暮らしていたので、言語を習得するには理想的な環境だった。

名 an idea based on the perfection of something

理想

例 The man has an **ideal** of love that is impossible to have in real life.

その男性には、現実生活で得るのは不可能な愛の理想がある。

0494語

□□□ 0495

valley

/ vǽli /

名 **a low area between hills or mountains**

谷

ⓘ 規模の大きな「峡谷」はcanyon。

例 There is a large river flowing through the middle of the **valley**.

谷の真ん中を流れる大きな川がある。

□□□ 0496

contract

/ kɑ́:ntrækt /

名 **a document that is signed by two or more people to show they have agreed to something**

契約、契約書

〈con-(共に)+tract(引き合う)〉

例 It is important to read through the whole **contract** before signing it.

契約書にサインする前に、全体をよく読むことが重要だ。

□□□ 0497

practical

/ prǽktɪkl /

副 practically ほとんど；実用的に
名 practice 実践

形 ① **useful or suitable**

実用的な

例 They asked the volunteers to wear clothes that were **practical**.

彼らはボランティアの人たちに、実用的な服を着てくるように頼んだ。

② **relating to what is real and not what is imagined**

現実的な

⇔ theoretical

例 The woman has 10 years of **practical** experience as a teacher.

その女性は教師として10年間の実務経験がある。

0498

entire

/ ɪntáɪər /

副 entirely 全体的に

形 **not leaving out any part**

全体の

≒ whole

例 The **entire** family goes to the beach for a party every summer.

家族全員で毎年夏にパーティーのためにビーチへ行く。

0499

dozen

/ dʌ́zn /

名 **12 things or people**

ダース

ⓘ 前に数詞がつくときはtwo dozen cans of beer（缶ビール2ダース）のように形容詞のように使う（dozensとはしない）。また「数十、多数」という意味もあり、その場合は、dozens ofで「数十の～、多数の～」という意味を表す。

〈do（2）+zen（10）〉

例 This recipe needs half a **dozen** eggs.

このレシピには卵が半ダース必要だ。

0500

tough

/ tʌ́f /

形 ① **not easy to do or deal with**

困難な、骨の折れる

≒ hard, difficult

ⓘ つづりに注意。「タフな」というカタカナ語にもなっている。

例 She has a **tough** time accepting when she is wrong.

彼女は間違うと、それをなかなか受け入れられない。

② **very strict**

厳格な

例 Roy is a very **tough** teacher, but all of his students like him.

ロイはとても厳格な教師だが、生徒たちはみんな彼のことが好きだ。

章末ボキャブラリーチェック

次の語義が表す英単語を答えてください。

語義	解答	連番
❶ showing how bad something is	terrible	0441
❷ belonging to the sex that can give birth or make eggs	female	0432
❸ to get someone to understand what you are thinking or feeling	communicate	0458
❹ to try very hard to do something that is not easy	struggle	0434
❺ thinking about things that are not good	negative	0490
❻ how tall or short something is	height	0474
❼ the money that is made in a business or investment after all the costs involved have been paid	profit	0418
❽ an amount that is taken off the usual price of something	discount	0483
❾ to do something because something has happened or been done	respond	0461
❿ an object or objects that you do not need to clearly name	stuff	0480
⓫ a statement or guide that says how to do something	instruction	0473
⓬ a group of people who are chosen to make decisions about something	committee	0440
⓭ the weather that is usual in a place or region	climate	0478
⓮ related to the buying and selling of goods and services	commercial	0438
⓯《------ to》to be a member of something	belong	0427
⓰ having a higher rank than someone in the same position	senior	0430
⓱ right for a purpose or situation	proper	0423
⓲ useful or suitable	practical	0497
⓳ without any doubt	indeed	0477
⓴ a way to do something that requires special knowledge or skill	technique	0433

語義	解答	連番
㉑ a person who organizes records and other documents in an office as their job	secretary	0475
㉒ not needing the help or support of other people or organizations	independent	0472
㉓ to match the size and shape needed (for something or someone)	fit	0422
㉔ not including someone or something	except	0436
㉕ to concentrate on something specific	focus	0482
㉖ happening or existing in the present time	current	0431
㉗ to make someone feel worried	concern	0454
㉘ an action that someone does to entertain people	trick	0464
㉙ an area that has a special purpose or characteristic	district	0451
㉚ a place, person, or thing from which you get something needed or wanted	source	0442
㉛ a tool that is used to do something specific	instrument	0481
㉜ often seen, heard, or experienced by many people	familiar	0412
㉝ to give someone your opinion about what should be done	advise	0469
㉞ an action that is against the law and that you can be punished for doing	crime	0468
㉟ to be likely to happen or be done, or to happen or be done often	tend	0435
㊱ the number of people who live somewhere	population	0404
㊲ to say something funny to make people laugh	joke	0405
㊳ something that you do regularly	habit	0439
㊴ a single thing, person, or group that is complete by itself but also is a part of something larger	unit	0479
㊵ to say or show that you will not do something that someone wants you to do	refuse	0492
㊶ connected to or made for one person	individual	0407
㊷ extremely important and needed	essential	0448
㊸ for that reason	therefore	0471

語義	解答	連番
㊹ a low area between hills or mountains	valley	0495
㊺ how long something is	length	0409
㊻ something you want to achieve	aim	0417
㊼ very small	tiny	0426
㊽ something that is given to someone or something because they did well at something	award	0457
㊾ to put something where it cannot be easily seen or found	hide	0403
㊿ something that helps someone or something have a higher chance of succeeding at something	advantage	0408
51 to let something happen or let someone do something	permit	0493
52 to finish studies at a school or college	graduate	0462
53 to recognize someone or something for who or what they are	identify	0476
54 a person who is paying a professional or an organization for a service	client	0419
55 a document that is signed by two or more people to show they have agreed to something	contract	0496
56 to take something that does not belong to you or that you are not allowed to have without asking permission	steal	0402
57 to put a new person or thing in the place or position of what was there before	replace	0413
58 a small, flat, and usually round piece of metal that is used as money	coin	0488
59 an amount of money that is used for a specific thing	fund	0460
60 a type of energy that provides the power needed to use lights, devices, and so on	electricity	0444
61 a person who has written something	author	0489
62 to happen	occur	0463
63 relating to soldiers and armed forces	military	0420
64 not leaving out any part	entire	0498

語義	解答	連番
(65) 《----- to》 to (briefly) talk or write about someone or something	refer	0421
(66) to plan or want to do something	intend	0415
(67) a symbol written or printed that is used as a sign for something else	mark	0446
(68) to provide something that is needed for someone or something	supply	0443
(69) hard and not in the form of a gas or liquid	solid	0484
(70) existing or happening before	previous	0428
(71) a person who has the job of watching over or protecting someone or something	guard	0470
(72) a type of person or thing	sort	0466
(73) to give a job to someone and pay them to do work	hire	0456
(74) 12 things or people	dozen	0499
(75) a specific part of something	element	0486
(76) very large, or including a lot of people or things	grand	0487
(77) having a soft and flat surface, without any rough areas or holes	smooth	0410
(78) long and not wide	narrow	0450
(79) a person who knows a lot about something specific or has trained to have a special skill	expert	0425
(80) the group of people who work on a ship, airplane, or train	crew	0459
(81) a member of the military or an army	soldier	0401
(82) to put an amount of something into or onto something	load	0467
(83) to say or accept that something is true, even though you do not want to	admit	0406
(84) to pull or cut something so that it is in different parts	tear	0455
(85) to think of someone or something in a particular way	regard	0491
(86) not easy to do or deal with	tough	0500

語義	解答	連番
(87) a small object produced by a plant from which a new plant can grow	seed	0445
(88) a place where people go to worship because it is connected to a holy person or event	shrine	0414
(89) the power to change the way people think or behave, or the way something is done	influence	0424
(90) an event or time during which something special happens	occasion	0411
(91) connected to the place a person was born or spent their childhood	native	0416
(92) to tell someone something, especially in an official way	inform	0465
(93) to hit someone or something hard	strike	0452
(94) a form of something that is slightly different from other forms of the same thing	version	0447
(95) the act of seeing someone or something	sight	0437
(96) to look at something carefully to find out more about it	examine	0449
(97) to make progress over time	advance	0485
(98) right for the situation or person	ideal	0494
(99) a way of thinking or doing things that has been done by a particular group of people for a long time	tradition	0453
(100) a piece of writing that talks about something in a magazine, newspaper, or online	article	0429

Stage 6

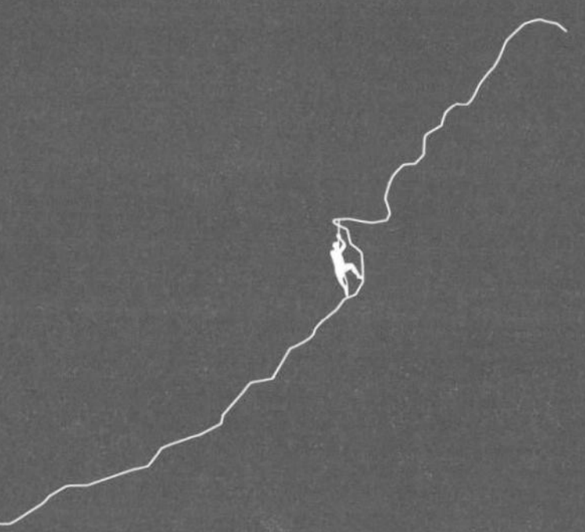

When the going gets tough, the tough get going.
困難なときが力の見せどき。

□□□ 0501

row

/ róʊ /

名 **a straight line made of people or things that are next to each other**

（横の）列

ⓘ in a row（1列になって；連続して）という表現も覚えておこう。five days in a rowで「5日連続して」。raw（生の）やlow（低い）と混同しないように注意。

例 The staff organized the chairs into three **rows** of six chairs each.

スタッフはいすを6脚ずつ横3列に並べた。

□□□ 0502

recommend

/ rèkəménd /

名 recommendation 推薦

動 **to tell people that someone or something is good and should be done or chosen**

～を推薦する、勧める

例 The waitress **recommended** the apple pie to the customers.

そのウエイトレスは、客にアップルパイを勧めた。

□□□ 0503

operate

/ ɑ́:pərèɪt /

名 operation 手術；作動
形 operational 使用できる

動 ① **to use and control something, such as a machine**

～を操作する

≒ run

〈opera（仕事）+-(a)te（動詞）〉

ⓘ「作動する、動く」という自動詞の意味もある。例：He bought a video camera that can operate underwater.（彼は水中でも動くビデオカメラを買った）

例 You need a special license to **operate** large machinery.

大型機械類を操作するには特別な免許が必要だ。

② **to do a surgery**

手術する

例 The only way to save his life was to **operate**.

彼の生命を守る唯一の方法は手術をすることだった。

□□□ 0504

repair

/ rɪpéər /

動 **to fix something that is broken or damaged**

〜を修理する

≒ mend

〈re-（再び）+pair（準備する）〉

例 His job is to **repair** broken refrigerators.

彼の仕事は壊れた冷蔵庫を修理することだ。

□□□ 0505

youth

/ júːθ /

形 young 若い
形 youthful 若々しい

名 **people who are young**

若者

例 Many of today's **youth** feel strongly about equal rights.

今日の若者の多くが権利の平等についてはっきりとした意見を持っている。

□□□ 0506

factor

/ fǽktər /

名 **something that is part of the reason something happens**

要因

〈fact（作る）+-or（もの）〉

例 There are many **factors** involved in the declining population of Japan.

日本の人口減少には多くの要因が関わっている。

□□□ 0507

survive

/ sərváɪv /

名 survival 生き残ること

動 **to continue living (after something)**

（〜を）生き残る

⇔ die, pass away

〈sur-（越えて）+vive（生きる）〉

例 Deep sea animals can **survive** in very extreme conditions.

深海の生き物たちは非常に過酷な条件下でも生き残ることができる。

0507語

□□□ 0508

divide

/ dɪváɪd /

名 division 分割

動 to separate something into multiple pieces

～を分割する

≒ split

⇔ unify, unite

〈di-(離れて)+vide(分ける)〉

例 She **divided** the candy evenly between everyone.

彼女は全員に均等にキャンディーを分けた。

□□□ 0509

region

/ ríːdʒən /

形 regional 地域の

名 a part of an area that is separate or different from other parts in some way

地域、地方

≒ zone

〈reg(統治する)+-ion(名詞)〉

例 Japan is divided into eight different **regions**.

日本は8つの異なる地域に分けられている。

□□□ 0510

transfer

/ trænsfə́ːr /

名 transference 移動、移転
形 transferable 移動［移転］できる

動 ① to make something go from one person, place, or object to another one

～を移動させる

≒ move

〈trans-(向こうに)+fer(運ぶ)〉

例 Keri used a phone app to **transfer** her money to another bank account.

ケリーは、別の銀行口座にお金を移すのに携帯電話のアプリを使った。

② to move (someone) to another place for work

転勤する；～を転任させる

例 He was **transferred** to Germany after two years at the company.

彼は入社して2年後にドイツに転勤になった。

 0511

lift

/ líft /

動 **to raise something or someone higher than they were before**

～を持ち上げる

≒ elevate

⇔ lower

ⓘ イギリス英語では名詞で「エレベーター」の意味もある。

例 Nelson **lifted** the ball over his head and threw it.

ネルソンは頭の上にボールを持ち上げて投げた。

□□□ 0512

royal

/ rɔ́ɪəl /

形 **relating to kings and queens**

王の、王室の

ⓘ loyal（忠実な）と混同しないように注意。

例 The British **royal** family might be the most famous family in the world.

イギリス王室は世界で最も有名な一家かもしれない。

□□□ 0513

victim

/ víktɪm /

名 **a person who has had something bad happen or done to them**

被害者

例 There were two **victims** in the car crash.

その自動車事故では被害者が2人いた。

□□□ 0514

combine

/ kəmbáɪn /

名 combination 組み合わせ、結合

動 **to put two or more things together**

～を組み合わせる、結合させる

≒ mix

ⓘ 〈combine A with B〉（AをBと結びつける）の形も押さえておこう。

🔑 〈com-（共に）+bine（2つのもの）〉

例 She **combined** the milk and sugar together to make icing for the cake.

彼女はケーキのアイシングを作るために牛乳と砂糖を混ぜ合わせた。

□□□ 0515

male

/ méɪl /

形 **belonging to the sex that cannot give birth or make eggs**

男性の、雄の

⇔ female

ⓘ mail（郵便）と同音。

例 The **male** penguins watch the eggs while the mothers return to the sea.

雄のペンギンは母親が海に戻っている間、卵の番をする。

□□□ 0516

seek

/ síːk /

動 **to look for someone or something**

～を探す、探し求める

ⓘ seek-sought-soughtと活用する。seek to *do*（～しようとする）という表現も覚えておこう。

例 The university is **seeking** a new president.

その大学では新しい学長を探している。

□□□ 0517

border

/ bɔ́ːrdər /

名 **the (often) invisible line that divides two areas, such as countries**

国境；境界

≒ boundary

例 Countries within the European Union have open **borders** with each other.

欧州連合の加盟国は、お互いに国境を開いている。

□□□ [illegible]

labor

/ léɪbər /

形 laborious 手間のかかる

名 **work that you do with your body or mind**

労働

≒ job

ⓘ イギリス英語ではlabourとつづる。

例 Manual **labor** is hard on the body.

力仕事は体に厳しい。

□□□ 0519

excuse

/ 名 ɪkskjúːs 動 ɪkskjúːz /

名 **a reason given to explain why something bad happened or was done**

言い訳

ⓘ 動詞と名詞の発音の違いに注意。

〈ex-（外に）+cuse（訴訟）〉

例 Oversleeping is a bad **excuse** for being late for work.

寝坊は仕事に遅刻した言い訳にならない。

動 **to forgive someone for doing something bad**

～を許す、容赦する

例 Her teacher **excused** her for forgetting to hand in her homework.

彼女の先生は、彼女が宿題を提出し忘れたことを許した。

□□□ 0520

basis

/ béɪsɪs /

名 **the important things, such as facts or ideas, from which another thing develops or can develop**

基礎

≒ base

ⓘ 複数形はbases。

例 Trust is the **basis** for a healthy relationship.

信頼は健全な関係の基本だ。

□□□ 0521

campaign

/ kæmpéɪn /

名 **a series of activities that are intended to produce a particular result**

（社会的・政治的な）運動

≒ movement

ⓘ gは発音しない。

例 The NGO did a **campaign** to raise awareness about plastic pollution in the oceans.

その非政府組織は、海のプラスチック汚染に関する意識を高めるキャンペーンをした。

□□□ 0522

recover

/ rɪkʌ́vər /

㊔ recovery 回復

動 ① to return to normal after a period of time that was difficult

回復する

〈re-（再び）+cover（覆う）〉

例 Some businesses never **recovered** from the 2008 financial crisis.

2008年の金融危機から回復することのなかった企業もある。

② to get something that was lost or stolen

～を取り戻す、回収する

例 The divers **recovered** treasure from the old sunken ship.

ダイバーたちは古い沈没船から宝を回収した。

□□□ 0523

broad

/ brɔ́:d /

動 broaden ～を広げる

形 large in size from one side to the other

（幅が）広い

≒ wide

⇔ narrow

例 The football player has very **broad** shoulders.

そのフットボール選手は肩幅がとても広い。

□□□ 0524

sink

/ síŋk /

動 to go down under the surface of something

沈む

⇔ float

ⓘ sink-sank-sunkと活用する。「流し、シンク」もこのsink。

例 Her ring **sank** to the bottom of the river after she dropped it into the water.

彼女は指輪を川に落としてしまい、それは川底に沈んだ。

0525

salary

/ sǽləri /

名 **the amount of money that someone is paid by their employer**

給料

ⓘ salは「塩」を意味する語根で、salt（塩）、salad（サラダ）なども同語源語。

例 She has a high monthly **salary** as a company CEO.

彼女は企業のCEOとして、高い月給を得ている。

0526

rumor

/ rúːmər /

名 **information or a story that is passed around but has not been proven to be true**

うわさ

ⓘ イギリス英語ではrumourとつづる。

例 There is a **rumor** going around that the mayor is dating a celebrity.

その市長は有名人と付き合っているといううわさが出回っている。

0527

loan

/ lóʊn /

名 **money that is lent to someone with the promise that it will be returned**

貸付、融資

ⓘ カタカナ語の「ローン」につられて「借りる」ことだと勘違いしないように注意。

例 It took her 10 years to pay back her student **loans**.

彼女は学生ローンを返済するのに10年かかった。

動 **to lend money to someone who promises to pay it back**

〈金〉を融資する

ⓘ 〈loan A B〉で「A（人）にB（金）を融資する」という意味を表す。

例 The bank **loaned** them money so that they could buy a house.

その銀行は、彼らが家を買えるように資金を融資した。

0528

sufficient

/ səfíʃənt /

動 suffice 十分である

形 **having or giving what is needed**

十分な

≒ enough

⇔ insufficient

〈suf-（下に）+fic（作る）+ient（形容詞）〉

ⓘ アクセントはfiの位置。

例 She has **sufficient** funds to buy a yacht.

彼女はヨットを買う十分な資金がある。

0529

abroad

/ əbrɔ́:d /

副 **in or to a country that is not yours**

外国へ、外国で

≒ overseas

〈a-（～に）+broad（広いところ）〉

ⓘ「外国の」はforeign、「外国」はforeign country。

例 She traveled **abroad** for the first time when she was 16 years old.

彼女は16歳のとき、初めて外国へ旅行した。

0530

stress

/ strés /

形 stressful ストレスを与える

動 **to say something strongly**

～を強調する

≒ emphasize

ⓘ アクセントはreの位置。

例 The doctor **stressed** the importance of sleeping enough to his patients.

その医師は患者に十分な睡眠を取ることの重要性を強調した。

名 **special attention that is given to something**

強調

≒ emphasis

ⓘ「（身体的・精神的）緊張、ストレス」の意味もある。

例 The writer put **stress** on the need to reform the prison system in her essay.

その作家はエッセイの中で刑務所の制度を改革する必要性に重点を置いた。

0531

establish

/ ɪstǽblɪʃ /

名 establishment 設立；組織

動 **to start or make something that is supposed to last**

～を設立する、確立する

≒ found

例 The city **established** a new school for blind children this year.

その市は今年、目の見えない子どもたちのために新しい学校を設立した。

0532

diet

/ dáɪət /

形 dietary 飲食物の

名 **the food that someone or something usually eats**

食事

ⓘ be [go] on a diet（ダイエットしている［する］）という表現も覚えておこう。大文字を使って the Diet と書くと「国会」の意味。

例 A healthy **diet** should include fruits and vegetables.

健康的な食事には果物と野菜が含まれていなければならない。

0533

succeed

/ səksíːd /

名 success 成功
名 succession 継承、相続

動 ① **to achieve something that you wanted to do**

成功する

⇔ fail

〈suc-（後に）+ceed（続く）〉

ⓘ succeed in（～に成功する）の形で押さえておこう。

例 The woman **succeeded** in convincing her boyfriend to go see the movie with her.

女性は、その映画を一緒に見に行こうとボーイフレンドを説得するのに成功した。

② **to get a job, title, or position from someone after they have died or retired**

（～の）あとを継ぐ

ⓘ succeed to（～のあとを継ぐ）の形も押さえておこう。

例 Gary will **succeed** his grandfather as owner of the candy store.

ゲリーは祖父のあとを継いで菓子店の店主になる。

□□□ 0534

formal

/ fɔ́ːrməl /

副 formally 正式に

形 **requiring or using serious and appropriate clothing or manners**

正式の、フォーマルな

⇔ informal

〈form（形）+-al（形容詞）〉

例 The queen of the country held a **formal** dinner at the palace.

その国の女王は宮殿で正式な晩さん会を開いた。

□□□ 0535

disappear

/ dìsəpíər /

名 disappearance 見えなくなること

動 **to stop being visible or existing**

いなくなる、見えなくなる

≒ vanish

⇔ appear

〈dis-（～ない）+appear（現れる）〉

ⓘ アクセントはpeの位置。

例 The deer **disappeared** into the forest.

そのシカは森の中へ消えた。

□□□ 0536

background

/ bǽkgràund /

名 ① **the events of the past that explain why something is the way it is now**

（出来事などの）背景

例 To understand the history lesson, the teacher gave the students a little **background** information about the war.

歴史の教訓を理解するために、その教師は生徒たちに戦争について少し背景知識を伝えた。

② **the things that have happened to you in the past and are part of who you are**

経歴

例 She talked about her academic **background** during her job interview.

彼女は採用面接中に自分の学歴について話した。

0537

ignore
/ ɪgnɔ́ːr /

形 ignorant 無知な、意識しない
名 ignorance 無知

動 **to do nothing to respond to someone or something or to pretend you do not see or hear someone or something**

～を無視する

〈i-（否定）+gnore（知る）〉

例 The tourists **ignored** the warning signs and entered the area anyway.

その旅行者たちは警告標識を無視して、その区域へ入っていった。

0538

target
/ tάːrgət /

名 **something that you are trying to do**

目標、目的

≒ aim, goal

例 The customer support team met their **target** of reducing complaints.

カスタマーサポートチームは、苦情件数の削減目標を達成した。

0539

doubt
/ dáʊt /

形 doubtful 疑わしい
副 doubtfully 疑わしげに

動 **to not be sure about something or think that it may not be true**

～を疑う、疑わしいと思う

ⓘ bは発音しない。that節が続く場合、「…ではないのではないかと思う」と訳すことが多い。例：Many people doubt that he would be a good leader.（多くの人は彼がよい指導者にはならないのではないかと思っている）

例 She had lied to him before, so he **doubted** her words.

彼女は以前彼にうそをついたことがあるので、彼は彼女の言葉を疑わしいと思った。

名 **a feeling of not being sure about something**

疑い

例 The doctor had no **doubt** that the surgery would be a success.

その医師は手術が成功することにまったく疑いを持っていなかった。

□□□ 0540

legal

/ lí:gl /

副 legally 法的に
動 legalize ～を合法化する
名 legality 合法性

形 relating to the law

法律の

ⓘ 名詞の前で使う。「合法的な」という意味も重要。

〈leg（法律）+-al（形容詞）〉

例 Some countries don't have a fair **legal** system.

公正な法制度がない国もある。

□□□ 0541

task

/ tǽsk /

名 something that someone has given you to do

（課せられた）仕事

≒ duty, job

例 The first **task** given to her at her new job was to read the manual.

新しい仕事で彼女に与えられた最初の課題は、マニュアルを読むことだった。

□□□ 0542

involve

/ ɪnvá:lv /

名 involvement 関わり、関与

動 ① to include something as a required part

～を含む、伴う

≒ contain

〈in-（中に）+volve（巻き込む）〉

例 The job **involves** a lot of travel between Tokyo and Bangkok.

その仕事には東京-バンコク間の多くの出張が含まれる。

② to make someone be a part of something

〈人〉を（～に）参加させる、巻き込む

ⓘ be involved in（～に参加する）の形で押さえておこう。

例 He tried to make sure his children were all **involved** in after-school activities.

彼は自分の子どもたちみんなを必ず放課後の活動に参加させようとした。

0543
alive
/ əláɪv /

形 **having life** — 生きている

⇔ dead

例 The woman stayed **alive** in the mountains by finding plants to eat.
その女性は食べられる植物を見つけて山中で生き延びた。

0544
reaction
/ riǽkʃən /

動 react 応答する

名 **the way someone acts or feels about something that happens or is said** — 反応、応答

≒ response

〈re-（再び）+act（行動する）+-ion（名詞）〉

例 Her **reaction** to the surprise birthday party was very good.
誕生日のサプライズパーティーに対する彼女の反応はとてもよかった。

0545
shine
/ ʃáɪn /

動 **to give off light** — 輝く

ⓘ shine-shone-shoneと活用する。「〈星が〉輝く」はtwinkle。

例 The moon **shone** brightly through the window.
窓越しに月が明るく輝いていた。

0546
despite
/ dɪspáɪt /

前 **used to say that something happened or is true although there was something else that might have prevented it** — ～にもかかわらず

例 **Despite** what people say, he is actually a good person.
人がどう言うかにかかわらず、彼は実はいい人物だ。

□□□ 0547

attach

/ ətǽtʃ /

名 attachment 付着物；愛着

動 ① to connect something to another thing

～を取りつける、貼りつける

⇔ detach

例 He **attached** a coupon to the brochure.

彼はそのパンフレットにクーポンを添えた。

② to connect a file, such as a document, to a message so that they can be sent together

〈ファイルなど〉を添付する

例 He forgot to **attach** his résumé to the e-mail before he sent it.

彼はメールを送る前に履歴書を添付し忘れた。

□□□ 0548

furniture

/ fə́ːrnɪtʃər /

名 the objects that are used to make a room usable

家具（類）

ⓘ 個々の家具ではなく家具類全体を指す語。「家具一つ」は a piece of furniture。

例 She went to the **furniture** store to buy a new bed.

彼女は新しいベッドを買いに家具店に行った。

□□□ 0549

ancient

/ éɪnʃənt /

形 of a time that was in the distant past

古代の

⇔ modern, contemporary

ⓘ aの発音に注意。

例 Many people study **ancient** Rome and Greece.

多くの人々が古代のローマとギリシャについて研究している。

0550

rare

/ réər /

㊖ rarely めったに～しない

形 **not common**

珍しい、まれな

≒ unusual

⇔ usual

ⓘ rare earth（レアアース、希土類元素）、rare metal（レアメタル、希少金属）などのようにカタカナ語にもなっている。

例 The little girl found a **rare** stone at the beach.

その小さな女の子はビーチで珍しい石を見つけた。

□□□ 0551

frame

/ fréɪm /

名 **an open object that holds another thing**

枠、額縁

ⓘ flame（炎）と混同しないように注意。

例 He painted the picture **frame** blue to match his curtains.

彼はカーテンに合うようにその絵の額縁を青く塗った。

□□□ 0552

obvious

/ ɑ́:bviəs /

副 obviously 明らかに

形 **easy to recognize or understand**

明らかな

≒ clear, apparent

〈ob-(～を遮って)+vi(a)(道)+-ous (形容詞)〉

例 For **obvious** reasons, many people don't share pictures of themselves online.

明白な理由から、多くの人々は自分の写真をオンラインでシェアしない。

□□□ 0553

stream

/ strí:m /

名 **an ongoing flow of people or things**

(人・ものなどの) 流れ

ⓘ ing形のstreaming（ストリーミング）はカタカナ語にもなっている。

例 There was a huge **stream** of people walking home after the concert.

そのコンサートの後には家路につく大勢の人々の流れがあった。

0553語

□□□ 0554

reply

/ rɪpláɪ /

動 **to say, write, or do something to answer something or someone**

返答する

≒ respond

〈re-（元に）+ply（たたむ）〉

例 He forgot to **reply** to the e-mail and his order was canceled.

彼はそのメールに返信するのを忘れ、彼の注文はキャンセルされた。

名 **something you say, write, or do to answer something or someone**

返答

≒ response

例 It took her all night to write a **reply** to the letter from her grandmother.

彼女は祖母からの手紙に返信を書くのに一晩かかった。

□□□ 0555

dramatic

/ drəmǽtɪk /

名 drama 劇
副 dramatically 劇的に

形 **sudden and extreme**

劇的な

ⓘ アクセントはmaの位置。

例 There was a **dramatic** increase in the price of food.

食品の価格が劇的に上がった。

□□□ 0556

stomach

/ stʌ́mək /

名 **the organ in your body where your food goes after you swallow it**

胃

ⓘ「胃痛、腹痛」はstomachache。

例 Some medicine will make your **stomach** hurt, so it's best to eat before taking it.

胃を傷める薬もあるので、薬を飲む前に何か食べておくのがベストだ。

□□□ 0557

rush

/ rʌ́ʃ /

動 to move or do something very quickly because you do not have much time

急いで行く、急いでする

≒ hurry

例 Marvin **rushed** to the train station so that he wouldn't be late for his date.

マーヴィンはデートに遅れないように駅に急いだ。

□□□ 0558

confidence

/ kɑ́ːnfədəns /

形 confident 確信した、自信のある

名 a feeling that you can do something or succeed at something

自信

〈con-（完全に）+fid(e)（信頼する）+-ence（名詞）〉

例 She has **confidence** in her ability to pass the test.

彼女は試験に合格する力があるということに自信がある。

□□□ 0559

argue

/ ɑ́ːrgjuː /

名 argument 議論

動 ① to give reasons why you are for or against something

…と主張する

ⓘ〈argue (that)...〉（…だと主張する）の形で押さえておこう。

例 They **argue** that the new law will hurt the environment.

その新しい法律は環境に害を与えると彼らは主張している。

② to speak in an angry way to someone because you do not agree with them

口論する、論争する

例 Her son **argued** with her about every rule in their house.

彼女の息子は、家でのあらゆる決まりごとについて彼女と口論になった。

□□□ 0560

definitely / défənətli /

形 definite 明らかな
動 define ～を定義する

副 in a way that is certain and without doubt

絶対に、確かに

≒ surely, certainly

ⓘ 会話では、1語で「確かに、その通りだ」という意味でも使われる。

例 There is **definitely** something eating our trash at night.

夜に私たちのごみをあさって食べている何かが絶対にいる。

□□□ 0561

aid / éɪd /

名 things that are sent or given to people in other countries or areas that need help

援助、支援物資

例 Countries around the world sent **aid** to the small nation after the earthquake.

地震の後、世界中の国々がその小さな国に支援物資を送った。

□□□ 0562

attitude / ǽtət(j)ùːd /

名 a way of thinking or acting

考え方、姿勢

ⓘ アクセントはaの位置。

例 He has a really bad **attitude** toward his teachers.

彼は教師たちに非常に悪い態度を取っている。

□□□ 0563

relax / rɪlǽks /

形 relaxed くつろいだ
形 relaxing くつろがせる
名 relaxation 息抜き、休息

動 to spend time resting or doing something you like, especially after working

くつろぐ、リラックスする

≒ unwind

〈re-（元に）+lax（緩める）〉

ⓘ「ストレス」はstress。

例 After a week at work, she decided to go to a hot spring to **relax**.

1週間の仕事の後、彼女はリラックスするために温泉へ行くことにした。

□□□ 0564

vote

/ vóut /

㊔ voting 投票

動 **to formally say who or what you choose to be or do something**

投票する

例 **Voting** in elections is an important way to make your voice heard.

選挙で投票をすることは、あなたの声を届けるための重要な方法だ。

名 **the formal choice you make regarding who or what someone or something should be or do**

投票

例 The U.S. voting system is complicated, so sometimes the person with the most **votes** still doesn't win the election.

アメリカの投票システムは複雑で、時に最も得票した人でも当選しないことがある。

□□□ 0565

aloud

/ əláud /

副 **in a way that others can hear clearly**

声を出して

⇔ silently

例 He always reads his writing **aloud** to check if it sounds natural.

彼はいつも、自分の書いたものが自然に聞こえるか確かめるために、声に出して読んでみる。

□□□ 0566

novel

/ nɑ́:vl /

形 **new and different from before**

目新しい

≒ original

〈nov（新しい）+-el（指小辞）〉

ⓘ「小説」という名詞の意味もある。

例 The young man is full of **novel** ideas to solve global warming.

その若い男性には、地球温暖化を解決する斬新なアイデアがたくさんある。

□□□ 0567

punish

/ pʌ́nɪʃ /

名 punishment 罰

動 **to make someone suffer because of something bad that they did**

～を罰する

例 The boy was **punished** for lying to his parents.

その男の子は両親にうそをついて罰を受けた。

□□□ 0568

license

/ láɪsəns /

名 **an official document or card that says that you are allowed to do or have something**

免許（証）

ⓘ イギリス英語ではlicenceとつづる。

例 In some countries, you can get a **license** to drive a car when you are 16 years old.

16歳になったら車を運転する免許が取れる国もある。

□□□ 0569

potential

/ pəténʃəl /

副 potentially 潜在的に

名 **someone's ability that can be improved and help them**

潜在能力、素質

≒ possibility

例 She has the **potential** to become the first female president of the country.

彼女はその国初の女性大統領になる可能性を秘めている。

形 **able to become real**

潜在的な、可能性のある

≒ possible

例 The investment has a lot of **potential** benefits, but a lot of risks as well.

その投資には多くの潜在的利益があるが、多くのリスクも伴う。

□□□ 0570

purchase

/ pə́ːrtʃəs /

動 **to buy something**

～を購入する

⇔ sell

〈pur-(求めて)+chase(追う)〉

ⓘ chaseの発音に注意。

例 Chris **purchased** his first car when he was 18.

クリスは18歳のときに初めての車を購入した。

□□□ 0571

nervous

/ nə́ːrvəs /

名 nerve 神経
副 nervously 神経質に

形 **having or showing feelings of worry or fear about something that might happen**

緊張した、不安な

≒ anxious, worried

〈nerve(神経)+-ous(形容詞)〉

⇔ calm, relaxed

例 Claude is **nervous** about flying without his parents.

クロードは両親に伴われずに飛行機に乗るのが不安だ。

□□□ 0572

thus

/ ðʌ́s /

副 **because of this**

それゆえ、従って

≒ therefore

例 He won the wrestling match, **thus** becoming the champion of the tournament.

彼はそのレスリングの試合に勝ち、したがって、トーナメントのチャンピオンになった。

□□□ 0573

trend

/ trénd /

名 **a way of being or doing something that is becoming more common**

傾向、動向

例 It is expensive to keep up with the yearly fashion **trends**.

毎年変わるファッションの傾向についていくのはお金がかかる。

0574

academic /ækədémɪk/

名 academy 協会、アカデミー

形 **relating to learning and education**

学問の、教育に関する

例 The young man got many **academic** awards when he graduated.

その若い男性は卒業するときに多くの学術的な賞をもらった。

0575

shadow /ʃǽdoʊ/

名 **a dark shape that appears somewhere when a person or thing is between that place and a source of light**

影

ⓘ「日陰」はshadeと言う。

例 She posed so that her **shadow** would look like a chicken.

彼女は影がニワトリに見えるようにポーズを取った。

0576

honor /ɑ́ːnər/

形 honorable 名誉の；尊敬すべき

動 **to think of or treat someone or something with respect and admiration, or to publicly show respect or admiration to someone or something**

～に栄誉を与える

ⓘ イギリス英語ではhonourとつづる。hは発音しない。

〈hon（名誉）+-or（名詞）〉

例 They were **honored** by the presence of their favorite musician at their wedding.

彼らは大好きなミュージシャンに結婚式に来てもらえるという栄誉を受けた。

名 **the respect you give to someone**

名誉、栄誉

例 The national rugby team brought **honor** to their country.

ラグビーの代表チームは自分たちの国に栄誉をもたらした。

□□□ 0577

comfort

/ kʌ́mfərt /

形 comfortable 心地よい
副 comfortably 心地よく

名 **a situation where you are relaxed and do not have any unpleasant physical feelings**

快適さ

⇔ discomfort

〈com-（完全に）+fort（力強い状態）〉

例 The girl read her favorite book in the **comfort** of her bed.

その女の子はベッドでくつろぎながらお気に入りの本を読んだ。

□□□ 0578

typical

/ típɪkl /

名 type 類型；種類

形 **normal or usual**

典型的な、代表的な

≒ common

ⓘ typiの発音に注意。

例 A **typical** day in the office is spent writing e-mails and answering phone calls.

その職場での典型的な1日は、メールを書いたり、電話対応をしたりして過ぎる。

□□□ 0579

pure

/ pjúər /

副 purely 純粋に
動 purify ～を浄化する

形 **not mixed with any other thing**

純粋な

例 That ring is made of **pure** gold.

その指輪は純金製だ。

□□□ 0580

theory

/ θíːəri /

形 theoretical 理論（上）の

名 **an idea that tries to explain facts or situations, but is not proven to be true**

理論、学説

ⓘ eの発音に注意。

例 Einstein is famous for his **theory** of relativity.

アインシュタインは相対性理論で知られている。

□□□ 0581

unfortunately

/ ʌnfɔ́ːrtʃənətli /

形 unfortunate 不運な、不幸な

副 used to say that something is sad, disappointing, etc.

不運にも、残念ながら

⇔ fortunately, luckily

ⓘ 同語源語のfortune（運；富）やmisfortune（不運）などの語も覚えておこう。

例 She was **unfortunately** not chosen to go to space.

残念ながら、彼女は宇宙へ行く人員には選ばれなかった。

□□□ 0582

billion

/ bíljən /

名 the number 1,000,000,000

10億

ⓘ「10億（人・個）の」という形容詞の意味もある。trillion（1兆）という語も覚えておこう。

例 There are **billions** of stars in the universe.

宇宙には何十億もの星がある。

□□□ 0583

arrange

/ əréɪndʒ /

名 arrangement 手配、準備

動 ① to plan or organize something before it happens

（～を）手配する、準備する

例 The man **arranged** for his wife to be sent flowers.

その男性は妻に花を送ってもらう手配をした。

② to organize something in a specific order or set something up to look nice

～を並べる、整理する

例 She **arranged** her books on the shelf in alphabetical order.

彼女は自分の本を棚にアルファベット順に並べた。

□□□ 0584

athlete

/ ǽθliːt /

形 athletic 運動の
名 athletics 運動競技

名 **a person who does sports or who is good at sports and physical exercises**

運動選手

ⓘ アクセントはaの位置。athlは「競う」を意味する語根で、triathlon（トライアスロン）などにも含まれる。

例 Many **athletes** dream of going to the Olympics.

多くの運動選手がオリンピック出場を夢見ている。

□□□ 0585

rely

/ rɪlάɪ /

形 reliable 信頼できる
名 reliance 依存；信頼

動 **to depend on something or someone for support or help**

頼る

ⓘ rely on（～に頼る）の形で押さえておこう。

〈re-（後に）+ly（縛る）〉

例 Pets **rely** on their owners to keep them safe.

ペットは自分の安全を確保する上で飼い主に頼っている。

□□□ 0586

convenient

/ kənvíːnjənt /

名 convenience 好都合、便利

形 ① **letting you do something easily**

便利な、楽な

⇔ inconvenient

〈con-（共に）+venient（来る）〉

例 It is more **convenient** to shower in the morning for some people.

朝にシャワーを浴びる方が楽な人もいる。

② **being somewhere that is easy to get to**

〈場所が〉便利のよい

例 That restaurant is in a **convenient** location.

あのレストランは便利のよい場所にある。

0587

experiment

/ ɪkspérəmənt /

形 experimental 実験（用）の

名 **a test that is done so you can see what happens and learn something from it**

実験

例 As a student, she got to do many small science **experiments**.

学生のとき、彼女は多くの小さな理科の実験をする機会があった。

0588

expense

/ ɪkspéns /

形 expensive 高価な

名 **the money that you use to buy something**

費用、出費

≒ cost

ⓘ at the expense of（～を犠牲にして）という表現も覚えておこう。

例 Those sandals are well worth the **expense**.

そのサンダルは費用に十分見合う価値がある。

0589

talent

/ tǽlənt /

形 talented 才能ある

名 **a natural ability to do something well**

才能

≒ gift

ⓘ 「テレビタレント」の意味はない。

例 She has a real **talent** for playing the piano.

彼女にはピアノを演奏する真の才能がある。

0590

escape

/ ɪskéɪp /

動 **to get away from a place or a person**

（～を）脱出する、逃げる

〈es-（外に）+cape（マント）〉

例 The prisoners tried to **escape** from prison, but they didn't succeed.

囚人たちは刑務所から脱走しようとしたが、うまくいかなかった。

0591

volume

/ vá:ljəm /

名 ① an amount of something — 量、数量

ⓘ カタカナ語の「ボリューム」同様、「音量」の意味もある。

例 If there is a high **volume** of sales, the book will get a second printing. — 大量に売れれば、その本は2刷になるだろう。

② a book that is part of a series — (書物の)巻

例 There are 23 **volumes** in this comic series. — この漫画のシリーズには23巻ある。

0592

session

/ séʃən /

名 a formal meeting or group of meetings in a court, government, etc. — 会合

〈sess (座る) +-ion (名詞)〉

例 The summer **session** of parliament ended last week. — 夏の国会は先週終わった。

0593

complex

/ kà:mpléks /

名 complexity 複雑さ

形 not easy to understand or made of many different parts — 複雑な

≒ complicated

⇔ simple, plain

〈com- (共に) +plex (編み込まれた)〉

ⓘ カタカナ語の「コンプレックス(=劣等感)」は英語ではinferiority complexと言う。

例 A car is made up of many **complex** parts. — 車は多くの複雑な部品でできている。

0594

decade

/ dékeɪd /

名 **a period of time that lasts 10 years**

10年間

ⓘ for decades（何十年もの間）という表現も覚えておこう。

〈dec-（10）+-ade（名詞）〉

例 She has been working as a nurse for over a **decade**.

彼女は10年以上、看護師として働いている。

0595

institution

/ ìnstət(j)úːʃən /

名 **an established organization**

機関、組織

〈in-（上に）+stit（建てる）+-ution（名詞）〉

例 The government needs to do more to support academic **institutions**.

政府は学術機関を支援するためにもっと努力する必要がある。

0596

observe

/ əbzə́ːrv /

名 observation 観察
名 observer 目撃者、観察者

動 **① to watch and listen to what is going on**

～を観察する

〈ob-（～の方を）+serve（注意して見る）〉

例 The scientists **observed** how the rats did puzzles to get food.

その科学者たちは、ラットが食べ物を得るためにどのようにパズルを解くかを観察した。

② to do what a rule or custom says you should

〈法など〉を順守する

≒ follow, obey

例 You cannot play the game if you aren't willing to **observe** the rules.

ルールを守る気がないなら、ゲームをすることはできません。

□□□ 0597

complain

/ kəmpléɪn /

名 complaint 不平、苦情

動 to say something that shows you do not like something or are annoyed by it

（…と）文句［不平］を言う

ⓘ〈complain (that)...〉（…と文句［不平］を言う）の形で押さえておこう。

例 The man **complained** that the room was too cold to sleep in.

その男性は、部屋が寒すぎて眠れないと苦情を言った。

□□□ 0598

desire

/ dɪzáɪər /

形 desirable 望ましい

名 a strong wish for something

願望

≒ longing

例 He has a **desire** to be a father.

彼には父親になりたいという願望がある。

□□□ 0599

impress

/ ɪmprés /

名 impression 印象
形 impressive 印象的な、感動的な

動 to make someone feel admiration or interest in something

～に感銘を与える

≒ touch

〈im-（中に）+press（押す）〉

例 She was **impressed** by how polite the children were.

彼女はその子どもたちの礼儀正しさに感銘を受けた。

□□□ 0600

warn

/ wɔ́ːrn /

名 warning 警告

動 to tell someone about something that could be dangerous or cause problems

〈人〉に警告する

≒ alert

ⓘ aの発音に注意。

例 The news reporter **warned** people that the roads would be icy after the snowstorm.

暴風雪の後は道路が凍結するだろう、とその記者は人々に警告した。

章末ボキャブラリーチェック

次の語義が表す英単語を答えてください。

語義	解答	連番
❶ to formally say who or what you choose to be or do something	vote	0564
❷ something that is part of the reason something happens	factor	0506
❸ relating to learning and education	academic	0574
❹ the money that you use to buy something	expense	0588
❺ an open object that holds another thing	frame	0551
❻ having or showing feelings of worry or fear about something that might happen	nervous	0571
❼ a situation where you are relaxed and do not have any unpleasant physical feelings	comfort	0577
❽ belonging to the sex that cannot give birth or make eggs	male	0515
❾ work that you do with your body or mind	labor	0518
❿ relating to kings and queens	royal	0512
⓫ to watch and listen to what is going on	observe	0596
⓬ to buy something	purchase	0570
⓭ to depend on something or someone for support or help	rely	0585
⓮ the organ in your body where your food goes after you swallow it	stomach	0556
⓯ to think of or treat someone or something with respect and admiration, or to publicly show respect or admiration to someone or something	honor	0576
⓰ information or a story that is passed around but has not been proven to be true	rumor	0526
⓱ in a way that others can hear clearly	aloud	0565
⓲ a test that is done so you can see what happens and learn something from it	experiment	0587
⓳ a feeling that you can do something or succeed at something	confidence	0558

語義	解答	連番
⑳ having or giving what is needed	sufficient	0528
㉑ people who are young	youth	0505
㉒ new and different from before	novel	0566
㉓ of a time that was in the distant past	ancient	0549
㉔ to include something as a required part	involve	0542
㉕ the number 1,000,000,000	billion	0582
㉖ to fix something that is broken or damaged	repair	0504
㉗ the (often) invisible line that divides two areas, such as countries	border	0517
㉘ a person who has had something bad happen or done to them	victim	0513
㉙ to get away from a place or a person	escape	0590
㉚ an established organization	institution	0595
㉛ not common	rare	0550
㉜ having life	alive	0543
㉝ to achieve something that you wanted to do	succeed	0533
㉞ the food that someone or something usually eats	diet	0532
㉟ the objects that are used to make a room usable	furniture	0548
㊱ to make something go from one person, place, or object to another one	transfer	0510
㊲ to put two or more things together	combine	0514
㊳ to make someone suffer because of something bad that they did	punish	0567
㊴ a formal meeting or group of meetings in a court, government, etc.	session	0592
㊵ used to say that something happened or is true although there was something else that might have prevented it	despite	0546
㊶ in or to a country that is not yours	abroad	0529
㊷ to say something that shows you do not like something or are annoyed by it	complain	0597

語義	解答	連番
43 a person who does sports or who is good at sports and physical exercises	athlete	0584
44 to go down under the surface of something	sink	0524
45 the events of the past that explain why something is the way it is now	background	0536
46 to separate something into multiple pieces	divide	0508
47 an official document or card that says that you are allowed to do or have something	license	0568
48 to move or do something very quickly because you do not have much time	rush	0557
49 a dark shape that appears somewhere when a person or thing is between that place and a source of light	shadow	0575
50 a straight line made of people or things that are next to each other	row	0501
51 to not be sure about something or think that it may not be true	doubt	0539
52 to give reasons why you are for or against something	argue	0559
53 a period of time that lasts 10 years	decade	0594
54 to raise something or someone higher than they were before	lift	0511
55 an amount of something	volume	0591
56 letting you do something easily	convenient	0586
57 in a way that is certain and without doubt	definitely	0560
58 to stop being visible or existing	disappear	0535
59 the way someone acts or feels about something that happens or is said	reaction	0544
60 to continue living (after something)	survive	0507
61 sudden and extreme	dramatic	0555
62 an idea that tries to explain facts or situations, but is not proven to be true	theory	0580
63 normal or usual	typical	0578

語義	解答	連番
❻❹ easy to recognize or understand	obvious	0552
❻❺ to plan or organize something before it happens	arrange	0503
❻❻ to return to normal after a period of time that was difficult	recover	0522
❻❼ to look for someone or something	seek	0516
❻❽ to give off light	shine	0545
❻❾ money that is lent to someone with the promise that it will be returned	loan	0527
❼⓿ not easy to understand or made of many different parts	complex	0593
❼❶ something that someone has given you to do	task	0541
❼❷ to say something strongly	stress	0530
❼❸ not mixed with any other thing	pure	0579
❼❹ to do nothing to respond to someone or something or to pretend you do not see or hear someone or something	ignore	0537
❼❺ to say, write, or do something to answer something or someone	reply	0554
❼❻ because of this	thus	0572
❼❼ used to say that something is sad, disappointing, etc.	unfortunately	0581
❼❽ a part of an area that is separate or different from other parts in some way	region	0509
❼❾ a strong wish for something	desire	0598
❽⓿ to tell someone about something that could be dangerous or cause problems	warn	0600
❽❶ a way of being or doing something that is becoming more common	trend	0573
❽❷ a natural ability to do something well	talent	0589
❽❸ a way of thinking or acting	attitude	0562
❽❹ to use and control something, such as a machine	operate	0503
❽❺ someone's ability that can be improved and help them	potential	0569

語義	解答	連番
㊗86 large in size from one side to the other	broad	0523
87 to tell people that someone or something is good and should be done or chosen	recommend	0502
88 to spend time resting or doing something you like, especially after working	relax	0563
89 to make someone feel admiration or interest in something	impress	0599
90 a reason given to explain why something bad happened or was done	excuse	0519
91 something that you are trying to do	target	0538
92 relating to the law	legal	0540
93 the important things, such as facts or ideas, from which another thing develops or can develop	basis	0520
94 to start or make something that is supposed to last	establish	0531
95 a series of activities that are intended to produce a particular result	campaign	0521
96 the amount of money that someone is paid by their employer	salary	0525
97 things that are sent or given to people in other countries or areas that need help	aid	0561
98 to connect something to another thing	attach	0547
99 an ongoing flow of people or things	stream	0553
100 requiring or using serious and appropriate clothing or manners	formal	0534

Stage 7

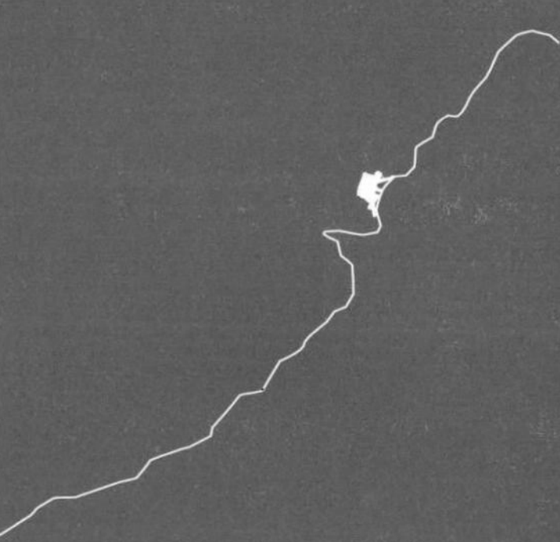

Where there's a will, there's a way.
志あるところに道あり。

□□□ 0601

raw

/ rɔ́ː /

形 ① **in a natural state**

加工していない、原料のままの

≒ crude

例 **Raw** silk can be used to make clothes.

生糸は服を作るのに使うことができる。

② **not cooked**

生の

例 Eating **raw** chicken is dangerous.

生の鶏肉を食べるのは危険だ。

□□□ 0602

label

/ léɪbl /

動 **to describe or name someone or something in a particular way**

～に（…の）レッテルを貼る

ⓘ aの発音に注意。「ラベル」、（大手レコード会社の意味の）「レーベル」もこのlabel。カタカナ語の「レッテル」はオランダ語letterから。

例 He was unfairly **labeled** a traitor by his coworkers for reporting his company's violation of the law.

彼は会社の法律違反を通報したことで、不当にも同僚から裏切り者のレッテルを貼られた。

□□□ 0603

religion

/ rɪlídʒən /

形 religious 宗教の

名 **an organized system of beliefs and rules about following a god or group of gods**

宗教

〈re-（再び）+lig（結ぶ）+-ion（名詞）〉

例 There are many different **religions** throughout the world.

世界各地には異なる宗教がたくさんある。

 0604

promote

/ prəmóʊt /

名 promotion 促進；昇進

動 ① **to help something develop, increase, or become well known**

～を推進する；
～を（販売）促進する

〈pro-（前に）+mote（進める）〉

例 The restaurant **promoted** its new menu using flyers.

そのレストランはチラシを使って新しいメニューを宣伝した。

② **to change the rank or position of someone to be higher or more important than it was before**

～を昇進させる

例 He was **promoted** to senior recruiter after two years of hard work.

彼は2年間熱心に働いた後、シニア・リクルーターに昇進した。

0606語

□□□ 0605

pour

/ pɔ́ːr /

動 **to fill a container with a liquid**

～を注ぐ、つぐ

ⓘ〈pour A B〉で「A（人）にB（飲み物）をついでやる」という意味を表す。

例 She **poured** her daughter a glass of orange juice.

彼女は娘にオレンジジュースを1杯ついだ。

□□□ 0606

obtain

/ əbtéɪn /

動 **to get something (with effort)**

～を得る、入手する

≒ earn, gain

〈ob-（～に向かって）+tain（保つ）〉

例 The lawyer **obtained** the information he needed to win the trial for his client.

その弁護士は、依頼人の裁判に勝つために必要としていた情報を入手した。

□□□ 0607

overall

/ 副 òʊvəró:l 形 óʊvərò:l /

副 **as a whole**

全体として、概して

〈over-（上に）+all（すべて）〉

例 She was nervous about presenting her project to the class, but did well **overall**.

彼女は自分の研究課題をクラスに発表するのに緊張していたが、全体としてはうまくいった。

形 **including everyone and everything involved in something**

全体の

例 The end-of-year bonus was decided by the **overall** performance of the whole team.

年末のボーナスは、チーム全員の全体的な業績によって決められた。

□□□ 0608

mental

/ méntl /

副 mentally 精神的に
名 mentality 心理（状態）

形 **relating to the mind**

精神の

⇔ physical

〈ment（心）+-al（形容詞）〉

例 People are starting to take **mental** health more seriously.

人々は心の健康を以前より重視し始めている。

□□□ 0609

passion

/ pǽʃən /

形 passionate 情熱的な

名 **a strong feeling of excitement or enthusiasm about something**

情熱

〈pass（苦しみ）+-ion（名詞）〉

例 She has always had a **passion** for learning languages.

彼女は言語を学ぶことに対してずっと情熱を持ち続けている。

□□□ 0610

opposite

/ áːpəzɪt /

動 oppose ～に反対する
名 opposition 反対

形 ① **completely different**

正反対の

⇔ same

🔑〈op-(反対に)+posit(e)(置く)〉

例 They're twins, but they have **opposite** personalities.

彼らは双子だが、性格は正反対だ。

② **at the other end or side of something, or across from it**

(位置が) 反対側の

例 There is a bank on the **opposite** side of the street.

この通りの反対側に銀行がある。

0612語

□□□ 0611

surround

/ səráʊnd /

形 surrounding 周囲の

動 **to be around every side of someone or something**

～を囲む

🔑〈sur(r)- (越えて) +ound (あふれる)〉

例 Their house is **surrounded** by bamboo.

彼らの家は竹に囲まれている。

□□□ 0612

propose

/ prəpóʊz /

名 proposal 提案
名 proposition 提案、申し出

動 **to offer an idea to someone or a group for them to think about**

～を提案する

≒ suggest

🔑〈pro- (前に) +pose (置く)〉

ⓘ「結婚を申し込む、プロポーズする」という意味もあるが、その場合は自動詞。

例 The man **proposed** that the city redesign the park to be better.

その男性は、市は公園を設計し直してもっとよくした方がよいと提案した。

0613

chemical

/ kémɪkəl /

副 chemically 化学的に
名 chemistry 化学

形 **relating to chemistry**

化学の、化学的な

ⓘ「化学物質、化学薬品」という名詞の意味もある。

〈chem（錬金術）+-ical（形容詞）〉

例 The young woman works in a **chemical** laboratory for the university.

その若い女性は、大学の化学研究室で働いている。

0614

pray

/ préɪ /

名 prayer 祈り；祈る人

動 **to speak to a god to ask for help or give thanks for something**

祈る

ⓘ prey（獲物）と同音。派生語のprayerは「祈り」の意味では[préər]、「祈る人」の意味では[préɪər]と発音が異なる。

例 His family **prayed** to God for his recovery.

家族は彼が回復するよう神に祈った。

0615

employ

/ ɪmplɔ́ɪ /

名 employment 雇用
名 employer 雇用者
名 employee 従業員

動 ① **to give someone a job where they will be paid money**

～を雇う

≒ hire

⇔ dismiss, fire

〈em-（中に）+ploy（抱え込む）〉

例 Her sister is **employed** at the bank.

彼女の姉は銀行に雇われている。

② **to use something for a specific reason**

〈手段〉を用いる

例 Aromatherapy is a commonly **employed** method of relaxation.

アロマテラピーはリラックスするのによく使われる手法だ。

0616

enable

/ ɪnéɪbl /

動 **to make it so that someone or something can do or be something**

～に（…）できるようにする

≒ allow

⇔ prevent

ⓘ 〈enable＋人＋to *do*〉（人が～できるようにする）の形で押さえておこう。

〈en-（～にする）+-able（できる）〉

例 Night classes **enable** people that work to continue their education.

夜間クラスのおかげで、仕事を持っている人も学業を続けることができる。

0617

mystery

/ místəri /

形 mysterious 不可解な、神秘的な

名 **something that is not easy to understand or explain**

謎、神秘

例 The northern lights were a **mystery** for hundreds of years.

オーロラは何百年もの間、謎だった。

0618

significant

/ sɪgnífɪkənt /

名 significance 重要性、意義
動 signify ～を意味する

形 ① **very important**

重要な、意義深い

⇔ insignificant

〈sign(i)（印）+fic（～にする）+-ant（形容詞）〉

例 The building of the Great Pyramids is a **significant** part of world history.

三大ピラミッドの建造は世界史の重要な一部だ。

② **large enough that it is noticed or has an effect on something**

かなりの

例 There will be **significant** changes to the way the company is run from April.

その企業の経営方法には4月からかなりの変更があるだろう。

0619

retire

/ rɪtáɪər /

名 retirement （定年）退職

動 **to stop working because you have reached the age when you do not have to work anymore**

引退する、（定年）退職する

〈re-（後ろに）+tire（引く）〉

例 Her grandfather never **retired** because he liked to work.

彼女の祖父は働くのが好きだったので決して引退しなかった。

0620

remind

/ rɪmáɪnd /

名 reminder 思い出させるもの、注意

動 **to make someone think about or remember something**

～に思い出させる

ⓘ 〈remind A of B〉（AにBを思い出させる）という形も押さえておこう。

〈re-（再び）+mind（気をつける）〉

例 He left a note to **remind** his daughter that her lunch was in the refrigerator.

彼は、冷蔵庫に昼食が入っていることを娘に思い出させるためにメモを残した。

0621

appeal

/ əpíːl /

形 appealing 魅力的な

動 **to be liked by or be attractive to someone**

（人の心に）訴える

例 That composer's music **appeals** to people of all ages.

あの作曲家の音楽はあらゆる年齢層の人々の心に訴える。

名 **a quality that makes someone or something liked**

魅力

例 The **appeal** of the movie was its beautiful animation.

その映画の魅力は美しいアニメーションだった。

 0622

crash
/ krǽʃ /

動 **to hit something hard and cause damage**

衝突する

ⓘ 擬音語からできた語で、音の近いclashも「衝突（する）」を意味する。

例 The car **crashed** into the light pole in front of the restaurant.

その車はレストランの前の街灯に衝突した。

□□□ 0623

somehow
/ sʌ́mhàʊ /

副 **in a way that is not clear**

どういうわけか

ⓘ「どうにかして」という意味もある。

例 They **somehow** got lost walking to the convenience store.

彼らはコンビニエンスストアへ向かって歩いていて、どういうわけか道に迷った。

□□□ 0624

muscle
/ mʌ́sl /

形 muscular 筋肉の

名 **a part of your body that produces movement**

筋肉

ⓘ cは発音しない。

例 He had to do **muscle** training after he broke his foot.

彼は足を骨折後、筋力トレーニングをしなければならなかった。

□□□ 0625

weigh
/ wéɪ /

名 weight 重さ

動 **to have a certain weight**

～の重さがある

ⓘ way（道；方法）と同音。

例 Tyler **weighed** 48 kg before getting married.

タイラーは結婚する前は48キロだった。

□□□ 0626

rough

/ rʌ́f /

形 ① **having a surface that is not smooth**

ざらざらした、粗い

⇔ soft

例 The texture of tree bark can be very **rough**.

樹皮の手触りはとてもざらざらしていることもある。

② **not detailed or exact**

大まかな

≒ approximate

例 The architect gave his client a **rough** draft of his plans for the new shopping mall.

その建築家は、新しいショッピングモールの設計図の大まかな草案をクライアントに見せた。

□□□ 0627

historical

/ hɪstɔ́ːrɪkəl /

名 history 歴史

形 **relating to history**

歴史に関する、歴史の

ⓘ historic（歴史的に重要な）という語も覚えておこう。

例 **Historical** research can teach us many important lessons.

歴史の研究は、多くの重要な教訓を私たちに教えてくれる。

□□□ 0628

survey

/ sə́ːrveɪ /

名 **an activity where people are asked questions about something to get information**

調査

≒ poll

〈sur-（上から）+vey（見る）〉

ⓘ「～を調査する」という動詞の意味もあるが、その場合、発音は[sərvéɪ]となる。

例 The company gave a **survey** to their customers to find out how to make their services better.

その企業はサービスを向上させる方法を探るために、顧客に調査をした。

0629

demonstrate

/ démənstrèɪt /

名 demonstration 証明

動 ① **to show something by providing clear evidence or proof**

～を証明する、実証する

≒ prove

🔑 〈de-（完全に）+monstr（見せる）+-ate（動詞）〉

ⓘ アクセントはdeの位置。

例 The lawyer **demonstrated** that the man was guilty of the crime.

弁護士は、その男性がその事件で有罪だということを証明した。

② **to show how something is done or works**

～を実演する

例 The scientist **demonstrated** how his new invention worked at the conference.

その科学者は会議で、彼の新しい発明がどのように動くかを実演した。

0630

ceremony

/ sérəmòʊni /

形 ceremonial 儀式の

名 **a formal social or religious event**

儀式、式典

ⓘ MC（司会者、司会進行役）はMaster of Ceremonyの略。

例 The whole town came to the opening **ceremony** for the new school.

町の全員が新しい学校の開校式典に集まった。

0631

possibly

/ pá:səbli /

形 possible 可能な
名 possibility 可能性

副 **used to say that something might happen or exist**

ひょっとすると

≒ maybe, perhaps

例 There is **possibly** life on other planets, but we don't know for sure.

ひょっとするとほかの惑星に生命がいるかもしれないが、確かにわかっているわけではない。

□□□ 0632

hardly

/ háːrdli /

副 **almost no** — ほとんど～ない

≒ barely

ⓘ hardly ever（めったに～ない）という強調表現も覚えておこう。

例 There was **hardly** any rain last summer. — 去年の夏はほとんど雨が降らなかった。

□□□ 0633

shade

/ ʃéɪd /

名 **an area that the light of the sun does not touch** — 日陰、木陰

ⓘ「影」はshadowと言う。

例 It is cooler in the **shade** than it is directly in the sun. — 直射日光の当たるところよりも日陰の方が涼しい。

□□□ 0634

relief

/ rɪlíːf /

動 relieve〈不安・苦痛〉を和らげる

名 ① **a good feeling that someone has after something bad stops or does not happen** — 安心、ほっとすること

ⓘ 美術用語のrelief（レリーフ；浮き彫り）も同じつづり。

〈re-(再び)+lief(持ち上げる)〉

例 Gail sighed in **relief** when the plane landed safely on the ground. — 飛行機が安全に地上に着地すると、ゲイルはほっとしてため息をついた。

② **things that are given to people who need help because something bad happened** — 救援、救助

例 The children raised money to donate to the hurricane **relief** effort. — 子どもたちはハリケーンの救援活動に寄付するためのお金を集めた。

□□□ 0635

suitable

/ sú:təbl /

動 suit ～に適する

形 **having what is right or needed for something**

適した、ふさわしい

≒ appropriate

〈suit(適する)+-able(できる)〉

例 He doesn't have any shirts that are **suitable** to wear to work.

彼は仕事に着ていくのにふさわしいシャツをまったく持っていない。

□□□ 0636

rapid

/ rǽpɪd /

副 rapidly 急速に
名 rapidity 急速さ

形 **happening without much time passing**

急速な

≒ fast, quick

⇔ slow

例 The **rapid** increase of water in the river worried everyone.

その川の水の急速な増加に誰もが心配した。

□□□ 0637

volunteer

/ vὰ:ləntíər /

名 **someone who does something for free because they want to**

ボランティア

ⓘ アクセントはteerの位置。「ボランティア活動をする」などの動詞の意味、volunteer work（ボランティアの仕事）のような形容詞の使い方もある。

例 She is a **volunteer** at the local nursing home.

彼女は地元の介護施設のボランティアだ。

□□□ 0638

wealth

/ wélθ /

形 wealthy 裕福な

名 **a large amount of money and things someone has**

富

≒ fortune

例 The family gained great **wealth** during the gold rush.

その家族はゴールドラッシュ中に莫大な富を得た。

0639

presence

/ prézns /

形 present 存在して

名 **the state of being somewhere**

存在

〈pre-（前に）+sence（存在）〉

例 The CEO's **presence** at the meeting made everyone nervous.

その会議でのCEOの存在は、みんなを緊張させた。

0640

prison

/ prízn /

名 prisoner 囚人

名 **a place where people have to stay because they committed a crime**

刑務所

≒ jail

ⓘ pris(e)は「捕まえる」を意味する語根で、enterprise（企て）、surprise（～を驚かせる）なども同語源語。

例 The man spent 10 years in **prison** for robbery.

その男性は窃盗罪で10年間刑務所で過ごした。

0641

settle

/ sétl /

名 settlement 入植（地）；解決

動 ① **to move somewhere new and make it your home**

定住する

例 Many Europeans **settled** in North America in the 1700s.

たくさんのヨーロッパ人が1700年代に北米に定住した。

② **to end something by agreeing to something**

～に決着をつける

≒ fix, set

例 The children **settled** their argument with a game of rock, paper, scissors.

子どもたちはじゃんけんをして口論に決着をつけた。

□□□ 0642

election

/ ɪlékʃən /

動 elect ～を選ぶ

名 an event in which people choose someone for a public position by voting

選挙

〈e-(外に)+lect(選ぶ)+-ion(名詞)〉

例 The U.S. presidential **election** is held every four years.

アメリカ大統領選挙は4年ごとに行われる。

□□□ 0643

neighborhood

/ néɪbərhʊ̀d /

名 neighbor 近所の人、隣人

名 a part of a town or city

地区、区域

ⓘ イギリス英語ではneighbourhoodとつづる。「近所」という意味もある。

例 Their new house is in a quiet **neighborhood** near the city center.

彼らの新しい家は、市の中心に近い閑静な地区にある。

□□□ 0644

fairly

/ féərli /

副 not extremely, but to a certain degree

かなり、まあまあ

≒ quite, pretty

ⓘ fair（公平な）の副詞としての「公平に」の意味もある。

例 Working in an office can be a **fairly** tiring job.

オフィスで働くのは、かなり退屈な仕事になり得る。

□□□ 0645

indicate

/ índəkèɪt /

名 indication 指示
形 indicative 示す

動 to show something

～を示す

≒ suggest

〈in-(中に)+dicate(指し示す)〉

例 Recent studies **indicate** that there are tiny pieces of plastic in our drinking water.

最近の研究は、私たちの飲み水に微小なプラスチックの破片が混入していることを示している。

□□□ 0646

deny

/ dınáı /

名 denial 否定

動 **to say that something is not true**

～を否定する

⇔ admit, confirm

〈de-(完全に)+ny(否定する)〉

ⓘ「〈要求など〉を拒否する」という意味もある。例：The bank denied their request for a loan.（銀行は彼らの融資の申請を拒否した）

例 She **denied** the rumor that she was going to retire.

彼女は自分が引退するといううわさを否定した。

□□□ 0647

dig

/ díg /

動 **to form a hole, tunnel, etc. by removing soil, snow, etc.**

〈穴・トンネルなど〉を掘る

ⓘ dig-dug-dugと活用する。

例 The workers **dug** a tunnel through the mountain to build the new highway.

作業員たちは、新しい幹線道路を建設するため、山にトンネルを掘った。

□□□ 0648

reward

/ rıwɔ́:rd /

形 rewarding やりがいのある

名 **something that is given to you because you have done something good**

報酬、報い

〈re-（後ろを）+ward（守る）〉

例 She was given a cash **reward** for winning the design contest.

デザインコンテストで優勝して彼女は賞金を与えられた。

動 **to give somebody something because they did well at something**

～に報いる

例 His parents **rewarded** him for doing well in school by taking him to Disneyland.

学校で頑張ったことに対して、両親は彼をディズニーランドに連れていくことで報いた。

□□□ 0649

cloth

/ klɔ́(:)θ /

名 **a material made by weaving threads together**　布

≒ fabric, textile

ⓘ clothe（〜に服を着せる）[klóuð]、clothes（衣服）[klóuz]と混同しないように注意。

例 Linen **cloth** is cooler to wear in the summer than wool.　リネンの布は夏に着るとウールよりも涼しい。

□□□ 0650

float

/ flóut /

動 **to stay on top of a liquid without sinking**　浮かぶ

例 One reason that ducks can **float** on water is the oil in their feathers.　カモが水に浮いていられる理由の一つは羽に含まれる油分だ。

□□□ 0651

reserve

/ rɪzə́ːrv /

名 reservation 予約

動 **① to save something for a specific reason**　〜を取っておく

ⓘ 〈reserve A for B〉（BのためにAを取っておく）の形で押さえておこう。

🔑〈re-（後ろに）+serve（取っておく）〉

例 They **reserve** their nice dishes for special dinners.　彼らは特別ディナー用に素敵な食器を取ってある。

② to organize something in advance so that you can use it or do something　〜を予約する

≒ book

例 He **reserved** a table at his wife's favorite restaurant for her birthday.　彼は妻の誕生日のために、妻のお気に入りのレストランの席を予約した。

0651語

□□□ 0652

injure

/ índʒər /

名 injury けが

動 **to hurt or cause damage to someone or something**

～にけがをさせる

例 She fell off her bike and **injured** her arm.

彼女は自転車で転倒して、腕をけがした。

□□□ 0653

freeze

/ fríːz /

名 freezer 冷凍庫

動 **to become hard because of the cold**

凍る

⇔ melt

i freeze-froze-frozenと活用する。「凍ったように動かなくなる」という意味もある。

例 The pond next to her house **freezes** every winter.

彼女の家の隣にある池は毎年冬になると凍る。

□□□ 0654

rank

/ rǽŋk /

動 **to put something or someone in a specific position based on their qualities**

～を格づけする、位置づける

i 「地位、ランク」という名詞の意味もある。

例 That university was **ranked** the top university in the country for the third year in a row.

その大学は3年連続で国内トップの大学に格づけされた。

□□□ 0655

contrast

/ kɑ́ːntræst /

名 **(the comparison of) the difference between two or more people or things**

対照、相違

i in [by] contrast（対照的に）という表現も覚えておこう。「～を対比させる」という動詞の意味もあるが、その場合、発音は[kəntrǽst]となる。

〈contra（対立して）+st（立つ）〉

例 He wrote an essay about the **contrasts** between the book and the movie.

彼は、その本と映画の相違についてエッセイを書いた。

□□□ 0656

clinic

/ klínɪk /

形 clinical 臨床の

名 a place smaller than a hospital where people get medical help

診療所

例 She goes to the **clinic** every month to get a check-up.

彼女は検診を受けるため、その診療所に毎月通っている。

□□□ 0657

transport

/ trænspɔ́ːrt /

名 transportation 輸送

動 to carry someone or something somewhere

～を輸送する、運ぶ

ⓘ「輸送」という名詞の意味もあるが、その場合、発音は[trǽnspɔːrt]となる。

〈trans-(向こうへ)+port(運ぶ)〉

例 Many goods are **transported** by train.

多くの品物が列車で輸送されている。

□□□ 0658

boring

/ bɔ́ːrɪŋ /

形 not interesting

退屈させる、つまらない

≒ tedious

⇔ exciting

ⓘ bore（～を退屈させる）の現在分詞が形容詞化したもの。

例 Doing the same thing every day gets **boring** after a while.

毎日同じことをしていると、しばらくして退屈になる。

□□□ 0659

severe

/ sɪvíər /

副 severely 厳しく、激しく
名 severity 厳しさ

形 very serious or bad

〈損害・苦痛などが〉ひどい、深刻な

≒ hard, harsh

⇔ mild

例 The storm caused **severe** damage to the building.

その嵐で建物はひどい損傷を受けた。

□□□ 0660

permanent

/ pə́ːrmənənt /

副 permanently 永続的に

形 **existing or continuing for a very long time or forever**

永続的な

≒ eternal

⇔ temporary

ⓘ 髪型の「パーマ」は英語でもpermと言う。元はpermanent waveの略語。

〈per-（最後まで）+man（留まる）+-ent（形容詞）〉

例 The museum opened a new **permanent** exhibit about dinosaurs.

その博物館は恐竜についての新たな常設展示を開設した。

□□□ 0661

defend

/ dɪfénd /

名 defense 防御
形 defensive 防御用の

動 **to work hard to keep someone or something safe**

～を守る、防御する

≒ protect, secure

⇔ attack

〈de-（離れて）+fend（打つ）〉

例 The soldiers **defended** the castle with their lives.

兵士たちは命がけで城を守った。

□□□ 0662

plain

/ pléɪn /

形 ① **simple and not decorated or complicated**

装飾のない、無地の

⇔ fancy

ⓘ plane（飛行機）と同音。

例 She wore a **plain** dress made of linen.

彼女はリネンでできた無地のワンピースを着ていた。

② **easy to notice or understand**

平易な

例 If you don't explain it to everyone in **plain** English, no one will understand.

みんなにそれを平易な英語で説明しないと、誰も理解できないでしょう。

□□□ 0663

vary

/ véəri /

形 variable 変わりやすい
名 variation 変化
名 variety 多様性

動 **to be or become different**

異なる、変化する

例 The color of gold jewelry **varies** depending on the quality of gold used.

金のジュエリーの色は、使われている金の品質によって変わる。

□□□ 0664

boss

/ bɔ́(:)s /

名 **the person who has the job of telling other workers what to do**

上司

⇔ subordinate

例 Her **boss** lets her work from home on Mondays.

上司は彼女に、月曜日に在宅勤務することを認めている。

□□□ 0665

stretch

/ strétʃ /

動 **to pull your body parts in a way that makes them long and tight**

手足を伸ばす

ⓘ「ストレッチ」というカタカナ語にもなっている。

例 It is important to **stretch** when you exercise.

運動するときはストレッチをすることが大切だ。

□□□ 0666

gallery

/ gǽləri /

名 **a room or building where you can look at art**

美術館、画廊

ⓘ ゴルフなどの「ギャラリー、見物人」もこのgallery。

例 You can enjoy art from local artists at the **gallery**.

その画廊では地元のアーティストの作品を楽しむことができる。

□□□ 0667

organize

/ ɔ́ːrgənàɪz /

名 organization 組織

動 ① **to plan and get ready for something**

〈イベントなど〉を計画する、準備する

≒ arrange

🔑〈organ(機関)+-ize(〜化する)〉

ⓘ イギリス英語ではorganiseともつづる。

例 The woman **organized** a party for her best friend's birthday.

その女性は親友の誕生日のためにパーティーを計画した。

② **to put things in a way that they are easy to find or can be used easily**

〜を整理する

例 It took him all day to **organize** his desk.

彼は机を整理するのに1日がかりだった。

□□□ 0668

wrap

/ rǽp /

動 **to cover something by putting something around it**

〜を包む

ⓘ 食品用の「ラップ」はふつうplastic wrapと言う。rap（(音楽の)ラップ）と同音。

例 Their family **wraps** Christmas presents in newspaper.

彼らの家では新聞紙でクリスマスプレゼントを包む。

□□□ 0669

domestic

/ dəméstɪk /

動 domesticate 〜を飼いならす

形 **relating to or made inside of a particular country**

国内の

⇔ foreign

🔑〈dom（家）+-estic（形容詞）〉

ⓘ「家庭内の」の意味もあり、domestic violence（家庭内暴力）、domestic waste（家庭ごみ）のように名詞の前で使う。

例 **Domestic** politics are deeply connected to the international economy.

国内政治は、世界経済と深くつながっている。

0670

import

/ 動 ɪmpɔ́ːrt 名 ímpɔːrt /

動 **to bring something into a country to be sold or used**

〜を輸入する

⇔ export

〈im-（中に）+port（運ぶ）〉

例 The small island country **imports** all of its oil.

その小さな島国は石油をすべて輸入している。

名 **something that is brought into a country to be sold or used**

輸入品

⇔ export

例 The main **import** of the country is salt.

その国の主な輸入品目は塩だ。

□□□ 0671

visual

/ víʒuəl /

名 vision 視力、視覚

形 **involving sight and your eyes**

視覚的な、視力の

〈vis(u)（見る）+-al（形容詞）〉

例 Some people are **visual** learners and find it easier to learn using pictures.

絵を使って学ぶ方が楽な視覚型の学習者もいる。

□□□ 0672

fellow

/ félou /

形 **describing people who are in the same group, situation, etc.**

仲間の、同僚の

ⓘ やや古い使い方だが、「男、やつ」という名詞の意味もある。

例 The class president gave a speech to his **fellow** students.

学級委員長は同級生にスピーチした。

0672語

□□□ 0673

adjust
/ ədʒʌ́st /

名 adjustment 調節

動 ① to change something a little bit to make it work better

～を調節する

〈ad- (～に) +just (正しい)〉

例 She **adjusted** the rearview mirror in her car so that she could see better.

彼女はもっとよく見えるように、車のバックミラーを調節した。

② to change to be better in a new situation

適応する、順応する

≒ adapt

例 It took a while for his eyes to **adjust** to the darkness of the hallway.

彼は廊下の暗さに目が適応するのにしばらくかかった。

□□□ 0674

literature
/ lítərətʃər /

名 something written that many people think is very good and worth respecting

文学

〈literat(e) (読み書きできる)+-ure (名詞)〉

例 The young man studied Korean **literature** at university.

その若い男性は大学で韓国文学を学んだ。

□□□ 0675

primary
/ práımèri /

形 prime 主要な
副 primarily 主として

形 most important

主要な、最も重要な

〈prim(e)(最初)+-ary(形容詞)〉

≒ main

⇔ secondary

例 The **primary** focus of the discussion was reducing pollution.

その議論の最も重要な焦点は、汚染を減らすことだった。

□□□ 0676

sudden

/ sʌ́dn /

副 suddenly 突然

形 **happening or done quickly in an unexpected way**

突然の

ⓘ all of a sudden（突然）という表現も覚えておこう。

例 There was a **sudden** crash of thunder, and then it started to rain.

突然の雷鳴が聞こえ、そして雨が降りだした。

□□□ 0677

amateur

/ ǽmətʃùər /

形 **doing something because you like it and not as your job**

アマチュアの

⇔ professional

ⓘ アクセントは語頭のaの位置。「アマチュア、素人」という名詞の意味もある。

例 Her friend is an **amateur** photographer.

彼女の友人はアマチュア写真家だ。

□□□ 0678

breathe

/ bríːð /

名 breath 息、呼吸

動 **to bring air into and out of your lungs**

呼吸する

ⓘ breath（息）の発音は[bréθ]。eaの発音が異なるので注意。

例 Humans cannot **breathe** underwater.

人間は水中では呼吸できない。

□□□ 0679

budget

/ bʌ́dʒət /

名 **an amount of money that is planned to be spent on a specific thing**

予算

ⓘ「安い」という形容詞の意味もあり、budget airline（格安航空会社）のように使う。

例 The prefectural government announced the new **budget** last night.

県は昨夜、新しい予算を発表した。

□□□ 0680

layer
/ léɪər /

名 **a part of something that lies over or under other parts of it**

層

例 Their wedding cake had five **layers**.

彼らのウェディングケーキは5層になっていた。

□□□ 0681

statue
/ stǽtʃuː /

名 **a figure of a person, animal, etc. that is made from stone, metal, etc.**

像

例 There is a large horse **statue** in front of the shopping mall.

そのショッピングモールの前には大きな馬の像がある。

□□□ 0682

suppose
/ səpóʊz /

名 supposition 推測

動 ① **to think that something is true or possible based on your current knowledge**

（たぶん）…だと思う、推定する

≒ guess, imagine

〈sup-（下に）+pose（置く）〉

i 〈suppose (that)...〉（（たぶん）…だと思う、推定する）の形で押さえておこう。

例 He **supposed** that it was possible for a cat and a dog to be friends.

彼は、猫と犬が友達になることは可能だろうと思った。

② **《be supposed to *do*》 to be expected, required, or allowed to do or be something**

～することになっている

例 Zac **was supposed to** be at the meeting by noon, but he missed the bus.

ザックは正午までにその会議に行くことになっていたが、バスに乗り損ねた。

0683

aspect

/ ǽspekt /

名 a part of something

側面、面

≒ side

ⓘ アクセントはaの位置。spectは「見る」を意味する語根で、perspective（観点）やinspect（～を詳しく調べる）なども同語源語。

例 Getting the job changed many **aspects** of his life.

その仕事に就いて彼の生活は多くの面で変わった。

0684

resident

/ rézɪdənt /

名 residence 住宅
形 residential 住宅用の
動 reside 住む

名 someone who lives in a particular place

住民

例 He has been a **resident** of Morioka for his whole life.

彼は生まれてからずっと盛岡の住民だ。

0685

consist

/ kənsíst /

形 consistent 一貫した

動《consist of》to be formed from some things or people

～から成る

〈con-（共に）+sist（立つ）〉

例 Breakfast at his house always **consists of** toast and orange juice.

彼の家では、朝食はいつもトーストとオレンジジュースだ。

0686

emotion

/ ɪmóʊʃən /

形 emotional 感情的な
副 emotionally 感情的に

名 a feeling such as love, joy, anger, etc.

感情

≒ sentiment

〈e-（外に）+motion（動くこと）〉

例 She has a hard time sharing her **emotions** with others.

彼女は他者に感情を伝えるのに苦労している。

□□□ 0687

annual

/ ǽnjuəl /

副 annually 年に1回

形 **happening once a year**

年1回の、毎年恒例の

〈ann (年) +-ual (形容詞)〉

例 The **annual** fireworks festival was canceled because of a typhoon.

毎年恒例の花火大会は台風のせいで中止になった。

□□□ 0688

origin

/ ɔ́:rədʒɪn /

形 original 元の、本来の
動 originate 〜を始める

名 **the point where something is created or starts**

起源

≒ root, source

ⓘ アクセントはoの位置。

例 The **origin** of the word "chef" is French.

chefという単語の起源はフランス語だ。

□□□ 0689

creature

/ krí:tʃər /

名 **a living thing, especially an animal**

生き物

ⓘ eaの発音に注意。「神によってcreateされたもの」が原義。

例 Many different **creatures** live inside the forest.

その森の中にはさまざまな生き物がたくさん住んでいる。

□□□ 0690

mode

/ móʊd /

名 **a way of doing something, or a type of thing**

方法、様式

≒ style

例 A bicycle is a **mode** of transportation that is better for the environment than cars.

自転車は車よりも環境によい交通手段だ。

□□□ 0691

critical

/ krítɪkəl /

名 critic 批評家
動 criticize ～を非難する

形 ① very important

重大な、決定的な

例 It is **critical** that everyone works together.

みんなが協力して取り組むことが非常に重要だ。

② showing that you do not like something

批判的な

例 Her parents were very **critical** of her decision to become a farmer.

彼女の両親は、農家になるという彼女の決断にとても批判的だった。

□□□ 0692

priority

/ praɪɔ́ːrəti /

形 prior 優先の、前の
動 prioritize ～を優先させる

名 something that needs to be done before something else because it is more important

優先事項

ⓘ「優先権」という意味もあり、give priority to（～に優先権を与える）のように使う。

例 The top **priority** for the company is customer satisfaction.

その会社の最優先事項は顧客満足だ。

□□□ 0693

insect

/ ínsekt /

名 a small animal with six legs and a body divided into three parts

昆虫

≒ bug

ⓘ「体にsect（切れ目）が入った動物」が原義。

例 An ant is a type of **insect**.

アリは昆虫の一種だ。

0693語

□□□ 0694

procedure

/ prəsíːdʒər /

動 proceed 進む、進行する

名 the way that something is done

手続き、方法

≒ process

〈pro-（前に）+ced（行く）+ -ure（名詞）〉

例 The **procedure** for applying for a car loan is very simple.

自動車ローンを申し込む手続きはとても簡単だ。

□□□ 0695

false

/ fɔ́ːls /

形 not true

正しくない、誤った

≒ wrong

⇔ correct, right

ⓘ aの発音に注意。

例 It is **false** to say that all birds can fly.

すべての鳥が飛べると言うのは正しくない。

□□□ 0696

decrease

/ 動 dìːkríːs　名 díːkriːs /

動 to get or make something smaller in size or number

減る；～を減らす

⇔ increase

ⓘ 品詞によってアクセントの位置が変わる。

例 They **decreased** the amount of garbage they produced by reusing plastic bags.

彼らはビニール袋を再利用することで、自分たちが出すごみの量を減らした。

名 the act of getting or making something smaller in size or number

減少

⇔ increase

例 The update to the product led to a **decrease** in customer complaints.

製品が更新されたことで、客の苦情が減少した。

□□□ 0697

category

/ kǽtəgɔ̀ːri /

動 categorize ～を分類する

名 **a group of things or people that are like each other**

カテゴリー、種類

例 There are many age **categories** for that sport.

そのスポーツには年齢別のカテゴリーがたくさんある。

□□□ 0698

initial

/ ɪníʃəl /

副 initially 初めに
名 initiative 主導権
動 initiate ～を始める

形 **happening at the start of something**

最初の

≒ first

⇔ final

〈in-（中に）+it（行く）+-ial（形容詞）〉

ⓘ「頭文字」という名詞の意味もあり、これがカタカナ語「イニシャル」になっている。

例 His **initial** reaction to the gift was surprise.

その贈り物に対する彼の最初の反応は驚きだった。

□□□ 0699

blame

/ bléɪm /

動 **to say that something bad that happened is someone's fault**

～を非難する、～のせいにする

ⓘ〈blame A for B〉（BをAのせいにする）の形で押さえておこう。

例 She **blamed** her brother for breaking her favorite toy.

彼女は大好きなおもちゃを壊したことで弟を責めた。

□□□ 0700

jam

/ ʤǽm /

名 **a situation in which something is so full that things can barely move**

混雑

ⓘ パンに塗るjam（ジャム）も同じつづり。

例 There was a large traffic **jam** on the highway because of an accident.

事故のため、幹線道路は大渋滞していた。

章末ボキャブラリーチェック

次の語義が表す英単語を答えてください。

語義	解答	連番
❶ the person who has the job of telling other workers what to do	boss	0664
❷ to bring something into a country to be sold or used	import	0670
❸ to stop working because you have reached the age when you do not have to work anymore	retire	0619
❹ something that is given to you because you have done something good	reward	0648
❺ to think that something is true or possible based on your current knowledge	suppose	0682
❻ to make it so that someone or something can do or be something	enable	0616
❼ to be liked by or be attractive to someone	appeal	0621
❽ to fill a container with a liquid	pour	0605
❾ a large amount of money and things someone has	wealth	0638
❿ not true	false	0695
⓫ relating to or made inside of a particular country	domestic	0669
⓬ describing people who are in the same group, situation, etc.	fellow	0672
⓭ an organized system of beliefs and rules about following a god or group of gods	religion	0603
⓮ to save something for a specific reason	reserve	0651
⓯ to say that something is not true	deny	0646
⓰ a place where people have to stay because they committed a crime	prison	0640
⓱ most important	primary	0675
⓲ to put something or someone in a specific position based on their qualities	rank	0654
⓳ involving sight and your eyes	visual	0671
⓴ happening once a year	annual	0687

語義	解答	連番
㉑ a group of things or people that are like each other	category	0697
㉒ simple and not decorated or complicated	plain	0662
㉓ a living thing, especially an animal	creature	0689
㉔ doing something because you like it and not as your job	amateur	0677
㉕ a part of something	aspect	0683
㉖ a strong feeling of excitement or enthusiasm about something	passion	0609
㉗ used to say that something might happen or exist	possibly	0631
㉘ something that is not easy to understand or explain	mystery	0617
㉙ someone who does something for free because they want to	volunteer	0637
㉚ to bring air into and out of your lungs	breathe	0678
㉛ (the comparison of) the difference between two or more people or things	contrast	0655
㉜ a part of a town or city	neighborhood	0643
㉝ a formal social or religious event	ceremony	0630
㉞ to say that something bad that happened is someone's fault	blame	0699
㉟ an event in which people choose someone for a public position by voting	election	0642
㊱ relating to the mind	mental	0608
㊲ an area that the light of the sun does not touch	shade	0633
㊳ to help something develop, increase, or become well known	promote	0604
㊴ an amount of money that is planned to be spent on a specific thing	budget	0679
㊵ not extremely, but to a certain degree	fairly	0644
㊶ to describe or name someone or something in a particular way	label	0602
㊷ to form a hole, tunnel, etc. by removing soil, snow, etc.	dig	0647

語義	解答	連番
㊸ to work hard to keep someone or something safe	defend	0661
㊹ relating to chemistry	chemical	0613
㊺ something that needs to be done before something else because it is more important	priority	0692
㊻ to be or become different	vary	0663
㊼ to carry someone or something somewhere	transport	0657
㊽ a situation in which something is so full that things can barely move	jam	0700
㊾ in a natural state	raw	0601
㊿ a good feeling that someone has after something bad stops or does not happen	relief	0634
51 《------- of》 to be formed from some things or people	consist	0685
52 to show something	indicate	0645
53 to cover something by putting something around it	wrap	0668
54 a figure of a person, animal, etc. that is made from stone, metal, etc.	statue	0681
55 to stay on top of a liquid without sinking	float	0650
56 an activity where people are asked questions about something to get information	survey	0628
57 to have a certain weight	weigh	0625
58 happening without much time passing	rapid	0636
59 a way of doing something, or a type of thing	mode	0690
60 to be around every side of someone or something	surround	0611
61 to become hard because of the cold	freeze	0653
62 to offer an idea to someone or a group for them to think about	propose	0612
63 a feeling such as love, joy, anger, etc.	emotion	0686
64 the state of being somewhere	presence	0639
65 not interesting	boring	0658
66 happening at the start of something	initial	0698

語義	解答	連番
(67) something written that many people think is very good and worth respecting	literature	0674
(68) to show something by providing clear evidence or proof	demonstrate	0629
(69) relating to history	historical	0627
(70) happening or done quickly in an unexpected way	sudden	0676
(71) having what is right or needed for something	suitable	0635
(72) a room or building where you can look at art	gallery	0666
(73) to hit something hard and cause damage	crash	0622
(74) having a surface that is not smooth	rough	0626
(75) someone who lives in a particular place	resident	0684
(76) to speak to a god to ask for help or give thanks for something	pray	0614
(77) completely different	opposite	0610
(78) as a whole	overall	0607
(79) very important	significant	0618
(80) a place smaller than a hospital where people get medical help	clinic	0656
(81) to change something a little bit to make it work better	adjust	0673
(82) a small animal with six legs and a body divided into three parts	insect	0693
(83) to get something (with effort)	obtain	0606
(84) a part of something that lies over or under other parts of it	layer	0680
(85) the way that something is done	procedure	0694
(86) to plan and get ready for something	organize	0667
(87) to move somewhere new and make it your home	settle	0641
(88) in a way that is not clear	somehow	0623
(89) existing or continuing for a very long time or forever	permanent	0660

語義	解答	連番
⓽⓪ almost no	hardly	0632
⓽⓵ to get or make something smaller in size or number	decrease	0696
⓽⓶ to make someone think about or remember something	remind	0620
⓽⓷ a material made by weaving threads together	cloth	0649
⓽⓸ to give someone a job where they will be paid money	employ	0615
⓽⓹ the point where something is created or starts	origin	0688
⓽⓺ to pull your body parts in a way that makes them long and tight	stretch	0665
⓽⓻ to hurt or cause damage to someone or something	injure	0652
⓽⓼ very important	critical	0691
⓽⓽ a part of your body that produces movement	muscle	0624
⓵⓪⓪ very serious or bad	severe	0659

Stage 8

Rome wasn't built in a day.
ローマは一日にして成らず。

□□□ 0701

strategy

/ strǽtədʒi /

名 **a plan that is designed to make something happen, often over a long period of time**

戦略

形 strategic 戦略上の

ⓘ 個別の「戦術」はtacticsと言う。

例 The marketing team had to think of a good **strategy** for selling the company's new product.

マーケティングチームは、その会社の新製品を売るためにうまい戦略を考え出さなければならなかった。

□□□ 0702

minor

/ máɪnər /

形 **not that important or large**

小さな、重要でない

名 minority 少数派

⇔ major

ⓘ「未成年者」という名詞の意味もある。

例 There was a **minor** scratch on the side of the car, but he bought it anyway.

車の側面に小さなひっかき傷があったが、彼はとりあえずその車を買った。

□□□ 0703

tight

/ táɪt /

形 ① **not easy to deal with because there is not enough time or money**

〈スケジュール・予算などが〉余裕のない

動 tighten ～をきつくする

例 They were on a **tight** schedule and had to work late every day.

スケジュールに余裕がなかったので、彼らは連日遅くまで働かなければならなかった。

② **fitting your body very closely**

〈服が〉きつい

⇔ loose

例 **Tight** jeans go in and out of popularity.

タイトジーンズは流行したり廃れたりする。

□□□ 0704

vitamin

/ váɪtəmɪn /

名 **a natural thing usually found in foods that helps make your body healthy**

ビタミン

ⓘ viの発音に注意。

〈vit(生命)+amin(アミノ酸)〉

例 They have added **vitamins** to the chocolate to make it healthier.

彼らはもっと健康によいものにするため、チョコレートにビタミンを添加した。

□□□ 0705

joint

/ ʤɔ́ɪnt /

形 **having two or more people or groups do something together**

共同の、合同の

≒ united

ⓘ「関節、継ぎ目」という名詞の意味もある。

例 They are the **joint** owners of a new coffee shop.

彼らは新しいコーヒー店の共同オーナーだ。

□□□ 0706

finding

/ fáɪndɪŋ /

名 **the results of research or an investigation**

発見したこと、研究の成果

ⓘ ふつう複数形で使う。

例 The research team published their **findings** online.

その研究チームは彼らの研究成果をオンラインで発表した。

□□□ 0707

reject

/ rɪʤékt /

名 rejection 拒否

動 **to not be willing to accept, believe, or think about something**

～を拒否する

≒ refuse, deny

〈re-(元に)+ject(投げる)〉

例 Even though she had no job, she **rejected** her parents' offer to give her some money.

彼女は仕事をしていなかったが、金をくれるという両親の申し出を断った。

□□□ 0708

capacity

/ kəpǽsəti /

名 ① **the number of people or things that can fit inside of something**

収容能力、容量

〈cap(つかむ)+-acity(名詞)〉

例 The school gym has a **capacity** of 1,000 people.

その学校の体育館は1,000人収容可能だ。

② **the ability to understand or do something**

能力

≒ capability

例 The company's **capacity** to build new cars is limited by the amount of steel available.

新車を作るその会社の能力は、手に入る鉄鋼の量によって制限される。

□□□ 0709

mood

/ múːd /

形 moody 不機嫌な

名 **the way someone feels at a particular time**

気分、機嫌

i 「雰囲気」は英語ではatmosphereと言う。

例 Being woken up from his nap put him in a bad **mood**.

彼は昼寝から起こされて機嫌が悪くなった。

□□□ 0710

signature

/ sígnətʃər /

動 sign ～に署名する

名 **your name written in the way that only you can write it**

署名、サイン

i 動詞のsignと異なり、gを発音する。有名人の「サイン」はautographと言う。

例 There is a place to write your **signature** on the back of all credit cards.

すべてのクレジットカードの裏側には署名を書く欄がある。

□□□ 0711

afford

/ əfɔ́ːrd /

形 affordable 入手可能な

動 ① **to be able to do something without anything bad happening**

～の余裕がある

ⓘ 〈afford to *do*〉（～する余裕がある）の形で押さえておこう。

例 She cannot **afford** to lose her job right now.

彼女には今すぐ仕事を手放す余裕はない。

② **to have enough money to pay for something**

～に払う［～を買う］余裕がある

例 Bell worked hard so that she could **afford** to buy a new watch.

ベルは新しい腕時計が買えるように熱心に働いた。

□□□ 0712

translate

/ trǽnsleɪt /

名 translation 翻訳
名 translator 翻訳家

動 **to change the words of one language into another language**

～を翻訳する

ⓘ 〈translate A into B〉（AをBに翻訳する）の形で押さえておこう。

例 Jennifer is going to **translate** that author's recent novel into English.

ジェニファーはその作家の最近の小説を英語に翻訳する予定だ。

□□□ 0713

circumstance

/ sə́ːrkəmstæ̀ns /

名 **something that affects a situation**

事情、状況

≒ condition

〈circum（周りに）+stance（立つ）〉

ⓘ ふつう複数形で使う。

例 The **circumstances** of the accident are not yet known.

その事故の状況はまだわかっていない。

0713語

□□□ 0714

revolution

/ rèvəlúːʃən /

形 revolutionary 革命的な

名 a (violent) attempt by a group of people to end one government and replace it with a new one

革命

〈re-（元に）+volut（回転する）+-ion（名詞）〉

例 The king and queen of France were overthrown during the **revolution**.

フランスの国王と王妃は革命の間に打ち倒された。

□□□ 0715

gap

/ gǽp /

名 a difference between two things or people

隔たり、間隔

ⓘ「ギャップ」はカタカナ語にもなっている。

例 The **gap** in the quality of life between the rich and poor gets larger every year.

裕福な人と貧しい人の生活の質の隔たりは、毎年大きくなっている。

□□□ 0716

inspire

/ ɪnspáɪər /

名 inspiration 着想、インスピレーション

動 ① to help someone think of an idea of what they want to do or make

～に着想を与える

例 The design for the building was **inspired** by Gothic churches in Europe.

その建物のデザインはヨーロッパのゴシック様式の教会に着想を得た。

② to make someone want to do or be something

〈人〉を奮い立たせる

≒ encourage

例 Hearing his grandmother's life story **inspired** him to become a poet.

祖母の人生の物語を聞いて、彼は詩人になろうと思った。

0717

tap

/ tǽp /

動 **to hit someone or something lightly, especially with your fingers**

（～を）軽くたたく

ⓘ 同じつづりで「蛇口」を意味する名詞もあり、tap water で「水道水」の意味。

例 He **tapped** the woman on the shoulder to get her attention.

彼は注意を引くためにその女性の肩を軽くたたいた。

0718

vast

/ vǽst /

形 **very great in amount or size**

広大な；莫大な

≒ huge

⇔ tiny

例 There are a **vast** number of reasons why you should lock your door.

ドアに鍵をかけるべき理由は非常にたくさんある。

0719

suggest

/ səgdʒést /

名 suggestion 提案

動 ① **to say an idea about what can be done, used, considered, etc.**

～を提案する

≒ propose

〈sug-（下から）+gest（持ち出す）〉

例 The child **suggested** that the family go on a picnic.

その子どもは、家族でピクニックに行こうと提案した。

② **to say something indirectly**

～を暗示する

例 He's trying to **suggest** that we should go tomorrow instead of today.

私たちは今日ではなく明日行くべきだと、彼はそれとなく言おうとしている。

□□□ 0720

crop

/ krɑ́ːp /

名 **something that is grown by farmers**

作物

例 Pineapples are one of the main **crops** grown in Hawaii.

パイナップルはハワイで栽培されている主要な作物の一つだ。

□□□ 0721

satisfy

/ sǽtəsfàɪ /

名 satisfaction 満足
形 satisfactory 満足な

動 **to make someone feel happy or pleased**

～を満足させる

⇔ dissatisfy

〈satis(十分な)+-fy(～にする)〉

例 The family was not **satisfied** by the quality of their dinner at the restaurant.

その家族は、そのレストランでのディナーの質に満足しなかった。

□□□ 0722

impressive

/ ɪmprésɪv /

名 impression 印象
動 impress ～に感銘を与える

形 **making people feel admiration by being good, skillful, large, etc.**

印象的な

〈im- (中に) +press (押す) + -ive (形容詞)〉

例 His violin skill is **impressive** for his age.

彼のバイオリンの技術は、彼の年齢にしては印象的だ。

□□□ 0723

melt

/ mélt /

動 **to (make something) change from a solid to a liquid, usually because of heat**

溶ける；～を溶かす

ⓘ「(塩などが水に) 溶ける」と言う場合はdissolveを使う。

例 She **melted** butter in the frying pan before adding the onions.

彼女は、玉ねぎを加える前にフライパンでバターを溶かした。

0724

mostly

/ móustli /

形 most ほとんどの

副 ① **almost entirely** — 主に、大部分は

≒ largely, mainly

例 The dinner was **mostly** ready to be served.

夕食は大部分が出す準備ができていた。

② **almost always** — たいてい

≒ usually

例 She **mostly** draws in black and white.

彼女はたいてい、白黒で絵を描く。

□□□ 0725

uniform

/ jú:nəfɔ̀:rm /

名 uniformity 一様性

形 **being the same at all times** — 均一の、一様な

≒ consistent

〈uni (1) +form (形)〉

ⓘ「制服、ユニフォーム」という名詞の意味もある。

例 The size of the cookies should be **uniform** so they cook at the same speed.

同じ速さで火が通るように、クッキーの大きさは均一にした方がよい。

□□□ 0726

affair

/ əféər /

名 **work or activities that are done for a specific reason, especially relating to business or politics** — 業務；情勢

≒ matter

〈af- (〜に) +fair (行う)〉

ⓘ ふつう複数形で使う。state of affairs (状況、情勢) という表現も覚えておこう。

例 They had an expert in foreign **affairs** on the news this morning.

今朝のニュースでは外交問題に詳しい専門家を招いていた。

0726語

0727

found

/ fáʊnd /

名 foundation 設立

動 **to start a group or organization that you want to last for a long time**

～を設立する

≒ establish

ⓘ found/fundは「基礎、底」を意味する語根で、fund（基金）、fundamental（根本的な）なども同語源語。

例 Their business was **founded** 30 years ago.

彼らの企業は30年前に設立された。

0728

lecture

/ léktʃər /

名 lecturer 講演者；講師

名 **a talk given to a group of people about a subject**

講演、講義

〈lect（読む）+-ure（名詞）〉

例 Over 100 people attended the **lecture** on Heian period history.

平安時代の歴史に関する講演に100人以上が出席した。

0729

eventually

/ ɪvéntʃuəli /

形 eventual 結果として起こる

副 **by the end**

ついに；いずれ

≒ finally

例 The rescued fox will **eventually** be released into the wild again.

救助されたキツネはいずれ、再び野生に放たれる。

0730

ordinary

/ ɔ́ːrdənèri /

副 ordinarily 普通に、通常

形 **normal or usual**

普通の

⇔ extraordinary

例 Most people are happy to live **ordinary** lives.

ほとんどの人々は普通の生活を幸せに送っている。

0731

owe
/ óʊ /

動 **to need to give money back to someone or an organization that you borrowed it from**

〈お金〉を借りている

ⓘ giveと同じように〈owe A B〉=〈owe B to A〉(AにBを負っている)の形をとる。

例 His sister never paid him back the money she **owed** him.

彼の妹は、彼に借りていたお金を決して返さなかった。

0732

soul
/ sóʊl /

名 **the spiritual part of someone that many people believe gives the body life**

魂

≒ spirit

例 Many people think that the **souls** of the dead come back to visit us.

死者の魂が私たちのもとを訪れるために戻ってくると、多くの人々が考えている。

0733

otherwise
/ ʌ́ðərwàɪz /

副 ① **if something did not happen or was false**

そうでなければ

例 It is important to tell people about this problem that might **otherwise** go unnoticed.

人々にこの問題について知らせることが重要で、さもなければ見過ごされてしまうかもしれない。

② **in all ways but one**

その他の点では

例 It was a little cold, but **otherwise** their vacation in Norway was great.

少し寒かったが、その他の点ではノルウェーでの彼らの休暇は素晴らしかった。

0734

behave

/ bɪhéɪv /

名 behavior 行動、振る舞い

動 to do things in a specific way

行動する、振る舞う

≒ act

例 The receptionist always **behaves** in a friendly way toward guests.

その受付係はいつも来客に対して親切に振る舞う。

0735

temporary

/ témpərèri /

副 temporarily 一時的に

形 continuing for a limited amount of time

一時的な

⇔ permanent, eternal

〈tempor(時間)+-ary(形容詞)〉

例 The young man got a **temporary** job as a delivery person.

その若い男性は配送員として一時的な仕事を得た。

0736

contribution

/ kɑ̀:ntrəbjú:ʃən /

動 contribute 寄与する

名 ① an action that causes something to happen, improve, etc.

貢献、寄与

≒ assistance

〈con-（共に）+tribut（与える）+-ion（名詞）〉

例 Researchers at Yale University have made many **contributions** to improving cancer treatments.

イェール大学の研究者たちはがん治療の向上に多大な貢献をしてきた。

② something that you give to help someone or something

寄付（金）

例 She makes a large **contribution** to the local food bank every year on her birthday.

彼女は毎年、自分の誕生日に地元のフードバンクに多額の寄付をしている。

0737

violence

/ váɪələns /

形 violent 暴力的な
動 violate 〈規則など〉に違反する

名 **the physical force that is used to hurt someone or cause damage**

暴力

例 Children have to learn to solve problems without **violence**.

子どもたちは暴力なしで問題を解決する方法を学ばなければならない。

0738

informal

/ ɪnfɔ́ːrməl /

副 informally 形式ばらずに、非公式に

形 **relaxed and not following strict rules**

形式ばらない、非公式の

⇔ formal

〈in-(否定)+formal(形式的な)〉

例 The class had an **informal** party at the end of the school year.

そのクラスは学年末に形式ばらないパーティーを開いた。

0739

debt

/ dét /

名 debtor 債務者

名 **money that you owe to someone or to an organization**

負債、借金

i bは発音しない。「債権者」はcreditor。

例 After his business failed, it took him years to pay back his **debt**.

事業に失敗した後、彼が借金を返済するのに何年もかかった。

0740

locate

/ lóʊkeɪt /

名 location 場所、位置

動 **to put or build something somewhere**

〈建物など〉を置く

i be locatedで「位置する、ある」という意味。

〈loc (場所) +-ate (動詞)〉

例 They decided to **locate** their new office closer to the train station.

彼らは駅のもっと近くに新しい事務所を置くことに決めた。

0741

conduct

/ 動 kəndʌ́kt 名 kɑ́ːndʌkt /

名 conductor 指揮者；車掌

動 to plan and do something

〈実験・調査など〉を行う

≒ carry out

〈con-（共に）+duct（導く）〉

例 They **conducted** an experiment to see how long it would take for bread to mold.

彼らは、パンにカビが生えるのにどれだけ時間がかかるかを観察する実験をした。

名 the way that someone behaves

行い、振る舞い

例 His **conduct** during the conference caused him to get fired from his job.

会議中の振る舞いのせいで、彼は仕事を解雇されることになった。

0742

delay

/ dɪléɪ /

動 to make something happen later or wait to do something

～を遅らせる、延期する

ⓘ「遅れ、延期」という名詞の意味もある。

〈de-（離れて）+lay（去る）〉

例 Devon decided to **delay** his trip to Greece until he had more money.

デヴォンは、もっとお金ができるまでギリシャ旅行を遅らせることに決めた。

0743

participate

/ pɑːrtísəpèɪt /

名 participation 参加
名 participant 参加者

動 to take part in something

参加する

ⓘ アクセントはtiの位置。participate in（～に参加する）の形で押さえておこう。

〈part(i)（部分）+cip（取る）+-ate（動詞）〉

例 She **participated** in an anime convention for the first time when she was 14 years old.

彼女は14歳のとき、アニメのコンベンションに初めて参加した。

0744

multiple / mʌ́ltəpl /

動 multiply ～を増加させる
名 multiplication 増加

形 **more than one**

複数の

⇔ single

〈multi (多くの) +ple (重ねる)〉

例 That couple has adopted **multiple** children.

その夫婦は複数の子どもたちを養子として迎えている。

0745

status / stǽtəs /

名 **the position or rank of someone or something compared to others**

地位

ⓘ [stéɪtəs] とも発音する

〈stat (立つ) +-us (状態)〉

例 His social **status** changed after the movie was released.

その映画が発表された後、彼の社会的地位は変化した。

0746

concept / kάːnsept /

動 conceive ～を心に抱く
名 conception 着想

名 **an idea about something**

概念、コンセプト

ⓘ「コンセプト」はカタカナ語にもなっている。

〈con- (完全に) +cept (取り入れられたもの)〉

例 She spent the first year of university studying the basic **concepts** of anthropology.

彼女は大学の1年目を人類学の基礎概念を学ぶことに費やした。

0747

bend / bénd /

動 **to use your strength to make something become curved**

～を曲げる

ⓘ bend-bent-bentと活用する。

例 He **bent** the wire into the shape of a bird.

彼は鳥の形に針金を曲げた。

0747語

□□□ 0748

charity

/ tʃǽrəti /

名 **an organization that helps people in need**

慈善団体

ⓘ charity concert（チャリティーコンサート）のように「慈善事業」の意味もある。

例 Gloria volunteers at a **charity** that helps adults learn to read.

グローリアは、大人が文字を読めるようになるのを支援する慈善団体でボランティアをしている。

□□□ 0749

precious

/ préʃəs /

形 **very important and too valuable to be wasted**

貴重な、重要な

〈preci（価値）+-ous（満ちた）〉

例 The government collects electronics to recycle the **precious** metals in them.

政府は、電化製品の中にある貴金属をリサイクルするため、電化製品を回収している。

□□□ 0750

debate

/ dɪbéɪt /

動 **to talk about something with someone who does not have the same opinion as you**

～を議論する

≒ argue

〈de-（完全に）+bate（打つ）〉

ⓘ 他動詞である点に注意。

例 People have been **debating** the meaning of the Bible for hundreds of years.

人々は聖書の意味について何百年も議論してきている。

名 **a discussion between people in which they talk about their different opinions on something**

討論会、議論

例 The **debate** between the two scholars lasted for several hours.

2人の学者の間で行われた討論は数時間続いた。

0751

soil

/ sɔ́ɪl /

名 the top part of the ground where plants grow

土、土壌

例 This **soil** is too wet for this plant to grow well.

この植物がうまく育つには、この土壌は湿り気が多すぎる。

0752

calculate

/ kǽlkjəlèɪt /

名 calculation 計算
名 calculator 計算機

動 to use math to find a number or answer to a question

～を計算する

ⓘ アクセントはcaの位置。

例 The students had to **calculate** the area of a circle on their test.

生徒たちはテストで円の面積を計算しなければならなかった。

0753

ease

/ íːz /

形 easy 簡単な、楽な

動 to become less bad, or to make something be better

(～を)緩和する、軽減する

ⓘ 「平易さ」「気楽さ」という名詞の意味もある。

例 The doctor gave him some medicine to help **ease** his pain.

医師は痛みを軽減するのに役立つ薬を彼に与えた。

0754

instance

/ ínstəns /

名 a particular case or example of something

事例、場合

ⓘ for instance (例えば) という表現も覚えておこう。

〈in-(中に)+stance(立つこと)〉

例 Saving the cat from the fire was a great **instance** of courage from the boy.

火事から猫を救い出したことは、その少年の勇気を示す優れた事例だ。

0755

mild

/ máɪld /

形 ① not strong or severe

穏やかな

⇔ harsh

例 She had to stay home from school because of a **mild** case of the flu.

彼女はインフルエンザの軽い症状があったため、学校に行かずに家で過ごさなければならなかった。

② not very cold

(気候が) 温暖な

≒ gentle

例 Compared to Moscow, the winters in Tokyo are rather **mild**.

モスクワと比べて、東京の冬はかなり温暖だ。

0756

seal

/ síːl /

動 to close something in a way that nothing will come out of it

～に封をする、～を密封する

ⓘ 同じつづりで、「アザラシ」を意味する名詞もある。「ステッカー」の意味の「シール」は英語ではstickerと言う。

例 He **sealed** the envelope with glue.

彼は封筒にのりで封をした。

0757

install

/ ɪnstɔ́ːl /

名 installation (機械などの) 取りつけ

動 to make something ready to be used somewhere

～を取りつける

≒ set up

⇔ uninstall

〈in- (中に) +stall (置く)〉

ⓘ ソフトウェアを「インストールする」という意味もあるが、英語のinstallはより広い意味で使う。

例 They **installed** a new air conditioner in the office.

彼らは職場に新しいエアコンを取りつけた。

0758

resolve

/ rɪzɑ́ːlv /

名 resolution 解決（策）

動 **to find the answer to a problem**

～を解決する

〈re-（元へ）+solve（解く）〉

例 The two friends weren't able to **resolve** their differences and stopped talking to each other.

その2人の友人は意見の相違を解決することができず、互いに話をするのをやめた。

0759

courage

/ kə́ːrɪdʒ /

形 courageous 勇気のある

名 **the ability to do something even when you are afraid or it is not easy**

勇気

≒ bravery

〈cour（心）+-age（名詞）〉

ⓘ courの発音に注意。

例 It took her a week to work up the **courage** to ask the man out on a date.

彼女は勇気を出してその男性をデートに誘うのに1週間かかった。

0760

financial

/ fənǽnʃəl /

名 finance 財政、融資

形 **relating to money**

財政上の、金融の

ⓘ アクセントはnanの位置。

例 The country is in a **financial** crisis.

その国は財政的危機にある。

0761

expose

/ ɪkspóʊz /

名 exposure さらすこと、暴露

動 **to put someone or something in a place or situation where they are not covered or protected**

～をさらす

ⓘ 「〈秘密など〉を暴露する」という意味もある。

〈ex-（外に）+pose（置く）〉

例 The color of the toy faded because it was **exposed** to the sun.

太陽にさらされたため、そのおもちゃの色は薄れた。

□□□ 0762

account

/ əkáʊnt /

形 accountable 説明責任がある
名 accountability 説明責任
名 accounting 会計

名 ① **a description or story about something that has happened**

説明、報告

ⓘ 〈take A into account〉（Aを考慮に入れる）という表現も覚えておこう。

〈ac-（～に）+count（数える）〉

例 The woman got in trouble for not giving an accurate **account** of what happened to the police.

その女性は起こったことの正確な説明を警察にしなかったせいで厄介なことになった。

② **a record held by the bank about how much money you keep there**

預金口座

例 Her parents opened a savings **account** for her when she was born.

彼女が生まれたとき、両親は彼女のための普通預金口座を開設した。

動 《account for》 **to give a reason or explain something to another person**

～を説明する

ⓘ account forには「～の割合を占める」という意味もある。

例 After years of searching, no one could **account for** the disappearance of the neighbor's cat.

何年も捜した後も、近所の猫の失踪について説明できる人は誰もいなかった。

□□□ 0763

attract

/ ətrǽkt /

名 attraction 魅力、引きつけるもの
形 attractive 魅力的な

動 **to make a person or thing go somewhere, do something, or be interested in something**

～を引きつける

≒ draw

〈at-（～に）+tract（引く）〉

例 The street performer's show **attracted** a large crowd of people.

大道芸人のショーは大勢の人々を引きつけた。

□□□ 0764

civil

/ sívəl /

形 civilian 一般市民の

形 relating to the people who live in a country

市民の、国民の

〈civ（市民）+-il（形容詞）〉

例 Everyone worked hard to protect their **civil** rights.

自分たちの市民としての権利を守るために誰もが熱心に取り組んだ。

□□□ 0765

broadcast

/ brɔ́ːdkæ̀st /

名 broadcasting 放送

動 to send out something by radio or television

～を放送する

≒ air

ⓘ broadcast-broadcast-broadcastと活用する。

〈broad（広く）+cast（投げられた）〉

例 That radio station **broadcasts** the news every night at 6 o'clock.

そのラジオ局は毎晩6時からニュースを放送している。

□□□ 0766

atmosphere

/ ǽtməsfìər /

形 atmospheric 大気の

名 ① the air that surrounds the Earth

大気

ⓘ アクセントは語頭のaの位置。

〈atmo(s)（空気）+sphere（球）〉

例 The good thing about wind power is that it does not release gases into the **atmosphere**.

風力のよい点は大気中にガスを放出しないというところだ。

② the way that a place or situation makes you feel

雰囲気

例 The **atmosphere** of the party was very lively.

パーティーの雰囲気はとても盛り上がっていた。

□□□ 0767

destination

/ dèstənéɪʃən /

動 destine ～を運命づける

名 **the place you are going or being sent**

目的地、行き先

〈de-（強意）+stin（立つ）+ -ation（名詞）〉

例 The final **destination** of the cruise was Sydney.

クルーズの最後の目的地はシドニーだった。

□□□ 0768

intelligence

/ ɪntélɪʤəns /

形 intelligent 聡明な、理解力のある

名 **the ability to understand or do new things**

知性、知能

i 「（敵軍などに関する）情報；諜報機関」という意味もある。

例 Someday, the **intelligence** of computers may be greater than that of humans.

いつかコンピュータの知能は人間の知能に勝るかもしれない。

□□□ 0769

wipe

/ wáɪp /

動 **to clean or dry something by rubbing it with a cloth, your hand, etc.**

～を拭く

i 「～するもの」を意味する-erがついたのが、wiper（ワイパー）。

例 He **wiped** his glasses clean with a small cloth.

彼は小さな布で眼鏡をきれいに拭いた。

□□□ 0770

index

/ índeks /

名 **something that shows how something else is changing or performing**

指標

i 本の「索引」の意味もある。「人差し指」はindex fingerと言う。

〈in-（上に）+dex（指し示す）〉

例 The public's spending is a good **index** of how the economy is doing.

一般の人々の支出は経済の状況を示すよい指標だ。

□□□ 0771

somewhat

/ sʌ́mwʌ̀t /

副 In a small amount or degree

幾分、多少

例 She felt **somewhat** silly for not understanding her teacher's question.

彼女は教師の質問がわからなかったことで、自分が少々愚かな感じがした。

□□□ 0772

estate

/ ɪstéɪt /

名 everything that belongs to a person

総資産、不動産

ⓘ real estate（不動産）という表現も覚えておこう。

例 The musician's **estate** is worth millions of dollars.

そのミュージシャンの総資産は、数百万ドルの価値がある。

□□□ 0773

puzzle

/ pʌ́zl /

名 puzzlement 困惑

動 to confuse someone or something, or be hard to understand

～を困惑させる

ⓘ zは2つ。名詞でカタカナ語の「パズル」の意味もある。

例 Hearing his owner's voice from the TV **puzzled** the dog.

その犬はテレビから飼い主の声が聞こえて困惑した。

□□□ 0774

constant

/ kɑ́:nstənt /

副 constantly 絶え間なく

形 happening all the time or repeatedly over a period of time

絶え間ない

〈con-(完全に)+stant(立つ)〉

例 The **constant** yelling of the neighbors kept him awake at night.

近所の人が絶え間なく叫ぶので、彼は夜中目が覚めたままだった。

□□□ 0775

strict

/ stríkt /

副 strictly 厳しく

形 ① **needing to be obeyed exactly**

〈命令・規則などが〉厳しい

≒ hard, harsh

例 If she doesn't follow a very **strict** diet, she'll get sick.

彼女はとても厳しい食事制限に従わなければ、病気になるだろう。

② **demanding that rules be followed**

〈人が〉厳格な

例 Her mother was not that **strict** with her.

母親は彼女に対してそれほど厳格ではなかった。

□□□ 0776

educate

/ édʒəkèɪt /

名 education 教育
形 educational 教育の

動 **to teach someone about something or train them in how to do something**

～を教育する

ⓘ アクセントは語頭のeの位置。

〈e-(外に)+duc(導き出す)+-ate(動詞)〉

例 Parents have to **educate** their children to know what is right and wrong.

親は子どもたちに何が正しくて何が間違っているかをわからせるために教育しなければならない。

□□□ 0777

capable

/ kéɪpəbl /

名 capability 能力

形 **having the abilities or qualities that are required to do something**

できる、能力がある

≒ able

ⓘ 「有能な」という意味もあり、He is a very capable worker and everyone trusts him.（彼はとても有能な社員で、誰もが信頼している）のように使う。

例 The little boy said that he was **capable** of carrying the large box by himself.

その小さな男の子はその大きな箱を一人で運べると言った。

□□□ 0778

absorb

/ əbzɔ́ːrb /

名 absorption 吸収

動 **to take in a liquid, gas, or other substance in a natural or gradual way**

～を吸収する

〈ab-（～から）+sorb（吸い込む）〉

例 The water was **absorbed** into the towel.

水はタオルに吸収された。

□□□ 0779

latter

/ lǽtər /

形 **coming or happening closer to the end of a period of time than to the beginning**

後半の、あとの

≒ later

⇔ former

ⓘ 名詞の前で使う。

例 She spent the **latter** half of her life helping animals as a vet.

彼女は人生の後半を、獣医として動物たちを助けて過ごした。

□□□ 0780

witness

/ wítnəs /

動 **to see something happen**

～を目撃する

〈wit(知っている)+ness(名詞)〉

例 Harriet **witnessed** a man steal her neighbor's package.

ハリエットは、男が近所の人の小包を盗むところを目撃した。

名 **a person who has seen something happen, especially a crime**

目撃者

例 The police could not find any **witnesses** to the theft.

警察はその盗難事件の目撃者を一人も見つけられなかった。

□□□ 0781

monitor

/ mɑ́:nətər /

動 **to watch and check someone or something over a period of time to see how they are doing**

～を監視する

ⓘ「(パソコンなどの) モニター」もこの monitor。

〈monit (忠告する) +-or (人)〉

例 The doctor **monitored** her condition after the surgery very carefully.

医師は手術の後、とても慎重に彼女の経過を観察した。

□□□ 0782

holy

/ hóʊli /

名 holiness 神聖

形 **relating to a god or religion**

神聖な

≒ sacred

〈hol (完全な) +-y (形容詞)〉

ⓘ holiday (休日) は〈holy (神聖な) + day (日)〉から。

例 The couple went to a **holy** temple to have their child blessed.

その夫婦は子どもに祝福を受けさせるために神聖な寺院へ行った。

□□□ 0783

approve

/ əprú:v /

名 approval 承認；賛成

動 ① **to officially accept something**

～を承認する、認可する

⇔ disapprove, deny, reject

例 The city **approved** the man's plans to open an ice cream shop.

市は、その男性がアイスクリーム店をオープンする計画を承認した。

② **to think that someone or something is good**

よいと認める、賛成する

⇔ disapprove

ⓘ approve of (～をよいと認める) の形で押さえておこう。

例 Her parents **approve** of what she has done with her life.

彼女の両親は彼女が人生でやってきたことを認めている。

□□□ 0784

household

/ háushòuld /

名 **the group of people who all live together in one house**

家族、世帯

〈house（家）+hold（中身）〉

例 The number of one-person **households** continues to increase.

単身世帯の数は増え続けている。

□□□ 0785

necessarily

/ nèsəsérəli /

形 necessary 必要な；必然的な

副 **《not necessarily》possibly but not certainly or always**

必ずしも～ない

ⓘ アクセントはsaの位置。

例 Smartphones are**n't necessarily** better, but they can do more than regular cell phones.

スマートフォンの方が必ずしも優れているわけではないが、通常の携帯電話よりも多くのことができる。

□□□ 0786

executive

/ ɪgzékjətɪv /

動 execute〈職務など〉を実行する

名 **a person who has a high position in an organization and manages others**

経営幹部、重役

例 The TV network **executives** canceled the show because it was becoming less popular.

そのテレビ局の幹部たちは、その番組の人気が落ちてきたので打ち切りにした。

□□□ 0787

harm

/ hɑ́ːrm /

形 harmful 有害な

名 **something that hurts or damages someone or something**

害

ⓘ「～を害する、傷つける」という動詞の意味もある。

例 The new tax law won't affect large companies, but it will cause **harm** to small businesses.

新しい税法は大企業には影響を与えないが、小企業には害を及ぼすだろう。

□□□ 0788

authority

/ əθɔ́ːrəti /

名 ① **people who have the power to make decisions and make people follow the rules**

官庁、当局

ⓘ この意味ではふつう複数形で使う。

〈author(作り出す)+-ity(名詞)〉

例 The local **authorities** are looking into the recent thefts in the neighborhood.

地元当局は最近地域であった盗難事件について捜査している。

② **a person who is an expert on something**

権威(者)、専門家

ⓘ「権威」という抽象的な意味もある。

例 He is an **authority** on classical Japanese literature.

彼は日本古典文学の権威だ。

□□□ 0789

genius

/ ʤíːnjəs /

名 **a very smart or talented person with a level of intelligence or talent that is extremely rare**

天才

例 The singer is a musical **genius**.

その歌手は音楽の天才だ。

□□□ 0790

illegal

/ ɪlíːgəl /

副 illegally 不法に

形 **against the law**

不法の、違法の

⇔ legal

〈il-(否定)+legal(合法の)〉

例 In many countries, it is **illegal** to use your cell phone while driving.

多くの国で、運転中に携帯電話を使用することは違法だ。

□□□ 0791

split

/ splít /

動 **to divide (something) into multiple parts**

～を割る、分割する；割れる

≒ separate

ⓘ split-split-splitと活用する。

例 The girl helped her father **split** the firewood.

その女の子は父親が薪を割るのを手伝った。

□□□ 0792

recall

/ rɪkɔ́:l /

動 **to remember something that happened in the past**

～を思い出す、覚えている

⇔ forget

〈re-（再び）+call（呼ぶ）〉

ⓘ カタカナ語の「リコール（不良品の回収）」もこのrecall。

例 She knew the man's face, but she couldn't **recall** his name.

彼女は男性の顔は知っていたが名前を思い出せなかった。

□□□ 0793

clerk

/ klə́:rk /

名 ① **a person who works in a store**

店員

例 He looked for the sales **clerk** to ask if he could try on some clothes.

彼は服を試着できるか尋ねるために店員を探した。

② **a person whose job is to keep track of records and documents and do other routine work in an office, shop, etc.**

事務員

ⓘ bank clerk（銀行員）、office clerk（事務員）のように、〈名詞＋clerk〉の形でよく使う。

例 She told the bank **clerk** that she had lost her debit card.

彼女はデビットカードを紛失したことを銀行員に伝えた。

0794

acid

/ ǽsɪd /

名 acidity 酸性

名 **a chemical, usually a liquid, that can have a sour taste or burn holes in or damage things**

酸

ⓘ「酸(性)の」という形容詞の意味もある。acid rain(酸性雨)という表現も覚えておこう。

例 Citric **acid** is used to make candy sour.

クエン酸は飴を酸っぱくするのに使われる。

0795

opponent

/ əpóʊnənt /

名 **a person or group that is against someone or something else in a contest or game**

(試合などの) 相手、対抗者

ⓘ「(戦争などの) 敵」はenemy。

〈op- (〜に対して) +ponent (置くこと)〉

例 The team's **opponents** were too strong, and they lost the basketball game.

そのチームの対戦相手はあまりにも強くて、彼らはバスケットボールの試合で負けた。

0796

sum

/ sʌ́m /

名 ① **an amount of money**

金額

例 His grandmother donated a large **sum** of money to a cancer charity.

彼の祖母はがんの慈善団体に多額のお金を寄付した。

② **the answer you get when you add numbers together**

合計、和

例 The **sum** of 15 and 27 is 42.

15と27の合計は42だ。

0797

largely
/ lɑ́ːrdʒli /

副 **not completely but mostly**

主に

≒ mainly

例 The members of the club are **largely** women.

そのクラブの部員は主に女性だ。

0798

horror
/ hɔ́ːrər /

形 horrible 恐ろしい
動 horrify ～を怖がらせる

名 **a strong feeling of fear and shock**

恐怖

ⓘ「(小説・映画などの) ホラー」もこのhorror。

〈hor (恐怖) +-ror (名詞)〉

例 He watched in **horror** as the river flooded his neighborhood.

彼は川が自分の住む地域で氾濫するのをぞっとして眺めた。

0799

scream
/ skríːm /

動 **to cry out in a loud and high voice because you are hurt or surprised**

金切り声を上げる

≒ shriek

例 The crowd started **screaming** when the singer walked onto the stage.

その歌手がステージに上がると、群衆はキャーキャー言い始めた。

0800

universal
/ jùːnəvə́ːrsəl /

形 **relating to everyone in the world or in a specific group**

全世界の；人類共通の；(集団内の) すべての人々の

≒ common, general, global

ⓘ「普遍的な」という意味もあり、universal truth (普遍的真理) のように使う。

〈uni (1) +vers (回転) +-al (形容詞)〉

例 Food is a **universal** need of all people.

食べ物はすべての人々に共通の必要品だ。

章末ボキャブラリーチェック

次の語義が表す英単語を答えてください。

語義	解答	連番
❶ to officially accept something	approve	0783
❷ to plan and do something	conduct	0741
❸ to make something happen later or wait to do something	delay	0742
❹ to put someone or something in a place or situation where they are not covered or protected	expose	0761
❺ to make something ready to be used somewhere	install	0757
❻ the physical force that is used to hurt someone or cause damage	violence	0737
❼ relaxed and not following strict rules	informal	0738
❽ your name written in the way that only you can write it	signature	0710
❾ to need to give money back to someone or an organization that you borrowed it from	owe	0731
❿ the spiritual part of someone that many people believe gives the body life	soul	0732
⓫ needing to be obeyed exactly	strict	0775
⓬ to clean or dry something by rubbing it with a cloth, your hand, etc.	wipe	0769
⓭ to divide (something) into multiple parts	split	0791
⓮ people who have the power to make decisions and make people follow the rules	authority	0788
⓯ a person or group that is against someone or something else in a contest or game	opponent	0795
⓰ a person who has a high position in an organization and manages others	executive	0786
⓱ a very smart or talented person with a level of intelligence or talent that is extremely rare	genius	0789
⓲ if something did not happen or was false	otherwise	0733
⓳ a natural thing usually found in foods that helps make your body healthy	vitamin	0704

語義	解答	連番
⑳ relating to everyone in the world or in a specific group	universal	0800
㉑ work or activities that are done for a specific reason, especially relating to business or politics	affair	0726
㉒《not -----------》 possibly but not certainly or always	necessarily	0785
㉓ a plan that is designed to make something happen, often over a long period of time	strategy	0701
㉔ having the abilities or qualities that are required to do something	capable	0777
㉕ the place you are going or being sent	destination	0767
㉖ to say an idea about what can be done, used, considered, etc.	suggest	0719
㉗ making people feel admiration by being good, skillful, large, etc.	impressive	0722
㉘ to teach someone about something or train them in how to do something	educate	0776
㉙ the air that surrounds the Earth	atmosphere	0766
㉚ continuing for a limited amount of time	temporary	0735
㉛ to do things in a specific way	behave	0734
㉜ having two or more people or groups do something together	joint	0705
㉝ to find the answer to a problem	resolve	0758
㉞ not strong or severe	mild	0755
㉟ by the end	eventually	0729
㊱ to send out something by radio or television	broadcast	0765
㊲ something that shows how something else is changing or performing	index	0770
㊳ not that important or large	minor	0702
㊴ to use math to find a number or answer to a question	calculate	0752
㊵ relating to a god or religion	holy	0782
㊶ a (violent) attempt by a group of people to end one government and replace it with a new one	revolution	0714

語義	解答	連番
㊷ relating to money	financial	0760
㊸ the results of research or an investigation	finding	0706
㊹ being the same at all times	uniform	0725
㊺ almost entirely	mostly	0724
㊻ coming or happening closer to the end of a period of time than to the beginning	latter	0779
㊼ to change the words of one language into another language	translate	0712
㊽ the ability to do something even when you are afraid or it is not easy	courage	0759
㊾ to help someone think of an idea of what they want to do or make	inspire	0716
㊿ not easy to deal with because there is not enough time or money	tight	0703
51 an action that causes something to happen, improve, etc.	contribution	0736
52 the group of people who all live together in one house	household	0784
53 to take in a liquid, gas, or other substance in a natural or gradual way	absorb	0778
54 a difference between two things or people	gap	0715
55 a strong feeling of fear and shock	horror	0798
56 to take part in something	participate	0743
57 an amount of money	sum	0796
58 to talk about something with someone who does not have the same opinion as you	debate	0750
59 a person who works in a store	clerk	0793
60 something that hurts or damages someone or something	harm	0787
61 money that you owe to someone or to an organization	debt	0739
62 normal or usual	ordinary	0730

語義	解答	連番
63 to watch and check someone or something over a period of time to see how they are doing	monitor	0781
64 to start a group or organization that you want to last for a long time	found	0727
65 to be able to do something without anything bad happening	afford	0711
66 the top part of the ground where plants grow	soil	0751
67 to remember something that happened in the past	recall	0792
68 relating to the people who live in a country	civil	0764
69 happening all the time or repeatedly over a period of time	constant	0774
70 the way someone feels at a particular time	mood	0709
71 the number of people or things that can fit inside of something	capacity	0708
72 very important and too valuable to be wasted	precious	0749
73 to confuse someone or something, or be hard to understand	puzzle	0773
74 a chemical, usually a liquid, that can have a sour taste or burn holes in or damage things	acid	0794
75 the ability to understand or do new things	intelligence	0768
76 something that affects a situation	circumstance	0713
77 to make a person or thing go somewhere, do something, or be interested in something	attract	0763
78 an idea about something	concept	0746
79 something that is grown by farmers	crop	0720
80 to use your strength to make something become curved	bend	0747
81 very great in amount or size	vast	0718
82 in a small amount or degree	somewhat	0771
83 the position or rank of someone or something compared to others	status	0745
84 everything that belongs to a person	estate	0772

語義	解答	連番
(85) to cry out in a loud and high voice because you are hurt or surprised	scream	0799
(86) to put or build something somewhere	locate	0740
(87) to close something in a way that nothing will come out of it	seal	0756
(88) to see something happen	witness	0780
(89) to (make something) change from a solid to a liquid, usually because of heat	melt	0723
(90) to become less bad, or to make something be better	ease	0753
(91) to make someone feel happy or pleased	satisfy	0721
(92) more than one	multiple	0744
(93) to not be willing to accept, believe, or think about something	reject	0707
(94) a talk given to a group of people about a subject	lecture	0728
(95) to hit someone or something lightly, especially with your fingers	tap	0717
(96) against the law	illegal	0790
(97) not completely but mostly	largely	0797
(98) an organization that helps people in need	charity	0748
(99) a description or story about something that has happened	account	0762
(100) a particular case or example of something	instance	0754

Stage 9

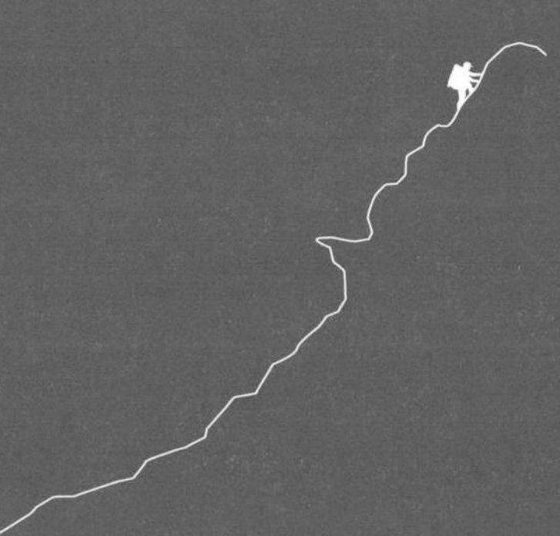

Put your best foot forward.
ベストを尽くせ。

0801

liquid

/ líkwɪd /

形 **not a solid or a gas and able to flow freely, like water**

液体の

ⓘ quiの発音に注意。「液体」という名詞の意味もある。

例 After getting her wisdom teeth removed, she could only eat **liquid** foods.

彼女は親知らずを抜いてもらった後、液状の食べ物しか食べられなかった。

0802

automatic

/ ɔ̀ːtəmǽtɪk /

副 automatically 自動的に

形 **having controls that allow something to work without a person to operate them**

自動の

⇔ manual

〈auto(自動で)+matic(動く)〉

例 Most cars these days have an **automatic** transmission.

最近のほとんどの車には自動変速機がついている。

0803

export

/ 動 ɪkspɔ́ːrt 名 ékspɔːrt /

動 **to send something from your country to another country to be sold**

～を輸出する

⇔ import

〈ex-(外に)+port(運ぶ)〉

例 Today, Canada **exports** a lot of oil.

現在、カナダはたくさんの石油を輸出している。

名 **something that is sent to another country to be sold there**

輸出品

⇔ import

例 The country's major **exports** include electrical machinery, clothing, and footwear.

その国の主な輸出品には電子機器、衣類、履物などがある。

□□□ 0804

analyze

/ ǽnəlàɪz /

名 analysis 分析

動 **to study something carefully so that you can understand or explain it**

～を分析する

ⓘ イギリス英語ではanalyseともつづる。

〈ana-（上に）+ly（解く）+-ze（動詞）〉

例 The chemist **analyzed** how the chemicals reacted to each other.

化学者は、その化学物質がどのように反応し合うかを分析した。

□□□ 0805

suspect

/ 動 səspékt 名 sʌ́spekt /

名 suspicion 疑い、疑念
形 suspicious 怪しい

動 ① **to think that something is probably true or will happen although you are not sure**

…ではないかと思う

≒ guess

ⓘ 〈suspect (that)...〉（…ではないかと思う）の形で押さえておこう。

例 She **suspects** that her daughter may be lying about skipping school.

彼女は、娘が学校をさぼったことについて嘘をついているのかもしれないと思っている。

② **to think that someone probably did something, especially a crime, although you are not sure**

～を疑う

⇔ trust

例 The woman is **suspected** in the murder of her neighbor.

その女性は近所の人の殺害事件で疑われている。

名 **a person who is thought to be guilty of something**

容疑者

例 The **suspect** was caught trying to leave the country.

その容疑者は出国しようとしたところを捕まった。

□□□ 0806

detect

/ dɪtékt /

名 detection 探知
名 detective 探偵

動 **to notice or discover something, especially something that is difficult to see, hear, etc.**

～を見抜く、検出する

〈de-（離れて）+tect（覆う）〉

例 The chef could **detect** every spice used in the dish just by tasting it.

そのシェフは料理を少し味見しただけで、使われているあらゆるスパイスを言い当てることができた。

□□□ 0807

alarming

/ əlɑ́ːrmɪŋ /

名 alarm 警報（器）

形 **causing worry or fear**

警戒すべき、憂慮すべき

例 The increase in strong storms every year is very **alarming**.

毎年ひどい嵐が増加しているのは大変憂慮すべきことだ。

□□□ 0808

moral

/ mɔ́ːrəl /

形 **relating to what is right and wrong**

道徳（上）の

≒ ethical

ⓘ 名詞の「道徳」はmoralsと複数形で表す。

例 There is a **moral** lesson in every good story.

あらゆるよい物語には道徳的な教訓がある。

□□□ 0809

occupy

/ ɑ́ːkjəpàɪ /

名 occupation 占領；職業
名 occupant 占有者

動 **to fill or use something**

～を占める

ⓘ「～を占領する」という意味もある。

例 Working **occupies** almost all of the young woman's time.

仕事がその若い女性の時間のほとんどすべてを占めている。

□□□ 0810

recipe

/ résəpi /

名 **directions on how to make food** 料理法，レシピ

ⓘ 語末のeのつづりに注意。

例 This **recipe** for apple pie calls for three green apples. このアップルパイのレシピには青リンゴが3つ必要だ。

□□□ 0811

shift

/ ʃíft /

動 **to change or make something change to a different opinion, belief, etc.** 〈意見などが〉変わる；〈意見など〉を変える

ⓘ カタカナ語の「シフト」と同じように「（交代制の）勤務時間」という名詞の意味もある。

例 Public opinion about the president has **shifted** from good to bad. 大統領についての国民の意見は、よいものから悪いものへと変わってきた。

□□□ 0812

bitter

/ bítər /

形 ① **having a strong flavor that is often not pleasant** 苦い

⇔ sweet

例 Coffee is too **bitter** for him to drink without adding sugar. コーヒーを砂糖なしで飲むのは彼には苦すぎる。

② **making you feel bad about something** つらい

例 The swim team suffered a **bitter** defeat at the latest competition. その水泳チームは最近の大会でつらい敗北を喫した。

□□□ 0813

insist

/ ɪnsíst /

名 insistence 主張

動 ① **to say something in a way that is hard to go against or disagree with**

…と主張する、言い張る

≒ claim

〈in- (上に) +sist (立つ)〉

ⓘ 〈insist (that)...〉(…と主張する、言い張る) の形で押さえておこう。

例 She **insisted** that she hadn't eaten all of the cookies.

彼女はクッキー全部は食べていないと言い張った。

② **to demand that something be done or happen**

…であることを要求する

ⓘ 〈insist (that)...〉(…であることを要求する) の形で押さえておこう。that節中の動詞は原形になる点に注意。

例 The manager **insisted** that everyone wear only white shirts to work.

そのマネージャーは誰もが職場に白いシャツだけを着てくるように要求した。

□□□ 0814

twist

/ twíst /

動 **to bend or turn something to make it have a different shape**

～をねじる

例 The man **twisted** the balloon into the shape of a mouse.

その男性は、風船をねじってネズミの形にした。

□□□ 0815

quantity

/ kwɑ́:ntəti /

名 **a number or amount of something**

量、数量

ⓘ Farmers in the area grow large quantities of potatoes [rice]. (その地域の農家は大量のジャガイモ [米] を育てている) のように、数えられる名詞にも数えられない名詞にも使う。

例 For some people, **quantity** is more important than quality when it comes to food.

食べ物については質より量が大切だ、と言う人もいる。

0816

tip

/ típ /

名 ① **a piece of information or advice that is useful**

秘訣、助言

≒ hint

ⓘ 同じつづりで「先端」という意味の名詞もある。

例 Her hairdresser gave her **tips** on how to style her hair better.

彼女の美容師は髪をより上手にスタイリングする秘訣を彼女に教えてくれた。

② **extra money that you give someone who has done a service for you**

チップ

例 The couple gave the waitress a 10 dollar **tip** for being so helpful.

その夫婦は、そのウエイトレスがとても親切にしてくれたので、10ドルのチップを渡した。

□□□ 0817

philosophy

/ fəlɑ́:səfi /

名 philosopher 哲学者

名 **the study of the nature and meaning of life, knowledge, and the universe**

哲学

〈philo（愛する）+sophy（知）〉

例 She has a degree in Chinese **philosophy**.

彼女は中国哲学の学位を持っている。

□□□ 0818

adapt

/ ədǽpt /

名 adaptation 適応

動 **to change how you act so that it is easier to do something in a particular situation**

適応［順応］する；～を適応［順応］させる

ⓘ adapt to（～に適応する）の形で押さえておこう。

〈ad-（～に）+apt（適した）〉

例 It takes some students many months to **adapt** to university life.

大学生活に適応するのに何か月もかかる学生もいる。

0818語

□□□ 0819

oppose

/ əpóuz /

名 opposition 反対
形 opposite 反対の

動 **to disagree with someone or something, or to try to stop them from succeeding**

～に反対する

⇔ support

〈op-（反対に）+pose（置く）〉

例 The whole town **opposes** the construction of the shopping mall.

町全体がショッピングモールの建設に反対している。

□□□ 0820

polite

/ pəláɪt /

副 politely 礼儀正しく
名 politeness 礼儀正しさ

形 **having good manners, or showing respect to other people**

礼儀正しい、丁寧な

⇔ impolite, rude

例 All of the children in their family are very **polite**.

彼らの家の子どもたちは全員とても礼儀正しい。

□□□ 0821

bother

/ bɑ́:ðər /

動 **to cause someone to be worried, annoyed, in pain, etc.**

〈人〉を悩ます、困らせる；〈人〉の邪魔をする

例 It's already been two years since the injury, but his foot still **bothers** him.

けがからすでに2年たつが、彼はまだ足に悩まされている。

□□□ 0822

core

/ kɔ́:r /

名 **the main or most central part of something, especially a problem or issue**

中核、核心

ⓘ「（果物の）芯」「（地球の）コア」などの意味もある。「（鉛筆の）芯」はlead［léd］。

例 The programmer spent many hours trying to find the **core** of the problem in his app.

そのプログラマーは、自分のアプリの問題の核心を見つけようとして何時間も費やした。

0823

trap

/ trǽp /

名 **something that is used to catch someone or something**

わな

ⓘ「(人を陥れるための)策略」という比喩的な意味でも使われる。

例 The hunter laid a **trap** for the bear that was seen in the village.

ハンターは、その村で目撃されたクマ用にわなをしかけた。

動 **to keep someone or something from getting away or getting lost**

〜を閉じ込める

例 The Earth's heat is **trapped** by the atmosphere.

地球の熱は大気に閉じ込められている。

0824

wound

/ wú:nd /

動 **to hurt someone or something, especially by making a hole in their skin with a weapon**

〜を傷つける、負傷させる

≒ injure

ⓘ ouの発音に注意。wind(曲がる)の過去分詞woundは[wáund]。

例 Hundreds of soldiers were **wounded** in the battle.

何百人もの兵士がその戦闘で負傷した。

0825

mission

/ míʃən /

名 **an important official job that someone has been given to do**

使命、任務

≒ task

〈miss(送る)+-ion(名詞)〉

例 The spy's **mission** was to find out where the money was kept.

そのスパイの任務は、その金が保管されている場所を突き止めることだった。

0826

meanwhile

/ míːnwàɪl /

副 **at the same time**

その間に

〈mean(中間)+while(〜の間)〉

例 You can feed the animals. **Meanwhile**, I'll make lunch for us.

動物たちにえさをあげて。その間に、私は昼食を作ります。

0827

loose

/ lúːs /

副 loosely ゆるく
動 loosen 〜をゆるめる

形 **not tightly attached to where it should be, or able to be separated from something**

ゆるい

⇔ tight

ⓘ seの発音に注意。

例 The ropes were too **loose**, and the couch fell off the back of the truck.

ロープがゆるすぎて、ソファーがトラックの後部から落下した。

0828

brief

/ bríːf /

名 brevity 短さ；簡潔さ

形 ① **not lasting for a long time**

短時間の

≒ short

⇔ lengthy

ⓘ 「〈人〉に（必要な）情報を伝える」という動詞の意味もある。

例 The team had a **brief** meeting about their monthly goals before starting work.

そのチームは仕事を始める前に、彼らの月間目標について短いミーティングをした。

② **not using many words**

簡潔な

≒ concise

例 Most people prefer to read **brief** emails rather than lengthy ones.

ほとんどの人は長ったらしいメールよりも簡潔なメールを読む方を好む。

□□□ 0829

pleasant

/ plézənt /

形 making you feel happy, comfortable, or satisfied

楽しい、心地よい

動 please ～を喜ばせる
形 pleased 満足した
名 pleasure 喜び

⇔ unpleasant

ⓘ eaの発音に注意。

例 He had a **pleasant** conversation with his mother on the phone last night.

彼は昨夜、電話で母親と楽しい会話をした。

□□□ 0830

boil

/ bɔ́ɪl /

動 to heat a liquid enough for it to start to bubble

～を沸かす、沸騰させる

ⓘ「〈食べ物〉をゆでる、煮る」という意味もある。「～するもの」を意味する-erがついたのがboiler（ボイラー）。

例 You must **boil** the water before adding the noodles.

麺を投入する前にお湯を沸かさなければならない。

□□□ 0831

principle

/ prínsəpl /

名 ① a law, rule, or theory that people have decided based on something

原理、原則

ⓘ principal（主要な）と同音。

例 The man learned the **principles** of writing when he was a university student.

その男性は大学生のとき、ライティングの原則を学んだ。

② a strong belief that influences what you do

主義、信条

例 It is against her **principles** to lie.

嘘をつくことは彼女の主義に反する。

□□□ 0832

fold

/ fóuld /

動 to bend part of something over itself

～を折りたたむ

ⓘ fold *one's* arms（腕を組む）のような使い方もある。また接尾辞 -foldは数詞について、fivefold（5倍の）のように使われる。

例 His least favorite chore is **folding** clothes.

彼が最も好きではない家事は服をたたむことだ。

□□□ 0833

stable

/ stéɪbl /

名 stability 安定
動 stabilize ～を安定させる

形 steady and not likely to change, move, or fail

安定した

⇔ unstable

例 The construction worker made sure the ladder was **stable** before climbing it.

建設作業員ははしごに登る前に、それが安定していることを確かめた。

□□□ 0834

humor

/ hjú:mər /

形 humorous おかしい、ユーモラスな

名 what makes something funny, or the ability to laugh at things that are funny

ユーモア

ⓘ イギリス英語ではhumourとつづる。発音に注意。

例 That comedian's type of **humor** is very popular with the public.

そのお笑い芸人のユーモアのタイプは、一般の人々にとても人気がある。

□□□ 0835

representative

/ rèprɪzéntətɪv /

動 represent ～を表す；～を代表する

名 someone who acts or speaks for someone else or for a group

代表者

例 A **representative** of the company spoke to the press about the scandal.

その会社の担当者が、その不祥事について報道関係者に語った。

0836

calm

/ kɑ́:m /

副 calmly 静かに
名 calmness 静けさ、落ち着き

形 not angry, excited, nervous, etc.

冷静な、落ち着いた

⇔ upset

ⓘ lは発音しない。「〈天候などが〉穏やかな」という意味もある。

例 He couldn't stay **calm** when he found out he was going to meet his favorite actress.

好きな女優に会うことになったと知ったとき、彼は落ち着いていられなかった。

動 to cause someone to become less angry, excited, emotional, etc.

～を落ち着かせる

ⓘ calm down（落ち着く）という表現も覚えておこう。

例 She **calmed** the baby by rocking him back and forth.

彼女は前後に揺らして赤ちゃんを落ち着かせた。

0837

mechanism

/ mékənìzm /

形 mechanical 機械の、機械仕掛けの

名 a process, system, or part of a machine or device that is used to produce a particular result

仕組み、装置

ⓘ アクセントはmeの位置。

例 The camera's shutter **mechanism** was in need of repair.

そのカメラのシャッター装置は修理の必要があった。

0838

concentrate

/ kɑ́:nsəntrèɪt /

名 concentration 集中

動 to completely focus on something and ignore everything else

集中する

ⓘ concentrate on（～に集中する）の形で押さえておこう。

〈con-（共に）+centr（中心）+-ate（動詞）〉

例 It was too loud in the café for her to **concentrate** on studying.

そのカフェはうるさすぎて彼女は勉強に集中できなかった。

0838語

□□□ 0839

invent

/ ɪnvént /

名 invention 発明
形 inventive 発明の、独創的な

動 to create something that has never been created before

～を発明する

〈in-（上に）+vent（出てくる）〉

例 The woman has **invented** a new way to recycle plastic.

その女性はプラスチックをリサイクルする新しい方法を発明した。

□□□ 0840

dynamic

/ daɪnǽmɪk /

名 dynamism 活発さ

形 always active or changing

活発な、活動的な

⇔ static, stagnant

ⓘ アクセントはnaの位置。

例 Tokyo is a very **dynamic** city to live in.

東京は住むにはとても活力に満ちた都市だ。

□□□ 0841

unite

/ ju(:)náɪt /

名 unity 統一

動 to make two or more people or things join together to become one thing

～を結合する

ⓘ 形容詞形united（団結した、連合した）は、the United States of America（アメリカ合衆国）、the United Kingdom（英国、連合王国）、the United Nations（国連）などに使われている。

例 The two teams were **united** to create the best soccer team in the country.

国内最強のサッカーチームを作るために、その2つのチームは統合された。

□□□ 0842

treasure

/ tréʒər /

名 something valuable that you hide or keep safe

宝もの、財宝

ⓘ eaの発音に注意。

例 The pirate hid his **treasure** on an island in the middle of the sea.

海賊は海の真ん中の島に財宝を隠した。

0843

fault

/ fɔ́:lt /

形 faulty 欠陥のある

名 **responsibility for something bad that happened**

(過失の)責任

例 The judge decided that the accident was not the man's **fault**.

裁判官は、事故はその男性の責任ではないと判決を下した。

0844

assume

/ əs(j)ú:m /

名 assumption 仮定

動 **to think that something is true without knowing for sure**

…と思う、想定する

≒ suppose

〈as- (～に) +sume (取る)〉

ⓘ 〈assume (that)...〉(…だと思う、想定する) の形で押さえておこう。

例 **Assuming** the roads aren't crowded, it should only take a few hours to get to Karuizawa from Tokyo.

道が混んでいないと想定すると、東京から軽井沢に到着するにはわずか数時間しかかからないだろう。

0845

besides

/ bɪsáɪdz /

前 **in addition to something**

～に加えて

ⓘ 前置詞のbeside (～のそばに) と混同しないように注意。

例 **Besides** hamburgers, the restaurant also makes great pizza.

ハンバーガーに加え、そのレストランではおいしいピザも作っている。

副 **in addition to what was said before**

そのうえ

≒ additionally, moreover

例 We have plenty of money for the trip, and **besides**, we've always wanted to visit Hawaii.

私たちには旅行のお金がふんだんにあり、そのうえ私たちはずっとハワイに行きたいと思っていた。

0845語

0846

steady

/ stédi /

副 steadily 着実に

形 ① **not changing (much) as time passes**

安定した、一定の

≒ constant, stable

〈stead（場所）+-y（形容詞）〉

例 Running at a **steady** pace is the key to finishing a marathon.

一定のペースで走ることがマラソンを完走する鍵だ。

② **growing, developing, etc. gradually and continuously in an even way**

着実な

例 Japan has seen a **steady** decline in population for over 10 years.

日本では10年以上にわたり、人口が着実に減少している。

0847

earthquake

/ ə́ːrθkwèɪk /

名 **an event in which the surface of the Earth shakes**

地震

〈earth（大地）+quake（揺れ）〉

例 Kumamoto Castle was damaged by the **earthquake** in 2016.

熊本城は2016年の地震で被害を受けた。

0848

architecture

/ ɑ́ːrkətèktʃər /

名 architect 建築家

名 **the study and art of designing and creating buildings**

建築（学）

ⓘ「建築物」はbuildingと言う。

例 She studies ancient Indian **architecture** at university.

彼女は大学でインドの古代建築を研究している。

0849

ruin

/ rú:ɪn /

動 to damage something to the point that it cannot be used or enjoyed anymore

～をだめにする、台無しにする

例 He **ruined** his favorite sneakers playing in the river.

彼は川で遊んでいて、お気に入りのスニーカーを台無しにした。

名 what remains of something that has been destroyed

廃墟、遺跡

i この意味では複数形で使う。

例 They turned the **ruins** of the castle into a park.

彼らは城の遺跡を公園に変えた。

0850

interior

/ ɪntíəriər /

形 located on the inside part of something

内部の、屋内の

⇔ exterior

i カタカナ語の「インテリア（室内装飾）」にあたるのはinterior decoration [design]。

例 The **interior** walls of the house are all covered in wallpaper.

その家の内部の壁はすべて壁紙で覆われている。

0851

profile

/ próʊfaɪl /

名 a short written description of someone or something

（人物・業績などの）紹介、プロフィール

i 発音、アクセントに注意。

〈pro-(前に)+file((糸を)紡ぐ)〉

例 The author's **profile** is on the inside cover of the book.

著者のプロフィールは本の表紙の内側にある。

□□□ 0852

urban

/ ə́ːrbən /

名 urbanization 都市化

形 **relating to cities and the people who live in them**

都市の、都会の

⇔ rural

例 Belinda grew up in the countryside and never did get used to **urban** life in the city.

ベリンダは田舎で育ち、その街での都会生活に慣れることは決してなかった。

□□□ 0853

empire

/ émpaɪər /

名 emperor 皇帝

名 **a group of countries or states that are controlled by one ruler or government**

帝国

ⓘ アクセントはemの位置。

例 The Roman **Empire** lasted for hundreds of years.

ローマ帝国は数百年間続いた。

□□□ 0854

manual

/ mǽnjuəl /

名 **a book that gives useful information about something and explains how things are done**

説明書、マニュアル

≒ guide

〈manu (手) +-al (形容詞)〉

例 He had to look in the **manual** to learn how to clean his new mixer.

彼は新しいミキサーの洗い方を知るために説明書を見なければならなかった。

形 **involving work that is done with the strength of your body**

体力を使う

ⓘ「手の、手動の」という意味もある。

例 Working as a farmer requires a lot of **manual** labor.

農家として働くには、肉体労働がたくさん必要だ。

0855
distant
/ dístənt /

名 distance 距離

形 **existing in a faraway place**

遠い

≒ remote

⇔ close, near

例 Maybe someday humans will be able to travel to **distant** galaxies.

人類はいつか、遠い銀河へ旅ができるようになるかもしれない。

0856
massive
/ mǽsɪv /

名 mass 塊

形 **very large or serious**

（大きさ・程度などが）巨大な

≒ huge

⇔ tiny, minute

例 His new SUV is so **massive** that he has trouble finding places to park it.

彼の新しいSUV車は大きすぎて、駐車する場所を見つけるのに苦労している。

0857
lately
/ léɪtli /

副 **in the period of time that is recent**

最近

≒ recently

ⓘ ふつう現在完了形と共に使う。「遅く」はlate。

例 There has been a lot of rain **lately**.

最近、たくさん雨が降っている。

0858
lonely
/ lóʊnli /

名 loneliness 寂しさ、孤独

形 **sad because you have no one to talk to or be with**

孤独な、寂しい

ⓘ -lyで終わるが形容詞。

例 The boy feels **lonely** during summer vacation because he cannot see his school friends.

その男の子は夏休み中、学校の友達に会えないので、寂しく感じている。

□□□ 0859

upset

/ ʌpsét /

形 **sad, disappointed, or angry because something bad has happened**

取り乱した、腹を立てた

⇔ calm

〈up-（上に）+set（置く）〉

例 She is **upset** that the event she wanted to go to was canceled.

彼女は、行きたかったイベントが中止されて腹を立てている。

動 **to make someone feel sad, worried, or another bad feeling**

～を動揺させる

ⓘ upset-upset-upsetと活用する。

例 He **upset** his mother by dying his hair green.

彼は髪の毛を緑色に染めて母親を動揺させた。

□□□ 0860

perspective

/ pərspéktɪv /

名 **a way of thinking about and understanding a specific thing**

観点、見方

≒ viewpoint

〈per-（通して）+spect（見る）+-ive（形容詞）〉

例 The story is told through the **perspectives** of five different characters.

その物語は、5人の異なる登場人物の視点から語られる。

□□□ 0861

superior

/ su(ː)pɪəriər /

名 superiority 優越、優位

形 **higher in quality**

（能力などが）優れた、（品質が）上等の

⇔ inferior

ⓘ superの比較級。superior to（～よりも優れた）の形で押さえておこう。

例 The quality of their chocolate is **superior** to that of the average company.

その会社のチョコレートの品質は、平均的な会社のものよりも高い。

□□□ 0862

visible

/ vízəbl /

形 **able to be seen**

目に見える

⇔ invisible

〈vis（見る）+-ible（できる）〉

例 The boat wasn't **visible** from the shore because of the fog.

その船は霧のために海岸からは見えなかった。

□□□ 0863

chairman

/ tʃéərmən /

名 **the person in charge of a meeting, committee, organization, etc.**

議長；（大企業などの）会長

ⓘ 性差別表現を嫌い、chairpersonあるいは単にchairと言うこともある。

例 The company **chairman** is planning to retire next year.

その会社の会長は来年引退する予定だ。

□□□ 0864

slight

/ sláɪt /

副 slightly わずかに

形 **very small in amount**

わずかな

≒ minor, tiny

例 There is a **slight** chance that it will rain tomorrow.

明日雨が降る確率はわずかだ。

□□□ 0865

unlike

/ ʌnláɪk /

形 unlikely ～しそうにない

前 **indicating that someone or something is different from another person or thing**

～と違って

⇔ like

〈un-（否定）+like（似ている）〉

例 **Unlike** many other mammals, human babies cannot walk when they are born.

ほかの多くの哺乳類と違い、ヒトの赤ちゃんは生まれたときに歩くことができない。

0866

bite

/ báɪt /

動 to press down or cut into someone or something with teeth

～をかむ、～にかみつく

ⓘ bite-bit-bittenと活用する。「かむこと」「軽食」という名詞の意味もある。

例 She was **bitten** by a snake during her hike.

彼女はハイキング中にヘビにかまれた。

0867

merchant

/ mə́ːrtʃənt /

名 a person who buys and sells (large amounts of) goods

商人

〈merch (商う) +-ant (人)〉

例 **Merchants** used to travel on the Silk Road to get goods to Europe.

商人たちはヨーロッパまで品物を運ぶためにシルクロードを移動したものだった。

0868

myth

/ míθ /

名 mythology 神話学

名 ① an ancient story used to explain natural events or early history

神話

例 Each culture has their own creation **myth**.

それぞれの文化には独自の創世神話がある。

② something that is believed by many people but is not true

(一般に信じられている) 俗説

例 Many people still believe the **myth** that getting money will solve all of their problems.

お金さえ手に入ればすべての問題は解決するという俗説をいまだに多くの人が信じている。

0869

marine

/ mərí:n /

形 relating to the sea and the plants and animals that live there

海の

ⓘ「陸の」はterrestrial。

例 The girl dreams of becoming a **marine** biologist when she grows up.

その女の子は大きくなったら海洋生物学者になるのが夢だ。

0870

paragraph

/ pǽrəgræ̀f /

名 a part of a piece of writing that starts on a new line, contains one or more sentences, and usually deals with a single subject

段落

例 The teacher asked the students to write three **paragraphs** about their summer vacation.

その教師は生徒たちに自分の夏休みについて3段落書くようにと言った。

0871

thief

/ θí:f /

名 a person who steals

泥棒

ⓘ「強盗」はrobberと言う。

例 The **thief** was never caught by the police.

その泥棒は一度も警察に捕まらなかった。

0872

beneath

/ bɪní:θ /

前 below something else

～の下に

⇔ above

例 The ground **beneath** the log was full of ants.

その丸太の下の地面にはアリがわんさかいた。

□□□ 0873

construct

/ kənstrʌ́kt /

動 **to build or make something, such as a road, building, or machine**

～を建設する

名 construction 建設
形 constructive 建設的な

〈con-(共に)+struct(建てる)〉

例 The bridge took almost four years to **construct**.

その橋は建設するのに4年近くかかった。

□□□ 0874

cure

/ kjúər /

動 **to make someone healthy again after they have been sick or injured**

〈人〉を治す

≒ heal

ⓘ〈cure A of B〉(AのBを治す)の形で押さえておこう。「〈病気〉を治す」という意味もある。

例 The doctors were able to **cure** him of his disease.

その医師たちは彼の病気を治すことができた。

□□□ 0875

barrier

/ bǽrɪər /

名 **something that keeps someone from doing something or makes something impossible to do**

障壁、障害

ⓘ「(通行・出入りなどを阻む)柵、フェンス」の意味もある。

例 Access to money is a **barrier** to a good education in many countries.

多くの国において、お金を調達できるかどうかがよい教育を受けるための障壁になっている。

□□□ 0876

poison

/ pɔ́ɪzn /

名 **something that can kill or hurt you if it enters your body**

毒

名 poisonous 有毒な

例 The woman went to the store to buy some rat **poison**.

その女性はネズミ用の毒を買いにその店へ行った。

□□□ 0877

elderly

/ éldərli /

形 **older than middle age**

年配の

ⓘ the elderly（年配の人たち）という表現も覚えておこう。

例 The program makes medical care more affordable for **elderly** people.

そのプログラムによって高齢者が医療を受けやすくなる。

□□□ 0878

cheer

/ tʃíər /

形 cheerful 陽気な

動 **to shout because something has made you happy or excited**

喝采する、声援を送る

ⓘ cheerleader（チアリーダー）の cheer。

例 The crowd **cheered** when the woman scored a goal.

群衆は女性がゴールを決めると歓声を上げた。

□□□ 0879

react

/ riǽkt /

名 reaction 反応

動 **to act in a specific way when something happens**

反応する

≒ respond

〈re-（再び）+act（行動する）〉

ⓘ 化学反応などにも使う。

例 The dogs **reacted** with joy when their owner returned from work.

犬は飼い主が仕事から戻ってくると喜んで反応した。

□□□ 0880

colleague

/ kɑ́:li:g /

名 **someone who works with you**

同僚

≒ coworker

〈col-（共に）+league（選ばれたもの）〉

例 She goes to lunch with her **colleagues** every Friday.

彼女は毎週金曜日に同僚たちとランチに行く。

□□□ 0881

exhibit

/ ɪgzíbɪt /

名 exhibition 展覧会、展示会

動 to show that you have or feel something, such as an ability, Interest, or symptom

〈感情・資質など〉を表に出す、見せる

≒ display

〈ex-（外に）+hibit（持つ）〉

例 The patient **exhibited** confusion and trouble remembering the names of family and friends.

その患者は家族と友人の名前を思い出そうとして混乱と困難を示した。

名 an object or objects that have been put out for people to look at

展示品

例 The museum has an interesting **exhibit** featuring items from ancient Egypt.

その博物館は古代エジプトの品を目玉とする興味深い展示品を収蔵している。

□□□ 0882

scholar

/ skɑ́:lər /

形 scholarly 学問的な；学者の

名 someone who has studied something for a long time and knows a lot about it

学者

ⓘ scholarship（奨学金）という語も覚えておこう。

〈schol（学校）+-ar（人）〉

例 She is a highly respected Shakespearean **scholar**.

彼女は高名なシェイクスピアの研究者だ。

□□□ 0883

agriculture

/ ǽgrɪkʌ̀ltʃər /

形 agricultural 農業の

名 the practice of farming, and the science behind it

農業

〈agri（畑）+culture（耕作）〉

例 The country doesn't have a lot of space for **agriculture**.

その国は農業をする場所がありない。

0886語

□□□ 0884

wisdom

/ wízdəm /

形 wise 賢い

名 **the ability to understand things and to know what is right**

賢明さ

〈wis(知っている)+dom(状態)〉

例 **Wisdom** is something that you gain from your life experiences.

賢明さとは、人生経験を通じて得るものだ。

□□□ 0885

grip

/ gríp /

動 **to grab or hold onto something tightly**

～をしっかりつかむ、握る

例 He **gripped** the railing as he looked over the edge of the building.

彼はビルのへりから見下ろすとき、手すりを握り締めた。

□□□ 0886

protest

/ 名 próʊtest 動 prətést /

名 **something said or done to show disagreement with or disapproval of something**

抗議

〈pro-(前に)+test(証言する)〉

例 There were **protests** about the new policies across the whole country.

新しい政策についての抗議が国全体で起こった。

動 **to show strong disagreement about or disapproval of something**

（～に）抗議する

ⓘ キリスト教旧教徒（Catholic）に抗議した人々がプロテスタント（Protestant）。

例 She **protested** against animal testing.

彼女は動物実験に抗議した。

□□□ 0887

decorate

/ dékərèɪt /

名 decoration 飾り、装飾
形 decorative 装飾的な

動 to make something or somewhere look nice by adding things to it

～を飾る

≒ adorn

〈decor (装飾) +-ate (動詞)〉

ⓘ アクセントはdeの位置。

例 She **decorated** her room with flowers.

彼女は自分の部屋を花で飾った。

□□□ 0888

forecast

/ fɔ́ːrkæ̀st /

名 a statement about what you think might happen in the future

予報、予測

≒ prediction

〈fore- (前もって) +cast (投げる)〉

ⓘ 「～を予測する」という動詞の意味もあり、forecast-forecast/forecasted-forecast/forecastedと活用する。

例 The weather **forecast** says that it will rain every day next week.

天気予報では来週は毎日雨だ。

□□□ 0889

apparent

/ əpǽrənt /

副 apparently 見たところ～らしい
動 appear 見える、現れる

形 ① easy to see or understand

明白な、明瞭な

≒ obvious, clear

〈ap- (～に) +par (現れる) + -ent (形容詞)〉

例 Sara seemed to be angry for no **apparent** reason.

サラは明白な理由もなく怒っているように見えた。

② seeming true when it may not be

見かけの

例 The **apparent** cause of the accident was drunk driving.

その事故の原因は、どうやら飲酒運転のようだった。

0890

entertain

/ èntərtéɪn /

動 **to do a performance for someone to bring them happiness, pleasure, etc.**

形 entertaining 面白い
名 entertainment 娯楽

～を楽しませる

〈enter-（間に）+tain（保つ）〉

例 The guests at the party were **entertained** by a band.

パーティーの招待客たちはバンドの演奏を楽しんだ。

0891

blank

/ blǽŋk /

形 **without anything on it**

白紙の、書き込みのない

ⓘ 試験問題では「空欄」という名詞の意味でもよく使われる。

例 The girl took out a **blank** piece of paper to draw on.

その女の子は絵を描くための白い紙を取り出した。

0892

consult

/ kənsʌ́lt /

動 **to go to someone to ask for their professional opinion**

名 consultant コンサルタント
名 consultation 相談

〈専門家〉に意見を求める

ⓘ consult a dictionary（辞書を引く）という使い方もある。

例 He needs to **consult** his accountant about filing his taxes.

彼は税金の申告について会計士に相談する必要がある。

0893

corporation

/ kɔ̀ːrpəréɪʃən /

名 **a (large) business or organization that legally has the rights and duties of an individual**

形 corporate 企業の

法人、企業

≒ company, firm

〈corpor（体）+-ation（名詞）〉

ⓘ cooperation（協力）と混同しないように注意。

例 He is a lawyer for a famous **corporation**.

彼は有名な企業の弁護士だ。

0894

conscious

/ kɑ́ːnʃəs /

形 **being aware of something**

⇔ unconscious

例 A teacher must be very **conscious** of how they act in front of their students.

名 consciousness 意識

意識している、自覚している

〈con-（共に）+sci（知っている）+-ous（形容詞）〉

教師は生徒たちの前でどのように振る舞うかをしっかり自覚していなければならない。

0895

interval

/ íntərvəl /

名 **the period of time between two events**

(i) アクセントは語頭のinの位置。

例 In experiments, there can be long **intervals** where nothing happens.

（時間の）間隔、休止期間

〈inter-（～の間）+val（城壁）〉

実験では、何も起こらない長い間隔が生じる場合がある。

0896

frontier

/ frʌntíər /

名 **the limits of what people know about something**

(i) アクセントはtierの位置。「国境」「辺境」という意味もある。

例 The **frontiers** of science are continuously growing.

（学問などの）最前線、未開拓分野

科学の最先端分野は拡大し続けている。

0897

grace

/ greɪs /

名 **a way of moving and acting that is smooth and not awkward**

≒ elegance

例 That woman always walks with **grace**.

形 graceful 優美な
形 gracious 丁重な、礼儀正しい

優雅さ、気品

その女性はいつも優雅に歩く。

□□□ 0898

available

/ əvéɪləbl /

動 avail ～に役立つ
名 availability 利用できること

形 ① **possible to get or use**

利用できる、入手できる

⇔ unavailable

〈avail（役に立つ）+-able（できる）〉

例 Those sneakers are **available** in larger sizes online.

そのスニーカーの大きなサイズはインターネットで入手できる。

② **free to do something**

手が空いている

例 The old man next door doesn't work, so he is always **available** to help his neighbors.

隣家の高齢男性は仕事をしていないので、いつも手が空いていて近所の人々を助けることができる。

□□□ 0899

declare

/ dɪkléər /

名 declaration 宣言

動 **to say something publicly in an official way**

～を宣言する、発表する

≒ announce

〈de-（完全に）+clare（明らかにする）〉

例 She **declared** that she would be running for mayor in the next election.

彼女は次の選挙で市長に立候補すると宣言した。

□□□ 0900

jewelry

/ ʤú:əlri /

名 **things, such as rings or necklaces, that you wear on your body to make yourself look nice**

宝石類、装身具

ⓘ 宝石類をまとめて表す語。一つひとつの宝石はjewelと言う。

例 She went to the **jewelry** store to get some new earrings.

彼女は新しいイヤリングを買いに宝飾品店へ行った。

章末ボキャブラリーチェック

次の語義が表す英単語を答えてください。

語義	解答	連番
❶ sad because you have no one to talk to or be with	lonely	0858
❷ to damage something to the point that it cannot be used or enjoyed anymore	ruin	0849
❸ a book that gives useful information about something and explains how things are done	manual	0854
❹ steady and not likely to change, move, or fail	stable	0833
❺ existing in a faraway place	distant	0855
❻ the main or most central part of something, especially a problem or issue	core	0822
❼ without anything on it	blank	0891
❽ the study of the nature and meaning of life, knowledge, and the universe	philosophy	0817
❾ a law, rule, or theory that people have decided based on something	principle	0831
❿ to make something or somewhere look nice by adding things to it	decorate	0887
⓫ a way of thinking about and understanding a specific thing	perspective	0860
⓬ the limits of what people know about something	frontier	0896
⓭ relating to cities and the people who live in them	urban	0852
⓮ a statement about what you think might happen in the future	forecast	0888
⓯ having good manners, or showing respect to other people	polite	0820
⓰ to make two or more people or things join together to become one thing	unite	0841
⓱ a group of countries or states that are controlled by one ruler or government	empire	0853
⓲ to change how you act so that it is easier to do something in a particular situation	adapt	0818

語義	解答	連番
⑲ to make someone healthy again after they have been sick or injured	cure	0874
⑳ to press down or cut into someone or something with teeth	bite	0866
㉑ something that is used to catch someone or something	trap	0823
㉒ to change or make something change to a different opinion, belief, etc.	shift	0811
㉓ in the period of time that is recent	lately	0857
㉔ directions on how to make food	recipe	0810
㉕ having controls that allow something to work without a person to operate them	automatic	0802
㉖ sad, disappointed, or angry because something bad has happened	upset	0859
㉗ an ancient story used to explain natural events or early history	myth	0868
㉘ an event in which the surface of the Earth shakes	earthquake	0847
㉙ an important official job that someone has been given to do	mission	0825
㉚ the ability to understand things and to know what is right	wisdom	0884
㉛ higher in quality	superior	0861
㉜ a number or amount of something	quantity	0815
㉝ to bend or turn something to make it have a different shape	twist	0814
㉞ a piece of information or advice that is useful	tip	0816
㉟ something that keeps someone from doing something or makes something impossible to do	barrier	0875
㊱ very small in amount	slight	0864
㊲ to grab or hold onto something tightly	grip	0885
㊳ at the same time	meanwhile	0826
㊴ located on the inside part of something	interior	0850

語義	解答	連番
㊵ to send something from your country to another country to be sold	export	0803
㊶ things, such as rings or necklaces, that you wear on your body to make yourself look nice	jewelry	0900
㊷ to bend part of something over itself	fold	0832
㊸ to fill or use something	occupy	0809
㊹ having a strong flavor that is often not pleasant	bitter	0812
㊺ causing worry or fear	alarming	0807
㊻ someone who acts or speaks for someone else or for a group	representative	0835
㊼ to go to someone to ask for their professional opinion	consult	0892
㊽ being aware of something	conscious	0894
㊾ to think that something is probably true or will happen although you are not sure	suspect	0805
㊿ to disagree with someone or something, or to try to stop them from succeeding	oppose	0819
51 something valuable that you hide or keep safe	treasure	0842
52 a (large) business or organization that legally has the rights and duties of an individual	corporation	0893
53 easy to see or understand	apparent	0889
54 in addition to something	besides	0845
55 not angry, excited, nervous, etc.	calm	0836
56 to shout because something has made you happy or excited	cheer	0878
57 the period of time between two events	interval	0895
58 possible to get or use	available	0898
59 a way of moving and acting that is smooth and not awkward	grace	0897
60 a short written description of someone or something	profile	0851
61 relating to the sea and the plants and animals that live there	marine	0869

語義	解答	連番
(62) the practice of farming, and the science behind it	agriculture	0883
(63) not lasting for a long time	brief	0828
(64) to do a performance for someone to bring them happiness, pleasure, etc.	entertain	0890
(65) to notice or discover something, especially something that is difficult to see, hear, etc.	detect	0806
(66) to hurt someone or something, especially by making a hole in their skin with a weapon	wound	0824
(67) the person in charge of a meeting, committee, organization, etc.	chairman	0863
(68) someone who has studied something for a long time and knows a lot about it	scholar	0882
(69) to heat a liquid enough for it to start to bubble	boil	0830
(70) able to be seen	visible	0862
(71) below something else	beneath	0872
(72) a part of a piece of writing that starts on a new line, contains one or more sentences, and usually deals with a single subject	paragraph	0870
(73) to build or make something, such as a road, building, or machine	construct	0873
(74) to act in a specific way when something happens	react	0879
(75) to say something publicly in an official way	declare	0899
(76) not changing (much) as time passes	steady	0846
(77) a person who steals	thief	0871
(78) very large or serious	massive	0856
(79) responsibility for something bad that happened	fault	0843
(80) to think that something is true without knowing for sure	assume	0844
(81) something said or done to show disagreement with or disapproval of something	protest	0886
(82) to say something in a way that is hard to go against or disagree with	insist	0813

語義	解答	連番
83 not tightly attached to where it should be, or able to be separated from something	loose	0827
84 making you feel happy, comfortable, or satisfied	pleasant	0829
85 always active or changing	dynamic	0840
86 to study something carefully so that you can understand or explain it	analyze	0804
87 to create something that has never been created before	invent	0839
88 what makes something funny, or the ability to laugh at things that are funny	humor	0834
89 older than middle age	elderly	0877
90 indicating that someone or something is different from another person or thing	unlike	0865
91 relating to what is right and wrong	moral	0808
92 to show that you have or feel something, such as an ability, interest, or symptom	exhibit	0881
93 to completely focus on something and ignore everything else	concentrate	0838
94 someone who works with you	colleague	0880
95 to cause someone to be worried, annoyed, in pain, etc.	bother	0821
96 a process, system, or part of a machine or device that is used to produce a particular result	mechanism	0837
97 something that can kill or hurt you if it enters your body	poison	0876
98 a person who buys and sells (large amounts of) goods	merchant	0867
99 not a solid or a gas and able to flow freely, like water	liquid	0801
100 the study and art of designing and creating buildings	architecture	0848

Stage 10

The best view comes after the hardest climb.
最高の景色は最も辛い登りの先にひらける。

□□□ 0901

mixture

/ míkstʃər /

動 mix ～を混ぜる

名 ① a combination of different things

混合

例 A **mixture** of young and old students attend the school.

その学校には若い生徒、年配の生徒が入り混じって通っている。

② something made by mixing other things together

混合物

例 Pour a small amount of the pancake **mixture** into a hot frying pan.

混ぜ合わせたパンケーキの生地少量を熱したフライパンに注いでください。

□□□ 0902

eager

/ íːgər /

名 eagerness 熱心さ、熱意

形 very interested and excited about something that you want to do or that will happen or be done

切望した

ⓘ 〈be eager (for A) to *do*〉（（Aが）～することを切望する）の形で押さえておこう。

例 She was **eager** for the next volume of her favorite book series to be released.

彼女は大好きな本のシリーズの次の巻が発売されるのを切望していた。

□□□ 0903

penalty

/ pénəlti /

名 a punishment for going against a law or rule

刑罰、罰則

ⓘ アクセントはpeの位置。

例 The construction company will face **penalties** if it doesn't finish the building on time.

その建設会社は期限通りに建築が終わらなければペナルティを科される。

0904

satellite

/ sǽtəlàɪt /

名 **a machine sent into space that moves around the Earth or other planets, moons, etc.**

人工衛星

ⓘ 月のような、天体の「衛星」も意味する。

例 The radio **satellite** was damaged by an asteroid.

その無線衛星は小惑星によって損傷を受けた。

□□□ 0905

brave

/ bréɪv /

副 bravely 勇敢に
名 bravery 勇敢さ、勇気

形 **feeling or showing that you are not afraid**

勇敢な

≒ courageous

⇔ cowardly

例 The young men that fought during the war had to be **brave**.

戦争中に戦った若い男たちは勇敢でなければならなかった。

□□□ 0906

shame

/ ʃéɪm /

形 shameful 恥ずべき

名 ① **a feeling of guilt, regret, or sadness that you get after you have done something bad or wrong**

恥ずかしさ

ⓘ It's a shame (that)... (…ということは残念だ) という表現も覚えておこう。

例 The **shame** she felt for lying to her parents was almost too much for her to bear.

両親に嘘をついたことで感じた恥ずかしさは、彼女には耐えられないほど大きかった。

② **dishonor or disgrace**

恥

例 His life of crime and drugs brought **shame** to his whole family.

犯罪と薬物にまみれた彼の生活は、家族全体の恥になった。

0907

bare

/ béər /

形 **not covered by clothes**

むき出しの、裸の

ⓘ bear（～に耐える）と同音。「裸の、裸体の」はnaked。

例 The children ran around on the grass in **bare** feet.

子どもたちは草の上をはだしで駆け回った。

0908

vessel

/ vésəl /

名 **a large boat**

船

ⓘ「血管」「（植物の）導管」という意味もある。

例 She is the captain of a large fishing **vessel**.

彼女は大型漁船の船長だ。

0909

polish

/ pɑ́:lɪʃ /

動 **to make something look shiny by rubbing it**

～を磨く

ⓘ 大文字のPolishは「ポーランド（人［語］）の；ポーランド語」の意味。

例 He got his shoes **polished** at the airport.

彼は空港で靴を磨いてもらった。

0910

accent

/ ǽksent /

名 **a way of pronouncing words that is shared among a group of people from a specific place**

なまり

≒ dialect

ⓘ「強勢、アクセント」という意味もある。

例 There aren't many different **accents** in that country, even though it is very large.

その国はとても広いが、なまりの種類はそれほど多くない。

0911

distinct

/ dɪstíŋkt /

動 distinguish ～を区別する
名 distinction 区別
形 distinctive 違いを示す

0913語

形 ① easy to see, hear, smell, feel, etc.

(感覚的に)はっきりした

≒ noticeable

〈di(s)-(離れて)+stinct(印をつける)〉

例 Coconut has a very **distinct** flavor.

ココナッツはとてもはっきりした風味がある。

② different in a way that is noticeable

別個の、まったく異なる

≒ separate

⇔ identical

例 That phrase has several **distinct** meanings.

その言い回しにはまったく異なる意味が複数ある。

0912

psychology

/ saɪkɑ́ːlədʒi /

形 psychological 心理的な
名 psychologist 心理学者

名 the science and study of the mind and how people act

心理学

ⓘ psychの発音に注意。

〈psycho(心)+logy(学問)〉

例 The study of **psychology** helps us understand why people do the things they do.

心理学の研究は、人はその人がする行動をなぜ取るのかを私たちが理解するのに役立つ。

0913

apologize

/ əpɑ́ːlədʒàɪz /

名 apology 謝罪

動 to say you are sorry for doing or saying something wrong

謝る

ⓘ イギリス英語ではapologiseともつづる。〈apologize to A for B〉(BについてAに謝罪する)の形で押さえておこう。

〈apo-(離れて)+log(言葉)+-ize(動詞)〉

例 Arthur **apologized** to his parents for breaking the front door.

アーサーは玄関のドアを壊したことを両親に謝った。

□□□ 0914

feature

/ fíːtʃər /

名 **an ability or quality that is important or interesting**

特徴

ⓘ future（未来）と混同しないように注意。

〈feat（作る）+-ure（結果）〉

例 This video camera has some extra **features** that the one you have doesn't.

このビデオカメラには、あなたの持っているものにはない追加機能がいくつかついている。

動 **to talk about something or someone in a way that is noticeable**

～を特集する

ⓘ「フィーチャーする」「フィーチャリング」というカタカナ語にもなっている。

例 The Sunday newspaper **featured** an article about the new emperor.

日曜日の新聞は、新天皇に関する記事を特集していた。

□□□ 0915

liberty

/ líbərti /

形 liberal 進歩的な；自由主義の

名 **the state of being free to say and do what you want**

自由

≒ freedom

〈liber（自由な）+-ty（名詞）〉

例 Many people don't have **liberty** in that country.

その国では多くの人々に自由がない。

□□□ 0916

virtual

/ vəːrtʃuəl /

副 virtually 実質的に

形 **existing or happening on computers or on the Internet**

仮想の

⇔ real, true

ⓘ「実質的な」という意味もある。

例 The band just announced that they will be having a **virtual** concert.

そのバンドはバーチャルコンサートを開催すると発表したところだ。

0917

dive

/ dáɪv /

動 **to move deeper or jump into water, especially with your arms and head going in first**

水に潜る；（頭から）飛び込む

ⓘ アメリカ英語では過去形にdoveも使う。「潜水；飛び込み」という名詞の意味もある。

例 She took a deep breath and **dived** into the water.

彼女は大きく息を吸って水の中に飛び込んだ。

0918

retail

/ ríːtèɪl /

名 retailer 小売業者

形 **relating to selling things to customers for them to use**

小売りの

ⓘ wholesale（卸売りの）という語も覚えておこう。

〈re-（再び）+tail（切る）〉

例 The couple decided to open a **retail** store to sell their pottery.

その夫婦は自分たちが作った陶器を売る小売店を開くことにした。

0919

relative

/ rélətɪv /

副 relatively 比較的
動 relate ～を関連づける

形 **compared to someone or something else**

相対的な

⇔ absolute

例 They discussed the **relative** benefits of the two marketing plans.

彼らは2つのマーケティング計画の相対的なメリットについて話し合った。

名 **someone who is part of your family**

親類（の人）

例 She grew up not knowing many of her **relatives**.

彼女は親類の多くを知らずに育った。

□□□ 0920

mobile

/ móʊbəl /

名 mobility 動きやすさ、可動性

形 able to be moved

動かせる、移動可能な

⇔ stationary

〈mob (動く) +-ile (できる)〉

i イギリス英語では「携帯電話」をmobile (phone)とも言う。

例 Unlike desktop computers, laptops are very **mobile**.

デスクトップコンピュータと違って、ノートパソコンはとても簡単に持ち運びできる。

□□□ 0921

update

/ ʌ̀pdéɪt /

形 updated 更新した、最新の

動 to change something so that it has the most recent information available

～を更新する

i 「最新情報」という名詞の意味もある。名詞の発音は[ʌ́pdèɪt]。

例 The company **updated** their website to include their new address.

その会社は新住所を掲載するためにウェブサイトを更新した。

□□□ 0922

advertise

/ ǽdvərtàɪz /

名 advertisement 広告

動 to show the public that something is being sold

～を広告する、宣伝する

例 She saw a new hair dryer **advertised** on TV and decided to buy it.

彼女は、新しいドライヤーがテレビで宣伝されているのを見て、それを買うことにした。

□□□ 0923

fiber

/ fáɪbər /

名 a thin thread of something that can be used to make things such as paper and cloth

繊維

i イギリス英語ではfibreとつづる。

例 Clothing made of natural **fibers** is cooler in the summer.

天然繊維でできた衣類の方が夏は涼しい。

0924

negotiate

/ nəgóuʃièɪt /

名 negotiation 交渉

動 **to talk about something formally to make an agreement about something**

交渉する

例 They contacted the seller to **negotiate** over the price of the item.

彼らはその品物の価格について交渉するためにその販売業者に連絡した。

0925

glue

/ glúː /

名 **something that is used to stick things together**

接着剤、のり

例 She used **glue** to stick the leaf to a piece of paper.

彼女はのりを使って紙にその葉っぱを貼りつけた。

0926

currency

/ kə́ːrənsi /

名 **the specific type of money a country uses**

通貨

i 原義は「流れること」。current（現在の；現在流通している）と同語源語。

例 Some foreign **currencies** are hard to get in that country.

その国では手に入れにくい外国通貨もある。

0927

laboratory

/ lǽbərətɔ̀ːri /

名 **a room or a building used for scientific experiments and tests**

実験室

i labと略されることもある。

〈labor（労働する）+-atory（場所）〉

例 The door to the **laboratory** is always locked when no one is in there.

実験室のドアは、中に誰もいないときはいつも鍵がかかっている。

0928

content

/ 名 kɑ́:ntent 形 kəntént /

動 contain ～を含む

名 **the information or amount of something that is within something else**

内容、中身

例 The **contents** of this magazine are meant for young women.

この雑誌の中身は若い女性向けだ。

形 **happy, satisfied, and not needing anything else**

満足して

≒ pleased

⇔ discontent

例 She is never **content** with second place.

彼女は2位では決して満足しない。

0929

phenomenon

/ fɪnɑ́:mənɑ̀:n /

形 phenomenal (自然)現象の; 驚くべき

名 **something that has happened and can be studied or observed but is not easy to understand**

現象

ⓘ 複数形はphenomena。

例 Many people continue to study the **phenomenon** of déjà vu.

多くの人々が「デジャヴュ」という現象について研究し続けている。

0930

diversity

/ dəvə́:rsəti /

形 diverse 多様な
動 diversify ～を多様化する

名 **a range of people or things that do not share much in common**

多様性

⇔ uniformity

〈di-(離れて)+vers(曲がる)+-ity (名詞)〉

例 Access to a **diversity** of opinions is helpful when making important decisions.

意見の多様性が得られることは、重要な決定をするときに役立つ。

□□□ 0931

delicate

/ délɪkət /

副 delicately 繊細に
名 delicacy 繊細さ

形 **easily broken or damaged**

(ものが) 壊れやすい、繊細な

≒ fragile

⇔ strong

ⓘ ateの発音に注意。アクセントはdeの位置。

例 Wine glasses are very **delicate**.

ワイングラスはとても繊細だ。

□□□ 0932

chat

/ tʃǽt /

動 **to talk to another person casually**

おしゃべりをする

ⓘ「おしゃべり、雑談」という名詞の意味もある。

例 Brenda spent a few minutes **chatting** with her husband about the weather before getting in the bath.

ブレンダはお風呂に入る前に数分、天気について夫とおしゃべりをした。

□□□ 0933

mass

/ mǽs /

形 massive 巨大な

形 **involving or affecting a large number of people**

大衆の、集団の

≒ widespread

例 There were **mass** demonstrations after the man's death.

その男性の死後、大規模なデモ活動があった。

名 **a large amount of something that does not have a specific shape**

塊

例 **Masses** of floating ice in the ocean are called icebergs.

海に浮かんでいる氷の塊は氷山と呼ばれる。

□□□ 0934

biology

/ baɪɑ́:ləʤi /

形 biological 生物学の
名 biologist 生物学者

名 **the science and study of things that are alive, such as plants and animals**

生物学

〈bio (生命) +logy (学問)〉

例 Her **biology** professor helped her find an internship.

彼女の生物学の教授は、インターンシップ先を見つけるのを手助けしてくれた。

□□□ 0935

nutrition

/ n(j)u(:)tríʃən /

形 nutritious 栄養のある
名 nutrient 栄養素

名 **the process of eating good food so that your body can be strong and healthy**

栄養摂取、食生活

〈nutr (養う) +-ition (名詞)〉

例 Good **nutrition** will help you live a long life.

良質な栄養は長生きするのに役立つ。

□□□ 0936

pale

/ péɪl /

形 **having a skin color that is whiter than usual**

青白い、青ざめた

例 Her skin is very **pale**, and she gets sunburnt easily.

彼女の肌はとても青白く、日焼けで炎症を起こしやすい。

□□□ 0937

horrible

/ hɔ́:rəbl /

名 horror 恐怖

形 **very bad or unpleasant**

ひどい、非常に嫌な

≒ terrible

〈hor (恐怖) +-rible (性質をもった)〉

例 The man gets a **horrible** headache whenever it rains.

その男性は雨が降るといつもひどい頭痛になる。

□□□ 0938

horizon

/ həráɪzn /

形 horizontal 水平の

名 **the line where the land or the ocean looks like it meets the sky**

地平線、水平線

例 They walked toward the **horizon**, hoping they would find a town soon.

彼らは町がもうすぐ見つかるだろうと期待しながら、地平線に向かって歩いた。

□□□ 0939

makeup

/ méɪkʌ̀p /

名 **the way that something is put together**

構造、構成

ⓘ「化粧（品）」という意味もある。

例 The ethnic **makeup** of the neighborhood is very diverse.

この近隣地域の民族構成はとても多様だ。

□□□ 0940

context

/ kɑ́:ntekst /

形 contextual 文脈上の

名 ① **the words that are used with a word or phrase, which help to explain its meaning**

文脈、前後関係

〈con-（共に）+text（織られたもの）〉

例 You cannot learn how to use new words if you don't understand the **context** in which they are used.

新しい語は、その語が使われる文脈を理解しなければ使い方を身につけることはできない。

② **the situation or conditions that exist when something happens**

状況、背景

例 Her new book puts recent events into a larger historical **context**.

彼女の新しい本は、最近の出来事をより大きな歴史的背景の中で捉えている。

□□□ 0941

vacuum

/ vǽkjuːm /

名 **a space that has little or no air or other gases in it**

真空

ⓘ アクセントはvaの位置。uが2つ重なる。vacは「からの」を意味する語根で、vacant（空虚な）、vacation（休暇）なども同語源語。

例 The food that is sent to the International Space Station is **vacuum**-packed.

国際宇宙ステーションに送られる食べ物は真空パックされている。

□□□ 0942

disappoint

/ dìsəpɔ́ɪnt /

名 disappointment 失望

動 **to make someone feel bad by being or doing less than was expected**

～を失望させる

⇔ satisfy

例 The remake of the movie **disappointed** all the fans.

その映画のリメイク版はファン全員を失望させた。

□□□ 0943

rude

/ rúːd /

形 **not having or showing respect for others**

失礼な、無礼な

≒ impolite

⇔ polite

例 Eating with your elbows on the table is **rude** in some cultures.

テーブルにひじをついて食べるのは無礼だとする文化もある。

□□□ 0944

virus

/ váɪrəs /

名 **a very small thing that makes people or animals sick and spreads among them**

ウイルス

ⓘ viの発音に注意。「細菌」はgerm、bacteriaと言う。

例 A lot of **viruses** spread through the air.

多くのウイルスは空気を介して広がる。

0945
troop
/ trú:p /

名 **a group of soldiers**
軍隊、部隊

例 The **troops** all gathered at the bottom of the hill to get ready to fight.
全軍が戦闘の準備をするために丘のふもとに集合した。

0946
pause
/ pɔ́:z /

名 **a period of time in which something is stopped for a short time before being started again**
小休止、途切れ

i 「ちょっと止める」という動詞の意味もある。pose（ポーズをとる）と混同しないように注意。

例 The lecture continued for two hours without **pause**.
レクチャーは途切れなく2時間続いた。

0947
utilize
/ jú:təlàɪz /
名 utilization 利用

動 **to use something to do a specific thing**
～を利用する、役立たせる

i イギリス英語ではutiliseともつづる。

例 The public library is **utilized** by almost all members of the community.
その公立図書館は地域のほとんど全員に活用されている。

0948
cope
/ kóʊp /

動 **to deal with something that is hard to manage and try to find a solution**
（うまく）対処する

≒ treat

例 The woman has learned to **cope** with the stress of her new job.
その女性は新しい仕事のストレスに対処できるようになった。

□□□ 0949

elite

/ ılíːt /

形 **belonging to a small and powerful group of people in a society**

エリートの、選り抜きの

ⓘ 「エリート」という名詞の意味もある。

例 Many children of **elite** politicians go to that school.

多くのエリート政治家の子どもたちがその学校に通っている。

□□□ 0950

statistics

/ stətístıks /

形 statistical 統計の

名 **a set of information shown in numbers**

統計

例 **Statistics** show that you are more likely to get hurt while driving a car than while riding in an airplane.

統計によれば、飛行機に乗っているときよりも車を運転しているときの方がけがをする可能性は高い。

□□□ 0951

purse

/ pə́ːrs /

名 **a bag used to carry money and other personal things when you go out**

ハンドバッグ、(女性の)財布

ⓘ 主に北米英語での使い方。イギリス英語では「(女性用の) 小銭入れ」を指す。

例 Carol was given a beautiful leather **purse** for her birthday.

キャロルは誕生日に美しい革の財布をもらった。

□□□ 0952

refrigerator

/ rıfrídʒərèıtər /

名 **a machine or room that keeps food and drinks cold**

冷蔵庫、冷蔵室

ⓘ fridgeという略語を使うことも多い。「冷凍庫」はfreezer。

例 He put the cake in the **refrigerator** so that the icing wouldn't melt.

彼はアイシングが溶けないようにケーキを冷蔵庫に入れた。

 0953

parallel

/ pǽrəlèl /

形 **describing the situation in which two things next to each other are the same distance apart and never touch**

平行の、並行した

ⓘ「平行線」という名詞の意味もある。

例 The river runs **parallel** to the expressway.

その川は高速道路と並行して流れている。

□□□ 0954

beg

/ bég /

動 **to ask someone for something in a very emotional way**

～に懇願する

≒ plead

ⓘ 〈beg (A) to *do*〉〈beg (A) that...〉（(Aに) ～するよう懇願する）の形で押さえておこう。

例 She **begged** her father to read her a bedtime story every night.

彼女は毎晩寝る前に読み聞かせをしてほしいと父親に頼んだ。

□□□ 0955

stiff

/ stíf /

動 stiffen ～を硬直させる

形 ① **painful or hard to use or move**

〈肩・足などが〉凝った、こわばった

⇔ flexible

例 His muscles were very **stiff** after running the marathon.

マラソンを走った後、彼の筋肉はとてもこわばっていた。

② **not friendly or relaxed**

堅苦しい

≒ formal

例 The man greeted the audience in a very **stiff** way.

その男性は聴衆にとても堅苦しい挨拶をした。

□□□ 0956

trash

/ trǽʃ /

名 **things that you do not need or cannot use and throw away**

ごみ、くず

≒ garbage

例 The crows got into the **trash** and made a big mess.

カラスはごみの中に入り込んで派手に散らかした。

□□□ 0957

thrill

/ θríl /

形 thrilling 興奮する、わくわくさせる

動 **to make someone feel very excited or happy**

〈人〉をぞくぞくさせる、わくわくさせる

例 The group was **thrilled** to see the dolphins jump out of the water.

一行はイルカが水中から飛び出すのを見てわくわくした。

□□□ 0958

dislike

/ dɪsláɪk /

動 **to not like something or someone**

～が嫌いである

≒ hate

〈dis-（否定）+like（好む）〉

例 Fabien **dislikes** the texture of fish.

ファビアンは魚の食感が嫌いだ。

□□□ 0959

pronounce

/ prənáʊns /

名 pronunciation 発音

動 **to make the sound of a word or letter with your voice**

～を発音する

〈pro-（前に）+nounce（宣言する）〉

例 Long words are hard to **pronounce**, even for native speakers.

長い単語はネイティブスピーカーでも発音が難しい。

0960
ambition
/ æmbíʃən /

名 something that you want to do or achieve

形 ambitious 野心のある、大志を抱いた

(強い) 欲求、目標

≒ desire

例 The woman has **ambitions** for a career in editing someday.

その女性はいつか編集の仕事に就きたいという目標がある。

0961
crowded
/ kráudɪd /

形 having a lot of people, or being filled with people or things

名 crowd 人込み

混雑した

例 Shinjuku Station is usually very **crowded**.

新宿駅は普段とても混雑している。

0962
civilization
/ sìvələzéɪʃən /

名 a human society that has become very developed and organized

動 civilize ～を文明化する
形 civilized 文明化された

文明

i イギリス英語ではcivilisationともつづる。cit/civは「市民」を意味する語根で、city（都市）、citizen（市民）、civil（市民の）などは同語源語。

例 We can learn a lot from the mistakes of ancient **civilizations**.

われわれは古代文明の失敗から多くを学ぶことができる。

0963
bless
/ blés /

動 to say a special prayer to make someone or something holy

形 blessed 祝福された

～を祝福する

例 The head of the family **blessed** their meal before they ate.

食事を始める前に、家長は家族の食事を祝福した。

□□□ 0964

ugly

/ ʌ́gli /

形 **not pretty or nice to look at**

醜い

⇔ beautiful

例 She thinks that pink is a very **ugly** color.

ピンクはとても醜い色だと彼女は思っている。

□□□ 0965

conquer

/ kɑ́ːŋkər /

名 conquest 征服
名 conqueror 征服者

動 **to use force to take control of a place, such as a country**

～を征服する

例 The Romans **conquered** many cities.

古代ローマ人は多くの都市を征服した。

□□□ 0966

dialogue

/ dáɪəlɔ̀(ː)g /

名 **a conversation between two or more people, especially one that appears in a book, film, etc.**

対話

ⓘ アメリカ英語ではdialogともつづる。「(国家・団体間での)意見交換、会談」という意味もある。

〈dia (間の) +logue (話)〉

例 The students have to listen to a **dialogue**, then answer three questions about it.

生徒たちは対話を聞き、それに関する3つの質問に答えなければならない。

□□□ 0967

vague

/ [illegible] /

形 **not clear in meaning**

あいまいな、漠然とした

≒ unclear, ambiguous

⇔ specific

例 The teacher's instructions were too **vague**, and all of the students were confused.

その教師の指示があまりにもあいまいだったので、生徒たちは皆困惑した。

□□□ 0968

obey

/ oʊbéɪ /

動 **to do what a person, law, rule, etc. tells you that you must do**

～に従う

形 obedient 従順な
名 obedience 従順さ

≒ follow

⇔ disobey

ⓘ 他動詞である点に注意。

〈ob-（～に）+ey（聞く）〉

例 He tries to **obey** all traffic laws while driving.

彼は運転中、すべての交通法規に従おうとしている。

□□□ 0969

luggage

/ lʌ́gɪʤ /

名 **the bags and suitcases you use when you travel**

手荷物

≒ baggage

〈lug(g)(引きずる)+-age(もの)〉

例 Depending on your flight, you may have to pay to bring **luggage** on the airplane.

フライトによっては、機内に荷物を持ち込むのに料金を支払わなければならないかもしれない。

□□□ 0970

bound

/ báʊnd /

形 ①《**bound to *do***》 **very likely to do or be something**

～するはずだ

ⓘ 元はbind（～を縛りつける）の過去分詞。

例 His mother is **bound to** be upset when she finds out he broke her favorite glass.

彼の母親は、お気に入りのグラスを彼が壊したと知ったら、腹を立てるはずだ。

②《**bound for**》 **going or planning to go to a specific place**

～行きの

例 That train is **bound for** Osaka.

その電車は大阪行きだ。

□□□ 0971

nuclear

/ n(j)úːkliər /

形 **relating to the energy made when atoms are split apart or joined together**

核の、原子力の

例 Many people don't agree with the use of **nuclear** energy.

多くの人が原子力の使用に賛同していない。

□□□ 0972

blossom

/ bláːsəm /

名 **a flower, especially of a fruit tree**

(果樹の)花

例 There is a festival in her hometown every year to celebrate the apple **blossoms**.

彼女の故郷の町では毎年、リンゴの花を祝う祭りがある。

□□□ 0973

disturb

/ dɪstə́ːrb /

名 disturbance 騒ぎ、騒動

動 **to keep someone from doing something, or interrupt someone while they are doing something**

～を乱す、～に迷惑をかける

≒ trouble, bother

〈dis-(完全に)+turb(混乱させる)〉

例 The company president told her secretary that she didn't want to be **disturbed** until after lunch.

その会社の社長は秘書に、昼食が終わるまで邪魔されたくないと伝えた。

□□□ 0974

dawn

/ dɔ́ːn /

名 **the time in the morning when the sun first begins to appear**

夜明け

≒ daybreak

⇔ dusk

ⓘ「発端」という比喩的な意味もある。

例 The sky at **dawn** was a beautiful red color.

夜明けの空は美しい赤い色をしていた。

□□□ 0975

inhabitant

/ ɪnhǽbətənt /

名 a person or animal that lives in a specific place

居住者、生息動物

動 inhabit ～に住む

〈in-（中に）+habit（保つ）+ -ant（人）〉

例 This city has more **inhabitants** than all of Ireland.

この市はアイルランド全土より住民が多い。

□□□ 0976

legend

/ lédʒənd /

名 a story about someone or something in the past that many people think is true but cannot be proven

伝説

形 legendary 伝説の、伝説的な

ⓘ「伝説的人物」の意味のカタカナ語「レジェンド」もこのlegend。

例 It is not known how much of the **legend** of Robin Hood is true.

ロビン・フッドの伝説がどの程度真実なのかはわからない。

□□□ 0977

mount

/ máʊnt /

動 ① to attach something to another thing

～をはめる、貼る

ⓘ「山」を意味するmountと同じつづり。

例 He **mounted** the shelf to the wall.

彼は壁に棚を取りつけた。

② to increase in amount

〈数量が〉増える、かさむ

例 Medical expenses **mount** up very quickly when you're in the hospital.

入院していると医療費がすぐにかさむ。

□□□ 0978

determine

/ dɪtə́ːrmən /

名 determination 決定
形 determined 断固とした

動 ① to (officially) decide something based on the information you have

…と結論を下す、決定する

≒ conclude, settle

ⓘ 〈determine (that)...〉（…と結論を下す、決定する）の形で押さえておこう。

〈de-（完全に）+termine（境界を定める））〉

例 The city **determined** that the building was no longer safe and had it torn down.

市はその建物がもう安全ではないと判断し、取り壊した。

② to discover something by getting information

～を特定する、究明する

例 Scientists still have not been able to **determine** what causes the disease.

科学者たちは、まだその病気の原因を特定できていない。

□□□ 0979

knit

/ nít /

動 to make something, especially a piece of clothing, using a special type of needles and thread

～を編む

ⓘ knit-knitted/knit-knitted/knitと活用する。kは発音しない。原義は「結び目（knot）を作る」。

例 His grandmother **knitted** him a sweater for Christmas.

彼のおばあさんは彼にクリスマスのためのセーターを編んでくれた。

□□□ 0980

mankind

/ mæ̀nkáɪnd /

名 all of the people on the Earth as one group

人類

≒ humankind

例 We must save our planet if we want to save **mankind**.

人類を救いたければ、私たちは地球を救わなければならない。

0981

antique / æntíːk /

形 **old and from a time before now** 骨董品の

ⓘ「骨董品」という名詞の意味もある。

〈ant(i)(昔の)+-que(～に関する)〉

例 **Antique** car shows are very popular in North America.
クラシックカーの見本市は、北米ではとても人気がある。

0982

beverage / bévərɪʤ /

名 **something that you can drink** 飲み物

例 This restaurant also serves alcoholic **beverages** after 6 p.m.
このレストランは午後6時からアルコール飲料も提供する。

0983

recognize / rékəgnàɪz /

名 recognition 認識
形 recognizable 認識[識別]できる

動 **① to know something is true or exists and accept it** ～を認める

≒ admit

〈re-(再び)+cognize(知る)〉

ⓘ イギリス英語ではrecogniseともつづる。

例 Until people **recognize** their own biases, things will not get better.
人々が自分の偏見を認識しない限り、状況はよくならないだろう。

② to know and remember someone or something because you have seen or met them in the past ～が(誰[何]か)わかる

≒ identify

例 She could **recognize** him even in a crowd because of his big, blue hat.
彼の大きな青い帽子のおかげで、彼女は人混みの中でも彼を見分けることができた。

□□□ 0984

aboard

/ əbɔ́ːrd /

副 **on, onto, or inside of a vehicle**

（列車・船・飛行機などに）乗って

〈a-（～に）+board（甲板）〉

例 Amber got **aboard** the train right before it left the station.

アンバーは電車が駅を出発する直前に乗った。

□□□ 0985

random

/ rǽndəm /

副 randomly 無作為に

形 **done, chosen, etc. without having a plan or pattern**

無作為の

≒ arbitrary

ⓘ at random（無作為に）という表現も覚えておこう。

例 The café played a **random** selection of music including jazz, hip-hop, and rock.

そのカフェはジャズ、ヒップホップ、ロックといった音楽を無作為に選んで流した。

□□□ 0986

guilty

/ gílti /

名 guilt 罪；罪悪感

形 **responsible for doing something bad or committing a crime**

有罪の

⇔ innocent

例 The man was found **guilty** of stealing his neighbor's car.

その男性は近所の人の車を盗んで有罪になった。

□□□ 0987

hug

/ hʌ́g /

動 **to put your arms around someone or something in a loving or friendly way**

～を抱き締める

≒ embrace

例 Linda **hugged** her dog when she got home from school.

リンダは学校から帰ってくると飼い犬を抱き締めた。

0988

pardon

/ pá:rdn /

動 to accept or forgive someone's behavior, even though it might be considered inappropriate

〈人〉を許す

≒ excuse

ⓘ I beg your pardon.（失礼ですが）のように、「許し」という名詞の意味もある。

例 **Pardon** me, but do you mind if I take this chair?

すみませんが、このいすに座ってもよろしいでしょうか。

0989

ecological

/ ì:kəlá:dʒɪkəl /

名 ecology 生態学

形 relating to plants and living things and how they relate to each other

生態（上）の

例 The **ecological** consequences of oil are now well known.

石油が生態系に及ぼす影響は今ではよく知られている。

0990

astronomy

/ əstrá:nəmi /

形 astronomical 天文学の
名 astronomer 天文学者

名 the science and study of stars, planets, and other things that are in outer space

天文学

〈astro（星）+nomy（法則）〉

例 There are many books on **astronomy** for kids at the bookstore.

その書店には子ども向けの天文学の本がたくさんある。

0991

humid

/ hjú:mɪd /

名 humidity 湿度

形 having a lot of moisture in the air

湿気の多い

⇔ dry

例 The place where she grew up is very **humid** in the winter.

彼女が育った場所は、冬はとても湿気が多い。

□□□ 0992

checkup

/ tʃékʌ̀p /

名 **an examination of someone by a doctor to see if they are healthy**

健康診断、検査

例 The man goes for yearly **checkups** to check the condition of his heart.

その男性は心臓の状態をチェックするために毎年健康診断に行っている。

□□□ 0993

skyscraper

/ skáɪskrèɪpər /

名 **a very tall building in a city**

超高層ビル

〈sky（空）+scraper（こするもの）〉

例 The **skyscrapers** in Manhattan can be seen from far away.

マンハッタンの超高層ビル群は遠くからでも見える。

□□□ 0994

mend

/ ménd /

動 **to make something that was broken able to be used again**

～を修理する、修繕する

≒ fix, repair

例 She took her watch to be **mended**.

彼女は腕時計を修理に出した。

□□□ 0995

folk

/ fóʊk /

形 **relating to the common people of a place**

民衆の、民俗的な

ⓘ lは発音しない。「人々」という名詞の意味もある。folklore（民間伝承）という語も覚えておこう。

例 I read a book on the **folk** culture of the Middle Ages.

私は中世の民俗文化に関する本を読んだ。

□□□ 0996

sightseeing

/ sáɪtsìːɪŋ /

名 **the activity of going to famous or interesting places somewhere**

観光

〈sight (名所) +see (～を見る) +-ing〉

例 Many people visit the town to try its famous foods and for **sightseeing**.

名産品を食べたり観光をしたりするために、多くの人がその町を訪れる。

□□□ 0997

reflect

/ rɪflékt /

名 reflection 反射、反省

動 **① to show or symbolize how someone feels about something**

～を反映する

〈re-(後ろに)+flec (曲げる)〉

例 Her new book aims to **reflect** the feelings of women everywhere.

彼女の新しい本はどこにでもいる女性の感情を反映しようとしている。

② to throw back something, such as light or sound from a surface

～を反射する

例 The color black doesn't **reflect** heat, so black clothes are hotter in the summer.

黒という色は熱を反射しないので、黒い服の方が夏は暑い。

③ to think carefully about something

熟考する

例 He used the two-week holiday to **reflect** on his career choices.

彼は2週間の休暇を使い、自分のキャリアの選択肢についてあれこれ考えた。

□□□ 0998

reasonable

/ ríːznəbl /

名 reason 理由；道理
副 reasonably 手ごろに

形 ① fair and sensible

理性的な、合理的な

⇔ unreasonable

例 A **reasonable** person wouldn't drink and drive.

理性的な人なら飲んだら車は運転しない。

② not very expensive

（値段が）手ごろな

例 That is a very **reasonable** price for that brand.

そのブランドにしてはそれはとても手ごろな値段だ。

□□□ 0999

ironically

/ aɪrɑ́ːnɪkəli /

形 ironic 皮肉な
名 irony 皮肉

副 in a way that is funny or strange because it is not what you expected it to be

皮肉なことに

例 **Ironically**, even though we have technology to help us, humans are working more than ever before.

皮肉なことに、われわれに役立つ科学技術があるにもかかわらず、人間はかつてないほどたくさん働いている。

□□□ 1000

upcoming

/ ʌ́pkʌ̀mɪŋ /

形 happening or appearing soon

来るべき

≒ forthcoming

例 The whole class is looking forward to their **upcoming** trip to the zoo.

もうすぐある動物園への遠足をクラス全体が楽しみにしている。

章末ボキャブラリーチェック

次の語義が表す英単語を答えてください。

語義	解答	連番
❶ painful or hard to use or move	stiff	0955
❷ all of the people on the Earth as one group	mankind	0980
❸ having a lot of people, or being filled with people or things	crowded	0961
❹ to move deeper or jump into water, especially with your arms and head going in first	dive	0917
❺ done, chosen, etc. without having a plan or pattern	random	0985
❻ a set of information shown in numbers	statistics	0950
❼ involving or affecting a large number of people	mass	0933
❽ a large boat	vessel	0908
❾ very bad or unpleasant	horrible	0937
❿ existing or happening on computers or on the Internet	virtual	0916
⓫ having a lot of moisture in the air	humid	0991
⓬ not pretty or nice to look at	ugly	0964
⓭ compared to someone or something else	relative	0919
⓮ to say you are sorry for doing or saying something wrong	apologize	0913
⓯ the process of eating good food so that your body can be strong and healthy	nutrition	0935
⓰ to attach something to another thing	mount	0977
⓱ to make something, especially a piece of clothing, using a special type of needles and thread	knit	0979
⓲ to keep someone from doing something, or interrupt someone while they are doing something	disturb	0973
⓳ not having or showing respect for others	rude	0943
⓴ a machine sent into space that moves around the Earth or other planets, moons, etc.	satellite	0904
㉑ the state of being free to say and do what you want	liberty	0915

語義	解答	連番
㉒ having a skin color that is whiter than usual	pale	0936
㉓ an examination of someone by a doctor to see if they are healthy	checkup	0992
㉔ to ask someone for something in a very emotional way	beg	0954
㉕ a human society that has become very developed and organized	civilization	0962
㉖ in a way that is funny or strange because it is not what you expected it to be	ironically	0999
㉗ to make something look shiny by rubbing it	polish	0909
㉘ a range of people or things that do not share much in common	diversity	0930
㉙ a very tall building in a city	skyscraper	0993
㉚ the way that something is put together	makeup	0939
㉛ a group of soldiers	troop	0945
㉜ a space that has little or no air or other gases in it	vacuum	0941
㉝ a combination of different things	mixture	0901
㉞ easily broken or damaged	delicate	0931
㉟ the specific type of money a country uses	currency	0926
㊱ the words that are used with a word or phrase, which help to explain its meaning	context	0940
㊲ the time in the morning when the sun first begins to appear	dawn	0974
㊳ something that is used to stick things together	glue	0925
㊴ to say a special prayer to make someone or something holy	bless	0963
㊵ the science and study of the mind and how people act	psychology	0912
㊶ to make the sound of a word or letter with your voice	pronounce	0959
㊷ a very small thing that makes people or animals sick and spreads among them	virus	0944
㊸ happening or appearing soon	upcoming	1000

語義	解答	連番
44 something that you can drink	beverage	0982
45 an ability or quality that is important or interesting	feature	0914
46 a conversation between two or more people, especially one that appears in a book, film, etc.	dialogue	0966
47 things that you do not need or cannot use and throw away	trash	0956
48 relating to the common people of a place	folk	0995
49 a period of time in which something is stopped for a short time before being started again	pause	0946
50 to make something that was broken able to be used again	mend	0994
51 the science and study of stars, planets, and other things that are in outer space	astronomy	0990
52 to not like something or someone	dislike	0958
53 a feeling of guilt, regret, or sadness that you get after you have done something bad or wrong	shame	0906
54 not covered by clothes	bare	0907
55 the information or amount of something that is within something else	content	0928
56 fair and sensible	reasonable	0998
57 a story about someone or something in the past that many people think is true but cannot be proven	legend	0976
58 to put your arms around someone or something in a loving or friendly way	hug	0987
59 responsible for doing something bad or committing a crime	guilty	0986
60 to use something to do a specific thing	utilize	0947
61 to show or symbolize how someone feels about something	reflect	0997
62 to use force to take control of a place, such as a country	conquer	0965
63 to change something so that it has the most recent information available	update	0921

語義	解答	連番
㊹ to talk about something formally to make an agreement about something	negotiate	0924
㊺ to accept or forgive someone's behavior, even though it might be considered inappropriate	pardon	0988
㊻ very interested and excited about something that you want to do or that will happen or be done	eager	0902
㊼ on, onto, or inside of a vehicle	aboard	0984
㊽ to do what a person, law, rule, etc. tells you that you must do	obey	0968
㊾ a way of pronouncing words that is shared among a group of people from a specific place	accent	0910
㊿ to make someone feel very excited or happy	thrill	0957
71 describing the situation in which two things next to each other are the same distance apart and never touch	parallel	0953
72 the science and study of things that are alive, such as plants and animals	biology	0934
73 the bags and suitcases you use when you travel	luggage	0969
74 to know something is true or exists and accept it	recognize	0983
75 belonging to a small and powerful group of people in a society	elite	0949
76 to (officially) decide something based on the information you have	determine	0978
77 something that has happened and can be studied or observed but is not easy to understand	phenomenon	0929
78 the line where the land or the ocean looks like it meets the sky	horizon	0938
79 a thin thread of something that can be used to make things such as paper and cloth	fiber	0923
80 the activity of going to famous or interesting places somewhere	sightseeing	0996
81 《----- to *do*》 very likely to do or be something	bound	0970
82 something that you want to do or achieve	ambition	0960
83 a punishment for going against a law or rule	penalty	0903

語義	解答	連番
84 a bag used to carry money and other personal things when you go out	purse	0951
85 to make someone feel bad by being or doing less than was expected	disappoint	0942
86 to talk to another person casually	chat	0932
87 a flower, especially of a fruit tree	blossom	0972
88 relating to plants and living things and how they relate to each other	ecological	0989
89 to deal with something that is hard to manage and try to find a solution	cope	0948
90 not clear in meaning	vague	0967
91 relating to selling things to customers for them to use	retail	0918
92 a room or a building used for scientific experiments and tests	laboratory	0927
93 a machine or room that keeps food and drinks cold	refrigerator	0952
94 feeling or showing that you are not afraid	brave	0905
95 easy to see, hear, smell, feel, etc.	distinct	0911
96 able to be moved	mobile	0920
97 a person or animal that lives in a specific place	inhabitant	0975
98 old and from a time before now	antique	0981
99 relating to the energy made when atoms are split apart or joined together	nuclear	0971
100 to show the public that something is being sold	advertise	0922

この索引には本書で取り上げた約2,140語句がアルファベット順に掲載されています。数字はページ番号を示しています。色の数字は見出し語として収録され、黒い数字は語句が派生語や類義語・反意語などとして収録されていることを表しています。

A

B

C

D

E

F

G

H

I

J

K

L

M

N

O

P

Q

R

S

T

Y

Z

［編者紹介］

ロゴポート

語学書を中心に企画・制作を行っている編集者ネットワーク。編集者、翻訳者、ネイティブスピーカーなどから成る。おもな編著に『英語を英語で理解する 英英英単語® 中級編／上級編／超上級編』、『英語を英語で理解する 英英英熟語 初級編／中級編』、『最短合格！ 英検® 1級／準1級 英作文問題完全制覇』、『最短合格！ 英検®2級英作文&面接 完全制覇』、『出る順で最短合格！ 英検®1級／準1級 語彙問題完全制覇［改訂版］』、『出る順で最短合格！ 英検®1級〜3級単熟語EX 第2版』（ジャパンタイムズ出版）、『TEAP単熟語Grip1500』（アスク出版）、『分野別 IELTS英単語』（オープンゲート）などがある。

本書のご感想をお寄せください。
https://jtpublishing.co.jp/contact/comment/

英語を英語で理解する

英英英単語® 初級編

2020年9月20日 初版発行
2024年4月20日 第6刷発行

編　者　ジャパンタイムズ出版 英語出版編集部&ロゴポート

発行者　伊藤秀樹

発行所　株式会社 ジャパンタイムズ出版
〒102-0082 東京都千代田区一番町2-2
一番町第二TGビル 2F
ウェブサイト　https://jtpublishing.co.jp/

印刷所　株式会社 光邦

Printed in Japan　ISBN 978-4-7890-1757-2